"The world is awash in agony endured by individuals and society alike as brutalizing power breaks free from the restraints of law, the civilizing recognition of our essential commonality. The authors of this gripping volume turn psychoanalytic inquiry to the study of specific outbreaks of heartbreaking violence against basic rights that cruelly torture and endanger life itself. There may be no more vital contribution psychoanalysis now can make than such as those in this selection of serious thinking about the suffering and sorrow threatening survival of person and group, indeed of humanity. This profoundly compelling contribution is a model for continued work if civilization is to last."

Warren S. Poland, *author*, Intimacy and
Separateness in Psychoanalysis

"The technical cooperation between the two areas of Psychoanalysis and Law is already much more advanced in practice all over the world than it is commonly studied theoretically and known in general. This seminal book opens a historical perspective on the official polyphonic recognition of the mutual implication and cooperative interaction of Psychoanalysis and Law. This has impressive consequences regarding social, political, and institutional life, and is dealt with at the highest scientific level, under the aegis of the International Psychoanalytical Association."

Stefano Bolognini, *Past President, International
Psychoanalytical Association*

"This remarkable work represents a milestone not only in the connection between psychoanalysis and law, but it also refers to current crucial issues, such as the work developed by the IPA in the Community Committees and the inspiring insertion of psychoanalysts in this area. Featuring a theoretical rigor and a completely refreshed view, the authors contribute with an outstanding critical examination of these subjects, providing a fruitful and indispensable reading for all those who seek to deepen their knowledge in the Psychoanalysis and Law field."

Virginia Ungar, *President* and Sergio Nick, *Vice President,
International Psychoanalytical Association*

GW00691169

Psychoanalysis, Law, and Society

Psychoanalysis, Law, and Society explores the connections between psychoanalysis and law, arguing that these are required not only for conceptual or theoretical needs in both fields, but also for the vast range of practical implications and possibilities their association enables.

The book is divided into four parts, each addressing a unique example of the interaction of legal and psychoanalytic work. It begins with matters that are as global as they are local: the challenge of caring for and aiding migrants, refugees, families, and individuals; the question of planetary survival; of the mistreatment and violence in military and secular conflicts; and the projects and processes of international governance. The middle two parts focus on the very wide-ranging problems of social violence as these target women and people of diversity. Then, on the penetration of law into the most intimate aspects of family life: adoption, divorce, child custody, and complex parental arrangements. In the last part, the contributions use this double vision (legal and psychoanalytic) perspective to explore basic processes in social and legal life.

Psychoanalysis, Law, and Society will be of great interest to psychoanalysts, psychoanalytic psychotherapists, as well as legal scholars.

Plinio Montagna, MD, is a psychoanalyst and past president of the Brazilian Society of Psychoanalysis of São Paulo and the Brazilian Federation of Psychoanalysis. He is the chair of the Committee of Psychoanalysis and Law for the International Psychoanalytical Association and former member of its Board of Representatives. He also works as a psychiatric and psychoanalytic expert in family courts in São Paulo.

Adrienne Harris, PhD, is a faculty member and supervisor for the New York University Postdoctoral Program in Psychotherapy and Psychoanalysis and at the Psychoanalytic Institute of Northern California. She is an associate editor of *Psychoanalytic Dialogues* and of *Studies in Gender and Sexuality*, and she is on the editorial boards of *Psychoanalytic Inquiry* and *American Imago*. She publishes in the areas of gender and development.

Relational Perspectives Book Series
Lewis Aron, Adrienne Harris, Steven Kuchuck & Eyal Rozmarin
Series Editors

The Relational Perspectives Book Series (RPBS) publishes books that grow out of or contribute to the relational tradition in contemporary psychoanalysis. The term *relational psychoanalysis* was first used by Greenberg and Mitchell[1] to bridge the traditions of interpersonal relations, as developed within interpersonal psychoanalysis and object relations, as developed within contemporary British theory. But, under the seminal work of the late Stephen A. Mitchell, the term *relational psychoanalysis* grew and began to accrue to itself many other influences and developments. Various tributaries – interpersonal psychoanalysis, object relations theory, self psychology, empirical infancy research, and elements of contemporary Freudian and Kleinian thought – flow into this tradition, which understands relational configurations between self and others, both real and fantasied, as the primary subject of psychoanalytic investigation.

We refer to the relational tradition, rather than to a relational school, to highlight that we are identifying a trend, a tendency within contemporary psychoanalysis, not a more formally organized or coherent school or system of beliefs. Our use of the term *relational* signifies a dimension of theory and practice that has become salient across the wide spectrum of contemporary psychoanalysis. Now under the editorial supervision of Lewis Aron, Adrienne Harris, Steven Kuchuck, and Eyal Rozmarin, the Relational Perspectives Book Series originated in 1990 under the editorial eye of the late Stephen A. Mitchell. Mitchell was the most prolific and influential of the originators of the relational tradition. Committed to dialogue among psychoanalysts, he abhorred the authoritarianism that dictated adherence to a rigid set of beliefs or technical restrictions. He championed open discussion, comparative and integrative approaches, and promoted new voices across the generations.

Included in the Relational Perspectives Book Series are authors and works that come from within the relational tradition, extend and develop that tradition, as well as works that critique relational approaches or compare and contrast it with alternative points of view. The series includes our most distinguished senior psychoanalysts, along with younger contributors who bring fresh vision. A full list of titles in this series is available at www.routledge.com/mentalhealth/series/LEARPBS.

[1] Greenberg, J. & Mitchell, S. (1983). *Object Relations in Psychoanalytic Theory.* Cambridge, MA: Harvard University Press.

Psychoanalysis, Law, and Society

Edited by Plinio Montagna and
Adrienne Harris

Routledge
Taylor & Francis Group

LONDON AND NEW YORK

First published 2019
by Routledge
2 Park Square, Milton Park, Abingdon, Oxon OX14 4RN

and by Routledge
52 Vanderbilt Avenue, New York, NY 10017

Routledge is an imprint of the Taylor & Francis Group, an informa business

British Library Cataloguing-in-Publication Data
A catalogue record for this book is available from the British Library

Library of Congress Cataloging-in-Publication Data
Names: Montagna, Plinio, 1948– editor. | Harris, Adrienne, editor.
Title: Psychoanalysis, law, and society / edited by
Plinio Montagna and Adrienne Harris.
Description: Milton Park, Abingdon, Oxon ; New York, NY : Routledge, 2019. |
Series: The relational perspectives book series |
Includes bibliographical references and index.
Identifiers: LCCN 2018060407 (print) | LCCN 2019003880 (ebook) |
ISBN 9780429202438 (Master) | ISBN 9780429511059 (Adobe) |
ISBN 9780429517914 (Mobipocket) | ISBN 9780429514487 (ePub3) |
ISBN 9780367194482 (hardback : alk. paper) |
ISBN 9780367194505 (pbk. : alk. paper) | ISBN 9780429202438 (ebk)
Subjects: LCSH: Social psychiatry. | Professional ethics.
Classification: LCC RC455 (ebook) |
LCC RC455 .P778 2019 (print) | DDC 616.89/14–dc23
LC record available at https://lccn.loc.gov/2018060407

ISBN: 978-0-367-19448-2 (hbk)
ISBN: 978-0-367-19450-5 (pbk)
ISBN: 978-0-429-20243-8 (ebk)

Typeset in Times
by Newgen Publishing UK

Plinio dedicates this book to his father, Haroldo, and to his mother, Yvonne.

Adrienne dedicates this book to her grandchildren Nevona, Nadav, Cedar, and Jake, rueful for the world we leave to them but confident of their deep skills and big hearts.

Contents

Contributors

Elizabeth Allured, PsyD, is on the teaching faculty at Suffolk Institute for Psychoanalysis and Psychotherapy, and Adelphi University's postgraduate training programs in Psychoanalysis and Psychotherapy. She has published articles on the environmental crisis from a psychoanalytic perspective, most recently in Contemporary Psychoanalysis: "Holding the Ungrievable: A Psychoanalytic Approach to the Environmental Crisis." Dr Allured has been presenting her ideas about this issue at international psychoanalytic conferences since 2007. She has a clinical practice in Port Washington, New York.

Ruth Axelrod Praes, PhD, is a clinical psychologist at the Mexican National Autonomous University. She was awarded by the National University with the Gabino Barreda Medal, and is a psychoanalyst and full member of the International Psychoanalytic Association, as well as a past Latin America board member of the IPA, and past co-chair of COWAP, Latin America 2013–2017. She is a past president of the Mexican Psychoanalytic Association (Asociación Psicoanalítica Mexicana – APM), 2014–2016; past director of the APM Institute, 2016–2018; and actual director of the Postgraduate Study Center of APM, 2018. She has published articles in several books on adoption, divorce, children of divorce, gender listening, trauma, and betrayal. She has worked in private practice for more than three decades.

Adrian Cesar Besuschio, MD, University of Buenos Aires, is a psychiatrist with the Health Ministry of Buenos Aires. He is an associate member of the Argentine Psychoanalytical Association, and of the International Psychoanalytical Association, as well as a member of the Espacio Fairbairn (APA). He is a specialist in Forensic and Occupational Medicine and is a member of the board of the Hospital J.T. Borda, a leading psychiatric hospital in Argentina.

Ghislaine Boulanger, PhD, is a psychologist and psychoanalyst in private practice in New York City and a member of the Relational Faculty at New York University's Postdoctoral Program in Psychotherapy and Psychoanalysis. Since the publication of her book *Wounded by Reality: Understanding and Treating Adult Onset Trauma* (The Analytic Press, 2007), she has taught and published extensively on the psychodynamic dilemmas facing adults who have survived violent and life-threatening events, and the clinicians who work with them. In 2006 Dr Boulanger founded WithholdAPADues for psychologists wishing to withhold their dues and subsequently to resign from the American Psychological Association in protest over the APA's collaboration with Bush-era detention policies in Guantanamo Bay and the CIA black sites.

Louis Brunet, PhD, is a psychoanalyst (IPA, CPS), psychologist, professor at Université du Québec à Montréal, and also past president of the Canadian Psychoanalytic Society. He has published more than 150 papers and seven books, including a book on forensic assessment: *L'expertise psycholégale. Balises méthodologiques et déontologiques, 2e édition* (Presses de l'Université du Québec, 2014).

Also: Casoni, D., Brunet, L. *La psychocriminologie. Apports psychanalytiques et applications cliniques* (Presses de l'Université de Montréal, 2003); *Comprendre l'acte terroriste* (Presses de l'Université du Québec, 2009); and *Profession psychologue* (Presses de l'Université de Montréal, 2009).

Rosa Corzo, PhD, is a training analyst and president of the Mexican Psychoanalytic Association (Asociación Psicoanalítica Mexicana – APM). She has carried out educational work both at the Psychoanalytic Institute and at the postgraduate courses at APM. She is the former founder and president of the Autism Mexican Society (SOMAC) and the Latin American Federation of Autism (FEPAL).

Gley P. Costa, MD, is a psychiatrist and psychoanalyst. He is a full member of the International Psychoanalytical Association and founding member and training analyst of the Brazilian Psychoanalytical Society of Porto Alegre. He also teaches at Mario Martins University Foundation. He is the author of a large number of psychoanalytic publications, including: *Conflitos da vida Real* (ed., Artmed, 2006), *O amor e seus labirintos* (ed. Artmed, 2007), and *A Clínica psicanalítica das psicopatologias contemporâneas* (ed., Artmed, 2015).

Ronald Doctor, MD, is a consultant psychiatrist in Medical Psychotherapy, West London NHS Trust; a member of the British Psychoanalytical Society; member of the IPA Committee of Psychoanalysis and Law; member of the British Psychotherapy Foundation; board member of the International Association for Forensic Psychotherapy; and Honorary Clinical Lecturer, Imperial College, London. He has edited two books: *Dangerous Patients: A Psychodynamic Approach to Risk Assessment and Management* (Karnac, 2003) and *Murder, a Psychotherapeutic Investigation* (Karnac, 2008). He has also published "History, Murder and the Fear of Death," *International Journal of Applied Psychoanalytical Studies* (2015).

Katie Gentile, PhD, is Professor of Gender Studies and chair of the Department of Interdisciplinary Studies at John Jay College of Criminal Justice (CUNY). She is the author of *Creating Bodies: Eating Disorders as Self-Destructive Survival* (2017) and the 2017 Gradiva award-winning *The Business of Being Made: The Temporalities of Reproductive Technologies, in Psychoanalysis and Cultures* (2016), both with Routledge. She is editor of the Routledge book series *Genders & Sexualities in Minds & Culture* and a co-editor of the journal *Studies in Gender and Sexuality*. She is on the faculty of New York University's Postdoctoral Program in Psychotherapy and Psychoanalysis and the Critical Social Psychology program at the CUNY Graduate Center.

Gabriele Gragnoli is a lawyer in Siena. He is one of the co-founders of the Civil Chamber of the Lawyers in Siena. He has written a number of articles, mostly on the juridical and ethical aspects in the law field, among which there is a contribution in "Comparative Confidentiality in Psychoanalysis" (BIICL – British Institute of International Comparative Law, IPA, London, edited by Penelope Garvey and Alexander Layton, 2004).

Adrienne Harris, PhD, is a faculty member and supervisor at New York University Postdoctoral Program in Psychotherapy and Psychoanalysis. She is a faculty member and a supervisor at the Psychoanalytic Institute of Northern California. She is an editor at *Psychoanalytic Dialogues*, and *Studies in Gender and Sexuality*. In 2012, along with Lewis Aron and Jeremy Safran, she established the Sandor Ferenczi Center at the New School University. With Lew Aron, Eyal Rozmaren, and Steven Kuchuck, she co-edited the Relational Perspectives Book Series (RPBS), a series now with over 100 published volumes. She is an editor of the IPA ejournal Psychoanalysistoday.com, which is developing cross-cultural communications among the five language groups in the IPA.

Alicia Beatriz Iacuzzi is a psychologist and psychoanalyst, a full member with educational role at the APA (Association Psychoanalytical Argentina), a full member of FEPAL and IPA, a member of COWAP, and consultant of the Committee of Psychoanalysis and Law. Prizes include the FELPAL 2004 and Prize Argentine Association of Mental Health 2006 and 2007. She is the author of *The Enigmatic Prison Labyrinths: A Psychoanalytic Itinerary* (2009) and *Crimes Against Sexual Integrity: Psychoanalytic Joints from the Shadows of Being in Prison* (2010).

Cynthia Ladvocat is a full member of Rio1 – Sociedade Psicanalítica do Rio de Janeiro; member of European Family Therapy Association; book organizer of "Guide to Adoption – Legal, Social and Family;" and author of *Myths and Secrets About the Origin of the Child in the Adoptive Family*.

Andrea Marzi, MD, is a psychiatrist and a full member of the International Psychoanalytical Association and Italian Psycho-analytical Society, where he holds several national and international tasks. He is also an active member of the ApsaA. He is a supervisor in institutions and in the National Health Service; he has been visiting fellow in Forensic Psychopathology, University of Cambridge; has worked in the Department of Forensic Psychopathology; and been a professor of Developmental Psychology in the University of Siena and in various schools of specialization in the Faculty of Medicine. He is on the editorial board of the Italian Rivista di Psicoanalisi.

He currently lives and works in Siena and is the author of several scientific articles in national and international journals. He is also the author of several books, including *Ciak Turns, Psychoanalysis in the Cinema* (Becarelli, 2013), *Post-modern. A Post to Decipher* (Becarelli, 2016, with other authors), and he is the author/editor of *Psychoanalysis, Identity, and the Internet* (Karnac, 2016).

Eliana Mello is a full member of Rio1 – Sociedade Psicanalítica do Rio de Janeiro and is a consultant of the Committee's Psychoanalysis and Law of International Psychoanalysis Association.

Plinio Montagna, MD, completed postgraduate studies in Social Psychiatry at the University of London. He holds a master's in Psychiatry, is a training analyst, and is the past president of the Brazilian Society of Psychoanalysis of São Paulo and the Brazilian Federation of Psychoanalysis. He is a former editor of the Revista Brasileira da Psicanálise, the chair of the Committee of Psychoanalysis and Law for the International Psychoanalytical Association, and former member of its Board of Representatives. He works as psychiatric and psychoanalytic expert witness in family courts in São Paulo.

Laura Orsi, Medical School-UBA, psychoanalyst-APA (Asociación Psicoanalítica Argentina), is a full member of the International Psychoanalytical Association (IPA). She is the coordinator of Social Media Commission in APA, a member of the Social Media Committee IPA and of the Psychoanalysis and Law Committee in IPA, and an advisor in the National Direction of Mediation and Participative Methods of Conflict Resolution, Ministry of Justice and Human Rights-Argentina. She is past director of publications in FEPAL, the secretary in the "Psychoanalysis Subjectivity and Community" chapter in APAAPSA, and coordinates the investigation group "Culture, Web Modernity, Technology and Psychoanalysis" in APA – Past Culture Assessment in Legislature in CABA (Baires). She has participated in several courses in gender leadership, empowerment, and social participation, and has been a member of the (WDN) Argentine Chapter since the beginning, working as a Network Communications Manager. She is the co-author of *Psychoanalysis and Society* (Ediciones Continente, 2007) and co-compiler and co-author of *Psychoanalysis and Society, New Paradigms in the Social* (Editorial Dunken, 2017).

Ann Pellegrini, PhD, is Professor of Performance Studies and Social and Cultural Analysis at New York University. She is also a candidate in adult psychoanalysis at IPTAR in New York City. A founding co-editor of the "Sexual Cultures" series at New York University Press, her own books include: *Performance Anxieties: Staging Psychoanalysis, Staging Race* (Routledge, 1997); *Love the Sin: Sexual Regulation and the Limits of Religious Tolerance*, co-authored with Janet R. Jakobsen (Beacon Press, 2004); and *Secularisms*, co-edited with Jakobsen (Duke University Press, 2008). Her most recent book – *"You Can Tell Just by Looking" and 20 Other Myths about LGBT Life and People*, co-authored with Michael Bronski and Michael Amico (Beacon, 2013) – was a finalist for the 2014 Lambda Literary Award for Best LGBT non-fiction. She was the 2007 Freud-Fulbright Visiting Scholar of Psychoanalysis at the Freud Museum-Vienna and the University of Vienna.

Vivian B. Pender, MD, is Clinical Professor of Psychiatry at the Weill Cornell Medical College and Training and Supervising Psychoanalyst at Columbia University, Center for Psychoanalytic Training and Research. She is a Trustee of the American Psychiatric Association. She has won honors and awards for her excellence in teaching medical students. At the United Nations she represents the International Psychoanalytical Association and the American Psychiatric Association. Until 2011, she chaired the NGO Committee on the Status of Women and now chairs the NGO Committee on Mental Health. During that time, she assisted in the establishment of UN Women. She is a volunteer Asylum Evaluator for Physicians for Human Rights. In 2015, she founded Healthcare Against Trafficking, Inc., a non-profit organization dedicated to promoting education and advocacy in the healthcare sector. She is a co-investigator on a Weill Cornell Department of Internal Medicine innovative grant to study "Experiences of Sex Trafficking Victims in Healthcare Settings." In 2017 she published a book chapter on violence against women and in 2018 published a chapter on women and leadership. She produced four documentaries of conferences at the United Nations on mental health, human rights, human trafficking, hatred, and violence. She is the editor of *The Status of Women: Violence, Identity and Activism* (Karnac, 2016).

Robert L. Pyles, MD, has twice been president of the American Psychoanalytic Association, president of the Massachusetts Psychiatric Society, has served on the Board of the International Psychoanalytical Association, and on many IPA committees. Since 1969 he has been on the faculty of Harvard Medical School. He has served for many years as a psychoanalytic and psychiatric forensic expert, often working with legal firms representing Harvard Medical School and the Harvard hospital system. For many years, he has worked in Washington, DC, with many congressmen, senators, and several presidents, representing the interests of psychoanalysis in the Halls of Congress. Among other activities, he is a consultant to US Major League Baseball and has run 47 marathons.

Gertraud Schlesinger-Kipp is a psychologist and psychoanalyst and since 1989 has run her own private practice in Kassel as a member of the German Psychoanalytical Association (DPV, IPA) and full member of the IPA. Since 1998 she has been a training analyst and supervisor. From 1995 to 2003 she was president of the Alexander-Mitscherlich-Institute for Psychoanalysis and Psychotherapy in Kassel, training institute of the DPV/IPA. From 2004 to 2010 she was a member of the board of the DPV, and from 2006 to 2008 president of the DPV. In the International Psychoanalytic Association (IPA) she was a member of the board from 2009 to 2011 and she was and is active in numerous committees, especially in the Committee on Women and Psychoanalysis (COWAP) since 2002 and as overall chair of COWAP from 2015 to 2017. She has numerous publications on subjects including: "Female development in life cycle," "Remembering of childhood during World War II," and psychotherapeutic approach with refugees.

Cândida Sé Holovko is a full member of IPA and the Brazilian Psychoanalytic Society of São Paulo (SBPSP); co-chair of COWAP for Latin America, 2014–2017; a liaison member of COWAP-IPA with SBPSP, 2005–2008; regional editor for the Latin American journal *Calibán* (2012–2014); member of the Institut de

Psychosomatique Pierre Marty de Paris; coordinator of a psycho-analytic psychosomatics group linked to the Institute of Paris; and chief editor of the institute's journal (*Jornal de Psicanálise*), 2009–2010, in which two volumes were dedicated to COWAP themes of masculinities/femininities (June and December, 2009). She co-edited three books on sexuality and gender at Karnac-London (2017), Blucher-São Paulo (2017), and Letra Viva-Buenos Aires (2016). She published on masculine and feminine psychosexuality, mind–body relations, and psychosomatics.

Rakesh Shukla has more than three decades of engagement with law, constitutional jurisprudence, human rights, and justice melded with training and practice in psychodynamic therapy. Explorations in the interface of law and psychoanalysis are a major area of engage-ment. Interventions in training of judges to minimize impact of unconscious biases, prejudices, and stereotypes in judicial decision-making constitute an important arena of work. His writings have been published in major newspapers as well as journals on law and psychology. Publications include "Bail Not Jail;" "Sex Work and Laws in South Asia;" "Equal Pay for Equal Work;" "Street Legal;" and "Halsbury's Laws of India on Misrepresentation and Fraud." He is a member of the Supreme Court Bar Association of India; affiliate, Indian Psychoanalytic Society; counselor, Delhi High Court Mediation and Reconciliation Centre; Consultant International Psychoanalytic Association Committee of Law and Psychoanalysis; and member of the Indian Association of Family Therapy.

Sverre Varvin, MD, DPhil, is a training and supervising analyst of the Norwegian Psychoanalytic Society. He is a professor at Oslo Metropolitan University. He has been working clinically and with research on traumatization and the treatment of traumatized patients, especially in the refugee field. He has done process and outcome research on psychoanalytic therapy, research on traumatic dreams, and on psychoanalytic training. He has twice been president of the Norwegian Psychoanalytic Society and he has held several positions in IPA, among others as vice-president and board member and chair of the IPA working group on terror and terrorism. He is presently chair of IPA China Committee. He has published articles and books on traumatization, refugees, terrorism, and on research on treatment process and outcome.

Luísa Branco Vicente, MD, is a specialist in Psychiatry and in Paedopsychiatry. She holds a doctorate in Psychiatry and Mental Health on the thematic "Depression in Child" (2000), from Faculdade de Medicina de Lisboa. She is a full member of IPA and didactic member of Teaching Commission of Portuguese Psychoanalytic, psychoanalyst of Children and Adolescents (FEP), president of the Teaching Commission and the Ethics Commission of the Portuguese Society of Psychoanalytical Group Psychodrama, chairman of the General Meeting of Portuguese Society of Psychosomatic, teacher of Faculdade de Medicina de Lisboa and investigator and coordinator in the areas of Medicine and Mental Health in Investigation Projects.

Estela V. Welldon is a psychoanalytical psychotherapist who worked for three decades at the Tavistock Portman Clinics NHS Trust. Presently she works in private practice and lectures worldwide. She is the author of: *Mother, Madonna, Whore: The Idealization and Denigration of Motherhood* (1988), which has been translated into 13 languages; *Sadomasochism* (2002); and *Playing with Dynamite: A Personal Approach to the Understanding of Perversions, Violence and Criminality* (2011). She is the main editor of *A Practical Guide to Forensic Psychotherapy* (1997); *Sex Now, Talk Later* (Karnac, 2016); and *Sadomasochism in Arts and Politics*. In 1997 she was awarded by Oxford Brookes University a DSc Honorary Doctorate of Science and in 2014 she was made an honorary member of the American Psychoanalytic Association for her work in helping to understand women who harm children. She has been the Visiting International Professor at Universidad Católica Lima Peru since June 2018, and she is also the director of the first Russian (Moscow) course on Forensic Psychotherapy, which has started in March 2019.

Acknowledgments

This project emerged from discussions in Buenos Aires during the IPA Congress in 2017. There at a meeting of the Psychoanalysis and the Law, chaired by Plinio Montagna, so many complex and exciting projects were discussed. This book is an outcome of that meeting and the inspiration generated by its attendees.

We would like to thank the IPA, through the Board, the President Virginia Ungar, the Vice President Sergio Nick and the Treasurer Andrew Brook for their support of this project. This support was both in encouragement and in funding, allowing us to develop and edit a series of papers that survey an international collection of legal/psychoanalytic problems.

We thank Lily Swistel and Charlotte Gartenberg, who did such careful deep editorial and translation work.

We are as always grateful to the Taylor and Francis Group who, in the midst of new and much enlarged responsibilities for publications and production, so carefully shepherded this project. Our thanks to Kate Hawes and Charles Bath in particular.

Adrienne thanks her colleagues on the Relational Perspectives Book Series – the late Lewis Aron, Steven Kuchuck, and Eyal Rozmarin – for their unfailing support and encouragement.

Plinio is grateful to two former Presidents of the IPA: Stefano Bolognini for endorsing the idea and creating the Committee of Psychoanalysis and Law of the International Psychoanalytical Association, and to Charles Hanly for his Outreach support in the IPA. He thanks also Lucas Weber Abramo for helping in the initial part of the work.

Introduction

Plinio Montagna and Adrienne Harris

To establish relations and work on the bridges between potentially allied fields is an unequivocal necessity of our time. Connections between psychoanalysis and law are required not only for conceptual or theoretical needs, but also for the vast range of practical implications and possibilities their association enables. This seems particularly true in this historic moment when so many aspects of human subjectivity – migration, exile, prejudices (racism, homophobia, misogyny, anti-semitism) – are proving so challenging to dissolve or transcend.

In this volume, we asked our authors to write on a problem of their choosing, within their particular, local situation. We think that has made it possible to go very deep but, at the same time, to offer useful ideas and concepts to many other allied but distinct situations. It was a decision to be deep and local in order to offer material and examples that those of us in many different circumstances can incorporate and tailor to our own circumstances.

The linkage between these two fields, psychoanalysis and the law, allow us to situate some complex contemporary questions in the context of a particular society, taking notice what aspects of a certain question may be common to most human contemporary organizations.

No one can live in a group in which law is not established. These are explicit principles that guide action and reaction. It is also clearly important that every individual life in a group and the group itself is influenced and affected by conscious and unconscious phenomena. This is the province and the particular contribution of psychoanalysis.

At the same time as we can grasp the scope of professional activities opened by the collaboration between these areas together, we will find these modes of thought and practice sometimes in synchrony and sometimes in conflict. The subject of the law and of the clinic are and are not identical. Here they are in conversation, often heated, always curious and engaged.

We live in a world where the spectrum of procedures in law is rather wide. What we might call the *judicialization* of life is present, possibly everywhere, and the influence of psychological and specifically psychoanalytical ways of seeing the human phenomena is also possibly ubiquitous.

To be aware of psychoanalytic thought may be influential to some parameters of legal studies and practices, as chapters of this book demonstrate. This happens not only by dismantling the rationality of behaviors, or bringing to the fore human drives and phantasies. Mainly, in the arena of practice, the valuable force of psychoanalysis is visible through assisting the understanding of meanings and interpreting apparently obscure motives in legal operations. This involves every side of a juridical process, encompassing also the lawmakers and the law representatives.

By the same token, to be acquainted with major or minor jurisprudences may contextualize psychoanalytical observations so that they may effectively contribute to broad interdisciplinary discussions of many different social and political themes in the contemporary world.

The linkage between the two fields is not new, it stems from the beginning of psychoanalytical development. In 1906 Freud published "Psycho-Analysis and the Establishment of Facts in Legal Procedures," where he draws an analogy between the criminal and the hysteric, as both are concerned with a secret, having something hidden. He emphasizes a common task for therapists and legal agents, which is to uncover the hidden psychical material.

His study of "The Schreber Case and Psychopathic Characters on the Stage," for example, is also relevant for juridical matters, and his papers assessing culture – such as "Totem and Taboo," "Moses and Monotheism," "Group Psychology and Analysis of the Ego," and "Civilization and its Discontents" – have relevant contributions to thinking human law and the individual.

We can say that repression is at the core of the installation of law. Its development goes around areas of repression, denial, prohibition, and interdiction.

At the same time the influential Austrian jurist and philosopher Hans Kelsen, who later emigrated to the USA and taught at the University of California, attended the meetings of Freud's group in Vienna and presented his text "State Concept and Social Psychology based on Totem and Taboo and Mass Psychology and Ego Analysis." His major work, *General Theory of Norms*, approximates psychoanalysis and law. Through investigating the origin of laws he proposes a "regressum infinitum," where each norm is determined by a higher one, until arriving at a fictional origin as the beginning, as the first law. This fictional origin was proposed by Freud in "Totem and Taboo."

A key element, both for psychoanalysis and for law, is the question of conflict. In psychoanalysis the conflict begins with Freud as intrapsychic, later extending to the interpsychic and intersubjective. Similarly, law is fundamentally related to conflicts between individuals, between groups or between individuals, groups, and the state.

Psychoanalysis shows that conflict can be manifest, that is, as it is shown in patient complaints, in people around them, or in the symptom itself and may be unconscious. This can be revealed by psychoanalytic work.

In its application in the area of law, one of the resources that psychoanalysis can offer will also be the clarification of the unconscious implicated in the conflicts at issue in a judicial dispute, or else in an act that will result in the need for judicial intervention.

The dynamics of interactions involving conflict implies the existence of opposition. Many times the particular good of each individual and the universal good are in opposition and have to be overcome, through law, by the advance in social organization.

If this topic has its powerful beginnings in the earliest conversations in psychoanalysis, it is also true that each era stirs up its own new sites of conversion, conversation, and conflict. This volume is divided into four parts, each addressing a unique site of the interaction of legal and psychoanalytic work. We begin with matters that are of global significance even as they are local. There is the challenge of caring for and aiding migrants, refugees, families, and individuals. There is the question of planetary survival, of the mistreatment and violence in military and secular conflict, and in the projects and processes of international governance.

The middle two parts focus on the very wide-ranging problems of social violence as these target women and people of diversity, on the one hand, and, on the other hand, the penetration of law into the most intimate aspects of family life – adoption, divorce, child custody, and complex parental arrangements. Here the law and psychoanalysis engage the most private and surely often unconscious forces in intimate life. These realms are more comfortably familiar for psychoanalysis and psychoanalysts. So here we see the potential advantage in the engagement of two disciplines in conversation. These kinds of interfaces between disciplines are accustomed to, on the one hand, intimacy and deeply private often unconscious realms (psychoanalysis), and, on the other hand, the most principled rational procedures designed to protect and adjudicate often in sites riddled with anguish and emotion. Here one feels the two disciplines need the engagement and must also find areas of difference and conflict.

In the last part of the volume, we look from the perspective of this double vision (legal and psychoanalytic) at basic processes in social and legal life. What is the role of forensics, of witnessing, of adjudicating subjectivity and citizenship in the life of communities and in our increasingly interrelated international community?

This book has been an unusual pleasure and privilege to work on. We hope that the reader experiences the pleasure and range of ideas in this volume and is inspired by the work that is reported and described in these chapters. Welcome to the work of an international group of psychoanalysts, thinking and working across many local situations. We note the range of topics relevant to thinking about psychoanalysis and the law, from the global to the local, the fate of large groups, and of endangered individuals

Questions related to global challenges

Introduction

Plinio Montagna and Adrienne Harris

In this part of the book we consider the legal *and* psychoanalytic elements in problems that are global in scale and importance, even as they also occupy local and specific experiences. We have found in putting together this collection of chapters, and their very different and also compatible authors, that sometimes we have to be very local in order to understand the intricacy of the situation, the general problem and the particular circumstances in which the psychoanalytic and the legal co-create and co-determine.

Nonetheless, in this part, we consider work which is relevant in so many parts of the world and must be seen as global problems, even as they are also local. We begin with two chapters on work with refugees. Both Sverre Varvin's work and Cândida Sé Holovko and Gertraud Schlesinger-Kipp's focus is deep and specific but the question of human rights violations, refugee protection, and support arises more and more, effecting both the Third World and the First World and engaging us in discussions which we must say we feel will only deepen and intensify over time. Varvin writes of the depth of anguish and pain for clinician and patient that arises in work with traumatized people, in and separated from their families as they face exile and extensive danger and isolation. How to work with individuals – and families – where the center of the world has fallen away, where vulnerability can appear endless. Varvin, importantly, reminds us that human rights are not simply abstract principles but codes of law and practice; these rights are anchored in legal activities and guarantees, which, of course, can be vulnerable, even as they are the legal centerpieces of the psychological work of care and support.

Sé Holovko and Schlesinger-Kipp add subtle clinical dimensions to the presentation of psychoanalytic psychodynamic work with people in states of exile and massive loss. Their work and the pain which they so powerfully represent remind us that the work is traumatic for the analyst/therapist and we need to consider how we take care of each other. Their presentation also demonstrates how fragile even the structures of help are, how vulnerable the psychological work is, even as in many sectors of the clinical situation psychological support is in place. It is manifest but it is vulnerable. People are too easily lost, even in a care-giving system.

Elizabeth Allured turns our attention to a problem that is inherently global and local: climate change and the demands, made on every one of us, to face the emotional and psychological implications of the threat to life that climate change constitutes. Here psychoanalysis is an essential tool, enabling us to notice the terror, the disabling denial and pervasive disavowal that has thus far had profound limits on work for change in our relationship to our environment.

This part, and indeed this volume, is anchored by the chapter Vivian Pender writes on the role of psychoanalysis institutionally and interactively in the United Nations (UN). Virtually every one of these chapters in this volume brings up an issue or a practice of a conflict (or all of the above) which can be imagined and explored by looking at the formal relationship between psychoanalysis and international legally constituted institutions. The International Psychoanalytical Association (IPA) is, as Pender notes, a non-governmental organization (NGO) to the UN, and she has played a consultative leadership role in this relationship. Its charge is to bring mental health issues and solutions to the UN and bring the work of the UN to our international psychoanalytic community.

The final chapter in this part, written by Ghislaine Boulanger, gives, as do many chapters in this volume, an analysis of the potential value of linking the legal and the psychological and the psychoanalytic, with a local, quite specific and, in this case, American situation. The discussions in America about the presence and utilization of torture and of the role of the psychologist expert in these practices has been shocking both professionally and among many of our citizens. But a collective commitment to conventions of war-making and conflict is not really solid and this chapter sounds a warning as it describes a political struggle waged in the profession and among all Americans.

Chapter 1

Psychoanalysis and the situation of refugees

A human rights perspective

Sverre Varvin

Introduction

Millions of people today experience human rights violations (HRV) worldwide. Many groups live under conditions that make them vulnerable and being exposed to HRV under such conditions can have devastating consequences. Those affected are people exposed to trafficking, violence in close relations (mostly women), abused and neglected children, victims of paramilitary groups and terrorist groups, violent religious groups, state-organized violence, those impacted by civil wars, and so forth. Many are forced to flee.

At the beginning of 2018, 68,5 million people are displaced worldwide due to conflict and persecution (this includes refugees and internally displaced people or IDPs). Of these, 28,5 million are refugees. There are 10 million stateless people who have been denied a nationality and access to basic rights such as education, healthcare, employment, and freedom of movement.

The magnitude of the problem is staggering. Approximately 44,400 were displaced every day in 2017 (UNHCR, 2018). One out of every 133 people in the world was displaced in 2017. Over the past five years, 50 families in Syria have been displaced daily and we have seen unimaginable suffering due to indiscriminate attacks on civilians. More than half of refugees and displaced persons are children. The suffering due to war and persecution today is enormous and we can expect serious consequences of massive traumatization in the years ahead, especially for coming generations.

For refugees, flight has become increasingly dangerous and death tolls are rising (UNHCR, 2016). Women are raped and abducted for prostitution; many are killed or die, for example at sea; children are violated and forced into the sex industry or slavery (there is increasing evidence that human trafficking networks cooperate with organized crime (Europol, 2016)) and many are maltreated and/or tortured by police, border guards, or organized crime during flight. One study from Serbia testifies to this sad situation: 220 refugees were examined and it appeared that torture and degrading treatments were more frequent during flight than in their country of origin (Jovanović, Trivunčić, & Đurašinović, 2015).

Conditions for refugees upon arrival are growing worse. Stranded in the refugee camps of Greece, Italy, Serbia, Bangladesh, and on islands outside Australia, thousands must survive with little or no access to healthcare, poor sanitation, insufficient food, and minimal human concern. In refugee camps near war zones, conditions have worsened since 2015 when UNHCR budgets were cut by more than half (Clayton, 2015). It is not unusual that there are political crises that involve frequent and cruel atrocities that seldom make headlines. There are several happening now, including the situation in Kongo, Yemen, and South Sudan, among others. Millions are displaced and humanitarian aid is insufficient.

Many refugees or asylum seekers describe their conditions *after arrival*, even in more affluent countries, as the worst part of their refugee journey. On a daily basis, they face long wait times, bureaucratic red tape, inactivity, and the possibility of being forced to return to their homelands. This is described by many as mental torture. There are reports that the mental and physical health of refugees today is deteriorating (Hassan, Ventevogel, Jefee-Bahloul, Barkil-Oteo, & Kirmayer, 2016), not only due to traumatization in their home countries but very much as a result of the conditions during flight (violence, torture, rape, slavery, and so forth) and due to the conditions offered refugees in centres at the border of Europe (Greece, Italy) and outside, for example in Libya.

It has repeatedly been shown that refugees as a group have endured many potentially traumatizing experiences before and during flight such as near-death experiences, seeing close ones maltreated or killed, tortured, raped, and so forth. These experiences represent gross human rights violations. Most research finds higher-than-average levels of known post-traumatic conditions in refugee populations, like PTSD, anxiety disorders, forms of depression, somatizing disorders, and psychotic disorders (see for example Alemi, James, Cruz, Zepeda, & Racadio, 2013; Apitzsch et al., 1996; Drozdek, Kamperman, Tol, Knipscheer, & Kleber, 2013; Kroll, Yusuf, & Fujiwara, 2011; Opaas & Varvin, 2015a, 2015b; Teodorescu, Heir, Hauff, Wentzel-Larsen, & Lien, 2012; Vaage et al., 2010; Vervliet, Lammertyn, Broekaert, & Derluyn, 2013). The complex traumatizing experiences of refugees may disturb personality functions, relational functions, affect regulation and somatic regulation (Allen & Fonagy, 2015; Allen, Vaage, & Hauff, 2006; Rosenbaum & Varvin, 2007; Schore, 2003; Varvin & Rosenbaum, 2011).

Those who develop mental health problems in exile often suffer from complex conditions with multi-layered aetiology, involving the circumstances of their exile and the aggravating factors accompanying displacement, which include poverty, poor housing, lack of social support, stressful acculturation processes, resulting in poor quality of life. Whole families may be affected and there are specific contingencies that make the transgenerational transmission of suffering more likely, for example, insufficient early care and traumatization of children and stressful family situations (Blanck-Cereijido & Grynberg Robinson, 2010; Daud, Skoglund, & Rydelius, 2005; de Mendelssohn, 2008; Krell, Suedfeld, & Soriano, 2011; Romer, 2012; Ruf-Leuschner, Roth, & Schauer, 2014; Silke & Möller, 2012; van Ee, Kleber, & Mooren, 2012; Wiegand-Grefe & Möller, 2012).

The consequences for refugees in the present situation are, in spite of a high degree of resilience, potentially very serious both for present and coming generations. It is important to understand and analyze the refugee crisis from a psychiatric, psychological and medical perspective, but also to see the situation as a consequence of serious violations of basic human rights. What many refugees and displaced persons have experienced and are experiencing would not happen if human rights, as formulated in internationally accepted conventions, are respected. The psychological matters at issue are moreover a consequence of the fact of the most basic rights having been violated in the first place. The psyche that has experienced these violations is one that is marked by disruptions in basic systems of attachment, basic trust, narcissistic imbalances, and major blows to conscious and unconscious dreams of future development. Understanding the ramifications of the violations of the patients in our consulting rooms is of paramount importance.

We must not think only in terms of mental health problems or diagnostic categories (e.g. PTSD), which of course may be useful; we need to consider the special circumstances of human rights violations.

Human rights matter

Violations represent grave problems for public health and also disturb the democratic foundations of a society. Healthcare systems in western countries have been affected in that a growing number of healthcare seekers have been exposed to HRV. Furthermore, healthcare workers have participated and still are participating in HRV in, for example, prisons.

In this chapter I will discuss a human rights perspective on mental health problems caused by HRV and how attacks on the fundamental right to be a human affect psychological functioning. I will first shortly present the international system of conventions that attempts to regulate and prohibit the violation of basic human rights.

What are human rights?

Every human being's uniqueness is what entitles them to ethical treatment and human rights. Human rights are situated on three pillars: ethics and moral principles, laws/conventions and declarations on human rights, and basic philosophical principles related to being human. Emphasizing the uniqueness of every human being has important implications; it opposes conceptions of human beings that would have them treated as a mass, or some groups as inferior or superior to others. There is a philosophical conception of man that informs human rights thinking, and creates ethical and moral imperatives. The conventions, laws, and declarations concerning human rights are built on these principles. Fundamental values are involved: the right to life, the integrity of the body, personal freedom, safety, the right to have property, the right to have a family and a private life, freedom of thought, freedom of belief, freedom of speech, the right to have work, and the right to health and welfare.

Human rights are thus moral principles or norms that describe certain standards for human life and are regularly protected as natural and legal rights in national and international law. There are several definitions of human rights and all concern rights to which a person is entitled simply because she or he is a human being. One broad definition may be that human rights are inalienable rights and freedoms; their protection secures all human beings' inherent dignity and lays the ground for freedom and justice (Stang & Sveaas, 2016).

They are applicable everywhere and at every time in the sense of being universal, and they are egalitarian in the sense of being the same for everyone.

The basis for modern human rights is the universal declaration formulated after the Second World War (UN, 1948).

Several conventions followed that specify these rights. Among others, these are:

International Covenant on Civil and Political Rights (1976)

This convention concerns "negative" rights in that these rights are not dependent on resources. These rights shall apply no matter the resources or circumstances. They concern a state's duty for example to provide freedom of speech, freedom of movement, freedom of religion, and proscribe torture. State adherence to the protection of these rights is supervised by the UN's committee on human rights.

International Covenant on Economic, Social and Cultural Rights (1976)

This convention concerns "positive" rights, that is, rights that require resources, for example, the right to work, pensions, a reasonable living standard. The convention recognizes the possible lack of resources, but there is a mandate to initiate measures and procedures to achieve these goals.

Convention Relating to the Status of Refugees (1951) with additional protocol 1967

This convention defines who has a right to be granted residence as a refugee in another country. It specifies the duties of countries when receiving refugees. It does not, however, mention the right to seek and admit persons' asylum. The Universal declaration from 1948, paragraph 14, says, however, that anybody has the right to seek asylum and accept asylum due to persecution.

There are several other conventions of concern for health workers, e.g. International Convention on the Elimination of All Forms of Racial Discrimination of 21 December 1965 (ICERD), Convention on the Elimination of All Forms of Discrimination against Women of 18 December 1979, Convention on the Rights of the Child of 20 November 1989 (CRC) (for further reference see www.eda.admin. ch/eda/en/home/foreign-policy/international-law/un-human-rights-treaties.html)

In the context of this article the Convention against Torture and Other Cruel, Inhuman or Degrading Treatment or Punishment from 1984 is of importance (UN, 1984).

This convention concerns protection against torture, the right to remedy and to justice, the right to reparation, compensation and in particular the right to rehabilitation. I will return to the question of torture. (It should be mentioned that other conventions also treat torture as a special case, e.g. the American Convention on Human Rights, the European Convention for the Prevention of Torture, the African Charter on Human and Peoples' Rights, The Convention for the Protection of Human Rights and Fundamental Freedoms).

These conventions/declarations and their underlying ethical principles function as guidelines for, among others, health workers in situations of conflict and who are under pressure, or in situations of dual loyalties (for example for health workers working in prisons) (Baldwin-Ragaven et al., 2002).

Why are human rights important for health workers?

Human rights are a concern for health workers for the following reasons: a) everyone's, including health workers' and patients', basic rights and dignity are dependent on human rights; b) health policies/programmes and all interventions can support or violate basic human rights; c) violations of human rights may have serious health consequences; d) endorsement of human rights promotes public health; and e) preventing health workers from participating in human rights violations is very important.

The last has been documented in recent history through the involvement of doctors in the Nazi genocide and euthanasia programs (Lifton, 2004), and the American Psychological Association's involvement in torture (Patel & Eikin, 2015). In the latter case, the torture and dehumanization of people supposedly connected with Al Qaeda and other terrorist groups were human rights violations sanctioned by state authorities. Health personnel failed to hinder or report torture, gave medical information to torturers, and even forged death certificates.

Dehumanization

Needless to say (but a reminder is important nevertheless), torture implies great health risk for the affected, for their families and larger communities, and for the foundation of society. Torture is the most dehumanizing treatment that is known. It often occurs in the context of other dehumanizing practices in political situations such as persecution, ethnic cleansing, and genocide. Today's refugees are especially exposed both in their country of origin and during flight.

Dehumanization is a process that is simultaneously socio-political and psychological; fundamental human characteristics are disavowed in other people, such that others are perceived as less than human or non-human. Consequently, actions resulting from dehumanization can threaten the basic rights of these "others" and endanger their lives and safety.

Dehumanization on a societal scale often goes hand-in-hand with xenophobia and lays the ground for malicious violations of basic human rights. This was the case in the genocides during the Balkan wars in the 1990s, during the genocide in Rwanda, during the genocide against Yazidis, to mention a few – and strong xenophobic political movements in the western world have, in the last decades, led to increasingly malignant behavior towards refugees/asylum seekers and ethnic minorities.

When xenophobia becomes part of a political or religious narrative and is used to foster intergroup conflict, unconscious processes, both at individual and group levels, are set in motion. These unconscious motivational forces are organized at primitive mental levels (i.e. undifferentiated and not well-structured) and involve fantasies that may be shared by many people in a group or community. Such fantasies are often related to common life themes such as sibling rivalry, the struggle between good and evil, or separation-individuation (Bohleber, 2007, 2010), but they are magnified in the xenophobic context where libidinal aspects are separated or split from aggression. Relationships and social fields usually characterized by mutuality are transformed into fields of projections where the other is cast in the role of the projected, unwanted parts of the self or of the group-self. As the other is perceived as "not human," not like "us," then inhumane and violent behavior may be justified (Varvin, 2017) as a fight/flight response (Bion, 1952).

There is thus a complex societal process that leads to atrocities (e.g. torture). The ground is prepared for the ignoring and more or less consciously violation of basic human rights as specified in human rights conventions. Dehumanizing processes deprive persons or groups of their political status and ultimately of their humanity. A man becomes only a man, that is, not a citizen protected by a state/nation. This "naked" status implies a loss of those characteristics that makes it possible for others to treat this person as a fellow human being (Mitmensch) (Arendt, 2017). Studies on processes leading to genocides demonstrate this with horrifying clarity (Crowe, 2013; Varvin, 1995; Yazda, 2017).

Torture

Torture may be defined as any act by which severe pain or suffering, whether physical or mental, is intentionally inflicted on a person for such purposes as obtaining from him or a third person information or a confession, punishing him for an act he or a third person has committed or is suspected of having committed.

The four Geneva Conventions on the law of war establish firm rules. The common Article 3 states:

the following acts are and shall remain prohibited at anytime and in any place whatsoever … violence to life and person, in particular murder of all kinds, mutilation, cruel treatment and torture; …

outrages upon personal dignity, in particular humiliating and degrading.

(ICRC, 1949)

The prohibition of torture or other ill-treatment could hardly be formulated in more absolute terms. In the words of the official commentary on the text by the International Committee of the Red Cross (ICRC), "no possible loophole is left; there can be no excuse, no extenuating circumstances" (ICRC, 1949).

In spite of this absolute "no," torture is practiced in more than half of the world's countries. There are undoubtedly countless people who are impacted by torture living in the world today, its direct victims and their communities. We don't know how many have been killed during torture.

Torture happens in what Lifton calls an ""atrocity-producing situation" – these are situations "so structured, psychologically and militarily, that ordinary people can readily engage in atrocities." And concerning doctors' participation, he states: "Even without directly participating in the abuse, doctors may have become socialized to an environment of torture and by virtue of their medical authority helped sustain it. In studying various forms of medical abuse, I have found that the participation of doctors can confer an aura of legitimacy and can even create an illusion of therapy and healing" (Lifton, 2004).

Article 14 in The Convention against Torture and Other Cruel, Inhuman or Degrading Treatment or Punishment states that: "Each state party shall ensure in its legal system that the victims of an act of torture obtains redress and has an enforceable right to fair and adequate compensation including the means for as full rehabilitation as possible."

There are a number of definitions of rehabilitation and of what is understood by services that aim at rehabilitation. The recently adopted General Comment number 3 to article 14 of the Convention Against Torture argues that rehabilitation "should be holistic and include medical and psychological care as well as legal and social services." Furthermore, rehabilitation "refers to the restoration of function or the acquisition of new skills required as a result of the changed circumstances of a victim in the aftermath of torture or ill-treatment.

It seeks to enable the maximum possible self-sufficiency and function for the individual concerned and may involve adjustments to the person's physical and social environment. Rehabilitation for victims should aim to restore, as far as possible, their independence, physical, mental, social and vocational ability; and full inclusion and participation in society" (UNCAT, 2012) (cited in Sveaass, 2013).

This is a strong statement, which implies that all who have been tortured should have the right to redress and rehabilitation wherever they are. By virtue of signing the convention, states are required to provide help and rehabilitation to the victims of torture residing within their borders.

Psychological effects of HRV and torture: what role can psychoanalysts have?

Being exposed to gross human rights violations, especially torture, affects basic systems of security, exposes the self to humiliation and shaming and sets forth a cascade of anxiety-provoking fantasies. More seriously, it gives the person a feeling of being outside of and not part of the human community. As Jean Amery wrote:

> I am certain that with the very first blow that descends on him he loses something we will ... call 'trust in the world'. Trust in the world includes ... the certainty that by reason of ... social contracts the other person will ... respect my physical ... being. The boundaries of my body are also the boundaries of my self. My skin surface shields me against the external world. If I am to have trust, I must feel on it only what I want to feel. At the first blow, however, this trust in the world breaks down. He is on me and thereby destroys me ... with the first blow ... a part of our life ends and it can never again be revived. ... Whoever was tortured, stays tortured. Torture is ineradicably burned into him.
>
> (Amery, 1998)

A patient came cautiously into the consulting room. He looked under the sofa, behind pictures and whispered, "He (the dictator) killed all my family". He was shivering, could hardly breathe properly and looked around with wide open eyes. I gave him tea. I asked about his daily and nightly life. Hesitatingly, stammering, he said he could hardly sleep, did not eat much and actually had no own place to live and had to be taken care of by friends. He was terrified all the time. Did not feel safe anywhere. I asked about what food he was eating, which he could not remember. When I asked what kind of food his mother had made for him and he started to remember, he started to cry and could relax a bit.

(Therapy session with author)

This man felt totally lost. He felt almost no safe anchoring in his internal world and the external reality was totally unsafe. He lost his familiarity of being a human being among other human beings and felt totally alienated. His way of being in the world is typical of persons who have survived gross human rights violations. It is a psychological situation reinforced by being in exile and, for many, by not having a proper legal status as a citizen. The next vignette concerns the situation of flight – and for the many who must live for years in bad refugee camps and wait for their asylum applications to be evaluated.

A father, stranded in Nauru outside Australia, wrote the following letter to United Nations Secretary-General Ban-Ki-Moon and Peter Thomson, president of the United Nations Summit on Refugees, held in New York on September 19, 2016:

We simply trusted what they told us. Yet over three years later we are still trapped in Nauru, like rare animals living in an Australian-made zoo.

After being brought to Nauru we spent almost 24 months in detention, before we were finally found to be genuine refugees. Since then I have not slept even one night without having recurring nightmares of those endless months living in a hot, mouldy tent. We became so alienated from our humanity, we were thoroughly transformed into a bunch of animals after years of living in the most appalling conditions possible.

(Herald, 2016)

These stories, of which there are many, illustrate the profound effect of being placed outside the common humanity. As Hanna Arendt described in her writing after the Second World War, people who are so mistreated, and deprived of basic rights, are subject to further dehumanizing treatment, as they are seen as less than human.

Miss A came to Norway as a refugee after having been arrested and spending time in prisons and concentration camps due to participation in a peaceful political movement in her home country. She had a daughter of 10 years. She lived in isolation, had few friends but managed to work part time. She suffered from posttraumatic problems with bad sleep, nightmares, anxiety of bodily pains. She had attempted treatment several times but they came to abrupt endings mostly because she felt humiliated and disrespected. She avoided close relationships, especially with men as she feared being treated with no respect and – as she later said – that it would be revealed that there was something fundamentally wrong with her.

The last was a pronounced fear in therapy. She felt she had to defend herself against a therapist whom she imagined could be dangerous. She resisted involving herself in the therapy, as she feared that during the process it would irrefutably be proven that she had been damaged for life. As she said: "That I cannot ever be a normal human being". It was revealed that that was what the torture team had repeatedly told her.

Her distrust and defensive attitude was present from the beginning of the therapy. She gradually became more depressed and expressed that hope for improvement was diminishing. During a period with suicidal ideation and intense distrust in the transference where the patient literally felt tortured by the therapist, it was revealed that there had been a medical doctor participating in the torture. She had been given medication to make her reveal secrets and the doctor had "supervised" how much torture she could stand. She realized soon after how much of her distrust had arisen from what she called "mixing up" present with past. This was a breakthrough in the therapy. A long working through followed where earlier determinants of her distrust, especially related to a difficult relation to her father was explored. It was also obvious that, in a work of nachträglich, her relation to father had been colored by the experiences with the male torturers.

(Varvin, 2003)

Conclusion

There is tremendous work to be done to improve the conditions of refugees, especially for seriously traumatized refugees – to provide proper re-humanizing conditions. The whole refugee system has to be revised internationally. The situation in most countries is geared towards keeping refugees out. Disproportionately more money is used in Europe on surveillance and border control in order to keep refugees out, than on providing good enough conditions and measures that would prevent trauma and retraumatization. Governments have for decades to a large degree failed to make refugees' flight safe and increasingly paved the ground for human smugglers profiting from organizing refugees' increasingly dangerous journeys. The conditions of refugee camps are appalling.

In this context some psychoanalysts have done important work on a larger scale (Volkan, 1999) and many provide psychological help for refugees both during flight and upon arrival (Lebiger-Vogel et al., 2015; Leuzinger-Bohleber, Rickmeyer, Tahiri, & Hettich, 2016). Psychoanalytic therapy is also provided in many places and there are prominent psychoanalysts that have developed good strategies for the treatment of severely traumatized persons (Henry Krystal, Dori Laub, and Sylvia Amati Sas, among others (Krystal, 1978; Laub, 2005; Sas, 1992)). Psychoanalytic therapy is not, however, offered to the extent that is necessary, especially as psychoanalytic psychotherapy is a very promising tool for what article 14 in the Convention on torture demands: redress and rehabilitation.

The humanizing potential of psychoanalysis is key to this crisis. There is increasing evidence that psychoanalytic therapies are effective for traumatized persons in comprehensive ways; they may help address crucial areas in the clinical presentation of complex traumatization (complex PTSD) that are not targeted by other currently empirically supported treatments. Psychoanalytic therapy has a historical perspective and works with problems related to the self and self-image.

It enhances the ability to modulate reactions to trauma through improved reflective functioning, and aims at internalization of more secure inner-working models of relationships. Our work utilizes the human therapeutic relationship to improve social functioning. Finally, and this is increasingly substantiated in several studies, psychodynamic psychotherapy for traumatized patients tends to result in continued improvement after treatment ends (Schottenbauer, Glass, Arnkoff, & Gray, 2008).

Psychoanalysis, psychoanalytic therapies, and psychoanalytically informed interventions in refugee camps have a broad and basically humanistic character in the sense of re-humanizing the individual, by facilitating the process of connection to others and by helping to re-establish basic human bonds. Dori Laub showed that a grave consequence of extreme traumatization is a breach in the bond to an empathic inner other (Laub, 1998, 2005). This special object relation is the basis for the experience of being connected to others – and for being and feeling like a human. This meaning is embedded in international declarations that concern human rights. Basic human rights, which include safety, the right to family, home, and protection, are integral to membership in the human community. These basic rights are givens, but not stable – they have to be fought for continuously in different arenas. Psychoanalysts have, in this fight, their specific tasks and obligations.

References

Alemi, Q., James, S., Cruz, R., Zepeda, V., & Racadio, M. (2013). Psychological distress in Afghan refugees: A mixed-method systematic review. *J Immigr Minor Health, 16*, 1247–1261. doi:10.1007/s10903-013-9861-1

Allen, J., & Fonagy, P. (2015). Trauma. In P. Luyten, L. Mayes, P. Fonagy, M. Target, & S. Blatt (Eds.), *Handbook of Psychodynamic Approaches to Psychopathology* (pp. 165–198). New York, London: Guilford Press.

Allen, J., Vaage, A.B., & Hauff, E. (2006). Refugees and asylum seekers in societies. In D.L. Sam & J.W. Berry (Eds.), *The Cambridge Handbook of Acculturation Psychology*. Cambridge: Cambridge University Press.

Amery, J. (1998). *At the Mind's Limits: Contemplations by a Survivor on Auschwitz and its Realities*. Bloomington, IN: Indiana University Press.

Apitzsch, H., Eriksson, N.G., Jakobsson, S.W., Lindgren, L., Lundin, T., Movschenson, P., … Sundqvist, G. (1996). A study of post-traumatic stress reactions among war refugees based on medical records. A standard model may support the treatment. [Swedish]. *93*(47), 4285–4288.

Arendt, H. (2017). *The Lawless and the Humble*. Copenhagen: Information forlag.

Baldwin-Ragaven, L., Bloche, M., Bryant, J., London, L., Orr, W., & Rubenstein, L. (2002). *Dual Loyalty & Human Rights in Health Professional Practice*. Boston, MA: Physicians for Human Rights; Cape Town, South Africa: Health Sciences Faculty, University of Cape Town.

Bion, W. (1952). Group dynamics: A review. *International Journal of Psycho-Analysis, 33*, 235–247.

Blanck-Cereijido, F., & Grynberg Robinson, M. (2010). Prejudice, transgenerational transmission, and neutrality. *The International Journal of Psychoanalysis, 91*(5), 1216–1219. doi:10.1111/j.1745-8315.2010.00293.x

Bohleber, W. (2007). Remembrance, trauma and collective memory. The battle for memory in psychoanalysis. *Int. J of Psychoanal, 88*, 329–352.

——— (2010). *Destructiveness, intersubjectivity and trauma*. London: Karnac.

Clayton, J. (2015). Funding shortage leaves Syrian refugees in danger of missing vital support. Series editor: L. Dobbs. Publisher: UNHCR. www.unhcr.org/news/latest/2015/6/558acbbc6/funding-shortage-leaves-syrian-refugees-danger-missing-vital-support.html (last accessed May 3, 2017).

Crowe, D.M. (2013). *War Crimes, Genocide, and Justice: A Global History. Palgrave Macmillan*. London: Palgrave Macmillan.

Daud, A., Skoglund, E., & Rydelius, P.A. (2005). Children in families of torture victims: Transgenerational transmission of parents' traumatic experiences to their children. *International Journal of Social Welfare, 14*(1), 23–32.

de Mendelssohn, F. (2008). Transgenerational transmission of trauma: Guilt, shame, and the "Heroic Dilemma." *International Journal of Group Psychotherapy, 58*(3), 389–401. doi:10.1521/ijgp.2008.58.3.389

Drozdek, B., Kamperman, A.M., Tol, W.A., Knipscheer, J.W., & Kleber, R.J. (2013). Seven-year follow-up study of symptoms in asylum seekers and refugees with PTSD treated with trauma-focused groups. *J Clin Psychol*. doi:10.1002/jclp.22035

Europol (2016). *Europol and Interpol issue comprehensive review of migrant smuggling networks*. www.europol.europa.eu/newsroom/news/europol-and-interpol-issue-comprehensive-review-of-migrant-smuggling-networks: Europol.

Hassan, G., Ventevogel, P., Jefee-Bahloul, H., Barkil-Oteo, A., & Kirmayer, L.J. (2016). Mental health and psychosocial wellbeing of Syrians affected by armed conflict. *Epidemiology and Psychiatric Sciences, 25*(2), 129–141.

Herald, S.M. (2016). Think Australia's treatment of refugees and asylum seekers is OK? Read this. An open letter from a refugee on Nauru to the leaders of the UN's Summit for Refugees and Migrants. *Sydney Morning Herald*. www.smh.com.au/comment/think-australias-treatment-of-refugees-and-asylum-seekers-is-ok-read-this-20160919-grjjz20160912.html.

ICRC (International Committee of the Red Cross) (1949). Geneva Conventions. www.icrc.org/eng/war-and-law/treaties-customary-law/geneva-conventions/overview-geneva-conventions.htm (last accessed June 13, 2018).

Jovanović, A., Trivunčić, B., & Đurašinović, V. (2015). The demographic picture, the assessment of the legal status and needs as well as examination the traumatic experiences of refugees who are in transit through Serbia. Retrieved from Belgrade Center for Human Rights and UNHCR:

Krell, R., Suedfeld, P., & Soriano, E. (2011). Child Holocaust survivors as parents: A transgenerational perspective. *American Journal of Orthopsychiatry*, *74*(4), 502–508.

Kroll, J., Yusuf, A., & Fujiwara, K. (2011). Psychoses, PTSD, and depression in Somali refugees in Minnesota. *Soc Psychiatry Psychiatr Epidemiol*, *46*, 481–493. doi:DOI 10.1007/s00127-010-0216-0

Krystal, H. (1978). Trauma and affects. *Psychoanalytic Study of the Child*, *33*, 81–116.

Laub, D. (1998). The empty circle: Children of survivors and the limits of reconstruction. *J Am Psychoanal Assoc*, *46*(2), 507–529.

――― (2005). Traumatic shutdown of narrative and symbolization: A Death Instinct Derivative? *Contemporary Psychoanalysis*, *41*(2), 307–326.

Lebiger-Vogel, J., Rickmeyer, C., Busse, A., Fritzemeyer, K., Rüger, B., & Leuzinger-Bohleber, M. (2015). FIRST STEPS – A randomized controlled trial on the evaluation of the implementation and effectiveness of two early prevention programs for promoting the social integration and a healthy development of children with an immigrant background from 0–3. *BMC Public Health*, *3*, 1–11.

Leuzinger-Bohleber, M., Rickmeyer, C., Tahiri, M., & Hettich, N. (2016). What can psychoanalysis contribute to the current refugee crisis? Preliminary reports from STEP-BY-STEP: A psychoanalytic pilot project for supporting refugees in a "first reception camp" and crisis interventions with traumatized refugees. *Int J of Psychoanal*, *97*(4), 1077–1093.

Lifton, R.J. (2004). Doctors and torture. *New England Journal of Medicine*, *351*(5), 415–416.

Opaas, M., & Varvin, S. (2015a). Relationships of childhood adverse experiences with mental health and quality of life at treatment start for adult refugees traumatized by pre-flight experiences of war and human rights violations. *J of Nerv and Ment Dis*, *203*(9), 684–695. doi:http://dx.doi.org/10.1097/NMD.0000000000000330

———— (2015b). Relationships of childhood adverse experiences with mental health and quality of life at treatment start for adult refugees traumatized by pre-flight experiences of war and human rights violations. *The Journal of Nervous and Mental Disease.* Retrieved from doi:10.1097/ NMD.0000000000000330

Patel, N., & Eikin, D. (2015). Professionalism and conflicting interests: The American Psychological Association's involvement in torture. *AMA Journal of Ethics, 17*(10), 924–930.

Romer, G. (2012). Transgenerational psychotraumatology. *Praxis der Kinderpsychologie und Kinderpsychiatrie, 61*(8), 559–563.

Rosenbaum, B., & Varvin, S. (2007). The influence of extreme traumatisation on body, mind and social relations. *Int J of Psychoanal, 88,* 1527–1542.

Ruf-Leuschner, M., Roth, M., & Schauer, M. (2014). Traumatized mothers – traumatized children? Transgenerational trauma exposure and trauma sequelae in refugee families. *Zeitschrift fur Klinische Psychologie und Psychotherapie: Forschung und Praxis, 43*(1), 1–16. doi:http://dx.doi.org/ 10.1026/1616-3443/a000237

Sas, S.A. (1992). Ambiguity as the route to shame. *73*(2), 329–341.

Schore, A. (2003). *Affect Dysregulation and Disorders of the Self.* New York and London: W.W. Norton & Company.

Schottenbauer, M., Glass, C.R., Arnkoff, D.B., & Gray, S.H. (2008). Contributions of psychodynamic approaches to treatment of PTSD and trauma: A review of the empirical treatment and psychopathology literature. *Psychiatry, 71*(1), 13–34.

Silke, W.-G., & Möller, B. (2012). The transgenerational transmission of traumatic experiences of the Second World War over three generations – A psychoanalytical perspective. *Praxis der Kinderpsychologie und Kinderpsychiatrie, 61*(8), 610–622.

Stang, E., & Sveaas, N. (2016). *Hva skal vi med menneskerettigheter? Betydningen av menneskerettigheter i helse– og sosialfaglig praksis (Why do we need human rigths? The importance of human rigths in health and social work practice.)* Oslo: Gyldendal Akademiske.

Sveaass, N. (2013). Gross human rights violations and reparation under international law: Approaching rehabilitation as a form of reparation. *Eur J Psychotraumatol, 4.* doi:10.3402/ejpt.v4i0.17191

Teodorescu, D., Heir, T., Hauff, E., Wentzel-Larsen, T., & Lien, L. (2012). Mental health problems and post-migration stress among multi-traumatized refugees attending outpatient clinics upon resettlement to Norway. *Scandinavian Journal of Psychology, 53,* 316–332.

UN (1948). The Universal Declaration of Human Rights. United Nations.

———— (1984). Convention against Torture and Other Cruel, Inhuman or Degrading Treatment or Punishment. United Nations.

UNCAT (2012). General comment nr. 3, on article 14 of the Convention against Torture.

UNHCR (2016). *UNHCR 2016. Figures at a glance.* Retrieved from www. unhcr.org/figures-at-a-glance.html.

UNHCR (2018). *Operational Portal. Refugee situation.* Retrieved 16.02.2018, from www.unhcr.org/globaltrends2017/#_ga=2.69151441.1548086208. 1551696018-282628868.1551696018.

Vaage, A.B., Thomsen, P.H., Silove, D., Wentzel-Larsen, T., Van Ta, T., & Hauff, E. (2010). Long-term mental health of Vietnamese refugees in the aftermath of trauma. *British Journal of Psychiatry, 196*, 122–125.

van Ee, E., Kleber, R.J., & Mooren, T.T. (2012). War trauma lingers on: Associations between maternal posttraumatic stress disorder, parent-child interaction, and child development. *Infant Mental Health Journal, 33*(5), 459–468. doi:http://dx.doi.org/10.1002/imhj.21324

Varvin, S. (1995). Genocide and ethnic cleansing: Psychoanalytic and social-psychological viewpoints. *Scandinavian Psychoanalytic Review, 18*(2), 192–210.

———— (2003). *Mental Survival Strategies After Extreme Traumatisation.* Copenhagen: Multivers.

———— (2017). Our relations to refugees: Between compassion and dehumanization. *The American Journal of Psychoanalysis,* 1–19.

Varvin, S., & Rosenbaum, B. (2011). Severely traumatized patients' attempt at reorganizing their relations to others in psychotherapy. In N. Freedman & M. Hurvich (Eds.), *Another Kind of Evidence* (pp. 167–182). London: Karnac.

Vervliet, M., Lammertyn, J., Broekaert, E., & Derluyn, I. (2013). Longitudinal follow-up of the mental health of unaccompanied refugee minors. *Eur Child Adolesc Psychiatry.* doi:10.1007/s00787-013-0463-1

Volkan, V. (1999). The Tree Model: A comprehensive psychopolitical approach to unofficial diplomacy and the reduction of ethnic tension. *Mind and Human Interaction, 10*(3), 142–210.

Wiegand-Grefe, S., & Möller, B. (2012). Die transgenerationale Weitergabe von Kriegserfahrungen aus dem Zweiten Weltkrieg über drei Generationen – eine Betrachtung aus psychoanalytischer Perspektive. *Prax. Kinderpsychol. Kinderpsychiat, 61*, 610–622.

Yazda (2017). An uncertain future for Yazidis: A report marking three years of an ongoing genocide. *Yazda.* www.yazda.org/an-uncertain-future-for-yazidis-a-report-marking-three-years-of-an-ongoing-genocide-yazda-september-2017/

Chapter 2

Speaking of sexual abuse with female refugees

Cândida Sé Holovko and Gertraud Schlesinger-Kipp

Introduction

The subject of this chapter, sexual abuse, has been one of the main topics studied by the Women and Psychoanalysis Committee (COWAP-IPA) since its very first steps. It is a well-established fact that sexual abuse is often perpetrated by relatives, boyfriends, friends or neighbors of women. Almost every minute a person may be suffering some sort of sexual violence in the world. Given such alarming data what can we as psychoanalysts do?

The psychoanalytical approach in this article intends to point out the importance of traumatic conscious and unconscious experience and its consequences on women's subjectivities and bodies, as well as the role of power and cultural differences in the sexual violence domain. Some studies have shown that working with victims of abuse evokes strong countertransference reactions in the therapist, which greatly affects intervention. Programs considered most effective usually involve the therapist's supervision and close attention to the process of dealing with the patient's traumatic situations.

At the pre-congress of IPA, Boston 2015, a group of psychoanalysts from various IPA Committees with the participation of the Committee of Women and Psychoanalysis; Committee on Children and Adolescents, the Committee on Law and Psychoanalysis and the UN Committee, met to create a Inter-Committee on IPA on Child Abuse, an unprecedented project.

It was shown that the earlier and closer the level of familiarity with the abuser the greater the pathological consequences, and also the sooner the psychotherapeutic intervention took place the more efficient the results.

It became clear at this meeting that there is a greater awareness of the importance of attention to child and adult sexual abuse at an international level, due to the greater value conferred to the protection of children and adolescents and the rights of women, but it has been observed that there is an increasing incidence of cases of sexual abuse which is difficult to interpret. The American psychoanalyst Kerry Novick, who attended this meeting, noted that:

> The general perception of an increase in the internal tension of adults in many countries, developed ones included – which is perhaps related to the rise of experiences of powerlessness in the modern world despite the paradoxical presence of expanded freedoms – may have as a reflection changes in abuse numbers in these countries. This led to the discussion of the specificity of the psychoanalytic understanding of its phenomenology and the impact of abuse on the victim and the abuser.
>
> (Novick, 2015)

At this meeting the term "victimator" was established for the person committing the abuse because they considered that the abuser can have also been the victim of frequent sexual abuse, that is often intergenerational, in their life stories. Durban (2017a) refers to the dynamics of the abuser conceptualizing it as the "victimizer complex." He affirms: "This complex involves several pathological identifications serving as a defense against archaic anxieties and can lead to tragically destructive behaviors directed at both the child and his environment" (p. 112).

According to this author, whenever the pathological precarious organization of the victim is disturbed, the compulsion to evacuate this abusive object may arise in another object perceived as weak or threatening, by opening children's feelings of profound helplessness and at the same time being able to live actively what was lived in a passive way.

In the contact with abused women we often find a reluctance to expose the abusive situation and to denounce their aggressor. We believe that the traumatic situation experienced, like those of many other victims of traumatic disruptive situations, produces a flood of non-metaphorical excitations in the mind of a woman that prevents the constitution of a representational chain that takes account of the lived; true holes in the tissue of representations. Approaching, remembering something that cannot be inscribed as verbal memory but marked in the body, usually produces an unnamed anguish that leads the victim to the avoidance of the story. We also believe that the guilt for what has been elicited in terms of sexual arousal in the woman's body is also another source that leads to the silence of abused women.

According to Tesone (2005), in the article "Incest: the stolen body," the abuser, in producing a bodily excitement not consented to by the abused woman, produces a traumatic effect on his victim who responds uncontrollably to external excitement, and the body itself becomes an external body:

> The excitation produced is a de-subjectifying excitation. Desire does not intervene, it is an encounter with a de-symbolizing event, a stolen excitement, for it triggers the drive excitement without the subject's consent. The body acquires a character of extraterritoriality, with its own forum that requires to be punished ... The enemy becomes not only the abuser but also the body itself lived as shame and even with contempt.
>
> (p. 108)

These experiences of abuse leave deep marks of much anguish and pain and increase suspicions that could already exist regarding the people in the surroundings that did not create the conditions for the protection of these young women. This can be a complication for psychotherapists who are willing to help and make room for a conversation and to enter into this universe of suffering.

We believe, as do many authors, that creating a climate of trust – so that the secret can be revealed and someone can witness the effects produced by this brutal experience – can generate in the violated woman feelings of anger and hate against the abuser, getting rid of the guilt that was mobilized by the abuser in the body of the victim.

We remember the words of Alizade (2011):

> The secret sets in as a perverse and intimidating pact ... They both engage in a guilty complicity that imprisons them. The deceived woman introjects the aggressor (Ferenzi 1933, p. 144) and

disappears as part of the external reality, transforming itself into something intrapsychic instead of extra psychic. This implies that movements toward otherness are limited due to constant exposure to malignant seductive exchanges.

(p. 24)

Experience with women on refugee camps
Gertraud Schlesinger-Kipp

A few years ago, Germany had to deal with great numbers of refugees who came to Europe in 2015 and 2016, fleeing the horrible experiences of war. There were many women and girls who had been under specific gender-related threats – from the time they were still in their homelands, through the whole period of flight and, finally and sadly, also in Europe's refugee camps.

In the Alexander-Mitscherlich-Institute's project in Kassel (IPA), Germany, about 25 psychoanalysts and psychotherapists put together a psychosocial and psychotherapeutic intervention on a free and voluntary basis in refugee camps in Kassel, mostly with women who were searching for shelter and asylum in Germany. The majority came from Syria, Afghanistan, Iraq, and Eritrea. The loss of identity, the pain of family conflicts, the gender-specific causes for escaping and the hope that came from the knowledge of the substantial difference in the actual freedom of western women are incredibly touching, for both therapists and translators. It was clear that the setting demanded a cultural and gender-sensitive approach. The limits and chances of what was sometimes a unique possibility of talking are presented in the case studies. Thus, the psychoanalysts and other voluntary professionals founded a Psychosocial Centre for refugees, where the work could take place.

Hana

Hana is 20 years old and visibly pregnant. She has mainly grown up in Sudan, in a refugee camp. She had then fled from Sudan and, in Libya, fell into the hands of Chad rebels. She had been detained in a camp. The male refugees were mistreated heavily and the women raped. She too had been raped repeatedly and injured as well. Eventually, she managed to pay her way out and flee across the Mediterranean.

Hana at first hesitates to talk about these incidents. She says that she always felt ashamed when asked about her pregnancy or the where-abouts of the father. She doesn't know who the father is. She seems very quiet, depressed, absent, very composed and controlled. She hints that she doesn't know how to accept the child. She didn't have anybody at her side. She slept poorly, though physically she had no problems with the pregnancy.

I take a long pause and think about what I could say to this friendly, humiliated woman. I tell her then that it shouldn't be on her to be ashamed, but on the perpetrators. And I say this twice very firmly, "You've gone through terrible experiences, but now you are going to have a child and this gives you a future." Hana relaxes somehow and describes her feelings of restrained shame. And she says: "I know that the father is still in Sudan."

The interpreter said that he often saw her sitting around the camp seeming totally absent. This is probably the reason why it took so long for her to be introduced to therapy, despite living in the camp for months – she does not attract attention.

After a while, Hana gave birth to her baby by caesarean section, with complications. When she came back to the camp after 14 days, everyone was very happy and excited and made a party. She was able to accept and take care of her baby and was breastfeeding very well. But as soon as she was alone she would have this empty lost look in her eyes again. She was transferred to a second settlement, quite far away, and the camp leader and interpreter visited her for the baptism of the child.

Sira

Sira comes from a country in Africa. During her escape she was captured in a European country by human traffickers and forced into prostitution. After a few months a man rescued her and took her to a city of the same country. The owner of the brothel found her there too. Finally she managed to escape to Germany. The European law says that refugees have to be transported back to the European country where they first entered (called the "Dublin Regulation," because this law was created in Dublin). Thus Sira got, after some time, the letter with her "transfer" to the country where she suffered these abuses. She fell into a state of panic, depression, suicidal impulses, dissociation. It was clear to her that the people would find her in this other country. In her belief they cast a spell on her and they would always get to her no matter what, until she died.

Also, she felt shame and guilt because of the forced prostitution. No one would ever forgive her, she would never be able to find a friend. In the sessions I always assured her that she was not guilty, and that human trafficking is a well-known practice and that these people are criminals, telling her that she managed to survive (she had scars all over her body) and escape from that horrible place. In the beginning Sira wasn't even able to go to church because of her feelings of guilt. She felt dirty and ashamed. And she had many physical consequences, maybe even Myasthenia. Nevertheless, she didn't do medical tests and she also left the psychiatric hospital where I sent her for shelter and treatment because of mistrust. She could only trust me because I was not an estate official. After some time she found a priest who talked to her and came back looking like another person, much freer and conscious of herself. She even made a friend and got a partner. As she got help from many institutions, and from me, the judge agreed to withdraw the "Dublin" transfer. Unfortunately, the therapy could not go on because she was transferred to another town in Germany. These things happen all the time. They are thoughtless, without sense and they keep many (mostly caritative and voluntary) helpers active but helpless.

I often have the impression – especially after the change of politics, and the atmosphere in German society to close the borders, to send the refugees back, to see them as enemies and as the possible perpetrators of some cruel attacks committed by refugees – that we therapists are only containers for the terrible stories of the refugees in their homeland, during their flight and also here in Germany through retraumatization. We offer contact and a human relationship but much too often we are also helpless against the politics and treatments. The fact that gender-specific reasons for fleeing have been legitimized for a long time is not very well known and is seldom carried through in court.

Kira

Kira is a young woman from Iraq. She is a very small and intelligent beautiful woman. She studied at university and married a man of her own choice. Together they converted to Christianity. If you do this you can be killed by your Muslim family. Why did they do it? I asked. She could no longer keep the faith in the Islamic religion after all that happened in its name. And in her country you have to have a religion. Because her family's life was threatened they had to escape from their country. In Germany they found asylum (many convert to Christianity to get asylum). After some time her husband began to beat her because she refused intimacy. She doesn't love him and he knew it before. She was never interested in sex, even before the marriage. She escaped to a women's shelter and got divorced but she still feels in danger. In her culture a woman can be killed if she leaves her husband. We often see that men from Islamic countries, who were quite liberal at home, are turning to old patriarchal behavior in exile, especially if they experience their wives approaching ideas of female rights and freedom. Kira cannot concentrate, has no joy in going out with friends, cannot pursue her studies, and is ruminating all the time. We agreed upon therapy sessions because of her depression, her sexual identity problems, and arranged a participation in establishing a group for women.

Some considerations about these women

The story of Hana (Schlesinger-Kipp, 2017) – who grew up in a refugee camp in the Sudan, went to another refugee camp in Libya, after being raped multiple times, and then was found by Gertraud in a refugee camp in Germany – makes us think about the numerous violent abuses suffered by this young woman throughout her life. She was prevented from very early on to develop one of the most basic experiences that ground the development of the feeling of being that is to have an environmental continuity with experiences of rooting in a stable, loving home. The constant changes of residence and the frequent rapes suffered, perforations in the corporal envelope in an age where the body is being resignified by the experience of adolescence and a pregnancy by sexual violence, brought this woman into a state of "soul emptiness," of deep depression similar to the psychic condition of "nowhere-ness" described by Durban (2017a). In this condition of "nowhere-ness" one observes the non-construction or destruction of a poor sense of home caused by severe and cumulative traumas. This author postulates that this condition causes the emergence of deeper archaic anxieties of being which deal with the very threats to our existence as bounded entities in body, time, space, and object, such as a state of dementalization, isolation, and withdrawal. These aspects were also observed in Hana by the helpers in the camp. (The interpreter said that he often saw her sitting around the camp seeming totally absent and practically passing unnoticed by the people around her.) Hana's difficulty in talking about her ailments and her guilt about the pregnancy illustrate many of the feelings found in sexually abused women. Gertraud tries with her emphatic words to facilitate de-identification with the incorporated abuser and paves the way for hope of a future figured by the baby that is coming. Having her story narrated in a welcoming environment, not only with the therapist and the interpreter but with several field employees who sympathized with her, allowed a closeness with the child expressed in the possibility of breastfeeding. We may think that perhaps she, supported by this environment of containment that was the German camp, was trying to recover her own helpless and suffering inner-baby through the care given to this new child. However, we know that a lot more analytical work would be necessary so that she could construct a subjectively structured experience with good internal objects that could relieve her of unthinkable anxieties. (She was able to accept and take care of her baby and was breastfeeding very well. But as soon as she was alone she would have this empty lost look in her eyes again, "nowhere-ness.")

In Sira's report we once again see the matter of the deep-seated guilt found in many women that are abused and pressed into the environment of prostitution. The feeling of having her body marked and dirtied by the sexual acts without consent reminds us of the ideas of the stolen body and the identification with the aggressor. Curious that in this account we see the force, the impact, and the importance of the presentation of new object relations, presented in the figure of the priest – who is a paternal-divine representative – and in the trust towards Gertraud, a maternal representative, containment and witness of her sufferings. These two people acknowledged the intrusions that her body and subjectivity suffered and thus contributed to a momentary return to a stable, protective, and loving environment. Durban (2017b) discusses "homelessness" – in people who have suffered severe traumas as they are forced to leave their homes in these forced emigrations – to remind us that the loss of the inner and outer home tends to trigger intense depressive feelings and paranoid-schizoid anxieties. Sira's belief that the abusers and traffickers of women would persecute her and find her no matter where she was, illustrate these terrible anxieties that threaten these people in the state of "homelessness."

As in many traumatic situations of sexual abuses in women we find in Sira the somatic illness (Myasthenia) expressing the break-in that was made in the psychic representational apparatus and in her bodily experiences. Smadja (2005) describes in these cases a process of somatic regression caused by a loss of narcissistic libido within the preconscious. In the case of Sira, the loss of cultural references, of the parents' house, of the country, the constant abuses of all orders created a traumatic situation due to the unprocessed charge of excitement that led to a failure of the psychic processes. In these situations, the psychic functioning becomes momentarily incapacitated to utilize its capacities of connections of the internal excitations and to turn them into representations of what was lived. "At this conjuncture the object libido that is unused in the psychic level will return to its somatic sources, in what we call somatic regression ... The consequence of this somatic regression movement is the installation of an abnormal amount of libido on certain organs and the inevitable physiological dysfunction that follows" (p. 38). In many psychotherapies with sexually abused women we find diseases such as anorexia, bulimia, or various somatizations.

In Kira, we witness the suffering of many female Muslim women who wish to live a westernized life different from the one marked by strong patriarchal traditions, especially in Muslim families. We see that changing values can produce deep wounds in the family's honor and that puts many of these women in situations of impossible choices as a result of shame and guilt. On shame, Schlesinger-Kipp (2017) states that:

> Shame about the experience of complete loss of identity, loss of one's own values and ego ideal – cannot be discussed and removed

in a normal conversation. Each person has their own "levels of shame": first, there is something that can be called "loss of face", which is to have fallen out of the natural social context. The next step is the shame of not having predicted the situation. Finally, there is the shame of being "drowned" by loss of identity and submission. The question would be how can this basic sense of shame be converted into useful signs to defend us from being penetrated by the disastrous inhumanity of our time?

(p. 167)

Stephan Streker's film (2016) "Noces" – a production from France, Belgium, Pakistan, Luxembourg – illustrates rather well the conflict of a Pakistani woman who has no right to her voice and own actions and is subjected to and condemned by extremes of tradition. Zahira, the protagonist, an 18-year-old girl living in France with her Pakistani family, is influenced by European culture and way of life. When she gets pregnant while being single, she has to face the conflicts and sufferings of an unwanted abortion and get married in the traditional way with an unknown man chosen by the family. After observing the long-distance marriage contract, with all the rituals of her culture, when she should move to Pakistan to meet and surrender – like all women – to her husband's cultural norms and desires, she decides in an act of independence to follow her own ways and a European way of life. This decision exposes all members of the family (father, mother, sisters, and brother) to dishonor, which may lead to the banishment and exclusion of all of them from their community of origin. We can ask ourselves, how can Zaira make the choice of living a life of her own in a situation like this, carrying the shame of the family, the blame for the father's heart attack and the suffering of all her beloved relatives?

Working with women in the German refugee camp arouses many countertransference reactions because of the shock of cultural patterns that are so deep-rooted and so foreign to the western mind. The process of changing cultural values for these women will certainly imply transgenerational dis-identifications that will affect the sense of being and continuity of belonging, which will always require a long and arduous work with very primitive anguish.

Migrations and uprooting

This uprooting experienced by these suffering women reminds us of another work with abused women described by Holovko and Paron (2017):

> This uprooting brings profound and serious consequences to the mental health of these women, who are forced to face new situations, where all their previous tradition is often inadequate, if not ill-seen. Simone Weil, in her book The Rooting (1949/2001) exposes what she calls the vital needs of the soul. Among the needs she describes, we highlight some such as: truth, order, security, equality, private property, collective property, etc.
>
> (p. 139)

Needs that are all violated in this trajectory of refugee women. These are women who experience the violence – such as physical ill-treatment, incest, sexual abuse, various deprivations, etc. – that were affected by it, but they could not transform it and symbolize it, freeing itself from this vicious circle. They left only another violence, which is the perpetuation of this tragic destiny.

The psychic experience of these women is of resentment, strong feelings of worthlessness are often present, experiencing loss of dignity, often causing: exhaustion, depression, guilt, self-harm, and antisocial attitudes. External conditions do not guarantee minimum rights, there is no environment that makes them feel human and favors conditions, including physical ones, to meet the needs of the body and the psyche.

Deprived of their basic needs, these people are often irretrievably disturbed in the constitution of their self and their psyche. According to Weil, uprooted beings would tend to fall "in an inertia of the soul almost equivalent to death ... or to engage in an activity that always tends to uproot, often by the most violent methods, those who are not yet so" (1949/2001, p. 46).

We believe that the work with this population should be twofold: on the one hand, recognizing the suffering they have been experiencing, witnessing and legitimizing their indignation at the injustices and aggressions lived, and on the other, creating the conditions so that these people can return to feel themselves worthy, finding a place of pertinence and hope in life.

In the paper (Holovko & Paron, 2017) with very poor women of the city of São Paulo, we described a type of service offered that is quite similar to this with refugee women in Germany narrated by Gertraud.

> Because that was not a situation of classical psychoanalysis, the framework had to be changed, namely: not managing the transference; not to favor regression; presenting to the members of the group the predominant affection to give them an exit from action; to encourage the internalization of new values. Analysts should be highly predictable because they are marginalized communities whose core characteristics are abandonment, exclusion or emigration.
>
> We did not work with transference or regression directly, but we used these concepts as well as our countertransference to understand the transferential phenomena that brought material to our interventions.
>
> (p. 142)

> In general, we tried to use these parameters, working with the present, in search of the construction of a meaning, a future. The past, as historical reference, has been included to be updated by the new configurations. The psychoanalytic intervention in the group functioned not only as a space of contention and psychic elaboration, but also as a solidarity community network that allowed the group to experience the feeling of belonging and having a place
>
> …
>
> The psychoanalytic listening of people deprived of the most basic needs of the soul defines a different setting from that of the practices, prioritizing less the transference of the meanings of the record of the lived experience in the past and more the transference to the future, in the search for meaning that gives a direction, a future project.
>
> (p. 145)

Safra (2006) affirms:

Usually, in our work we are aware of how transference is affected by the meanings of the past. However the transference situation is also signified by the future. In this case the analyst is placed in the place of what the analysand aspires to accomplish and to find.

(p.87)

Analysts testifying to the report of these refugee women (Ana, Sira, and Kira) have given legitimacy to these now shared memories creating a real, less phantasmatic experience; a path to symbolization.

Now, more than ever, psychotherapeutic experiences such as these – with the collaboration of dedicated psychoanalysts – need to be increased in number and scope to minimize these terrible sufferings and to help huge numbers of marginalized, alienated communities that are deprived of the right to their own subjectivity.

References

Alizade, M. (2011). O incesto verbal (*Verbal Incest*). In *Revista Psicanalítica, Rio de Janeiro, 12*(1), 17–26.

Durban, J. (2017a). Home, homelessness and nowhere-ness in early infancy. *Journal of Child Psychotherapy, 43*(2), 175–191.

———— (2017b). O "complexo do vitimador" e suas vicissitudes no abuso de crianças (The "victimizer complex" and child abuse). In Holovko & Cortezzi, Blucher (Eds.), *Sexualidade e Gênero. Desafios da Psicanálise*. São Paulo, 111–140.

Holovko, C., & Paron, E.G. (2017).Violência e Escuta analítica: trabalhando com mulheres da periferia de São Paulo (Violence and Analytic Listening: working with women from the favelas). In Revista Trieb/ Sociedade Brasileira de Psicanálise do Rio de Janeiro, edição especial, 139–114.

Novick, K. (2015). First Inter-Committee on Child Abuse meeting at the IPA 2015 Boston pre-congress. Unpublished.

Safra, G. (2006). Hermenêutica na situação clínica. O desvelar da singularidade pelo idioma da pessoa. (Hermeneutics in the clinic. Unveiling singularity through one's dialect). São Paulo: Sobornost.

Schlesinger-Kipp, G. (2017). Encontro terapêutico com mulheres refugiadas na Alemanha In Sexualidades e Gênero: Desafios da psicanálise, Holovko & Cortezzi. Editora Blucher. (155–177) Hana (p. 168).

Smadja, C. (2005). *La vida operatória. Estudios Psicoanalíticos* (La Vie opératoire: Etudes psychanalytiques, Broché, 2001). Traducción de Cristina

Rolla y José Maria Franco Vicário, Editorial Biblioteca Nueva, S.L., Madrid, 2005.

Streker, S. (2016). 'Noces.' Film produced in France, Belgium, Pakistan, and Luxembourg.

Tesone, J.E. (2005). Incesto: o corpo roubado (Incest: the stolen Body). In Revista Ide, *41*, 107–114.

Weil, S. (2001). O enraizamento (*The rooting*). Trad. Maria Leonor Loureiro-Bauru. São Paulo: Edusc (trabalho original publicado em 1949).

Chapter 3

The tragedy of the earth's commons

Psychoanalytic perspectives on climate change and the law

Elizabeth Allured

Introduction

Greed, secrecy, and competitive strivings have been with us long before the time of Esau and Jacob. Conflicting legal claims to resources have concerned land use rights, water rights, mineral rights, or rights to the airspace above skyscrapers in New York. Securing legal rights over resources has repeatedly instigated armed conflicts, and the genocide of indigenous peoples. There is currently widespread human and non-human suffering due to overuse, misuse, and abuse of earth's land, sea, and atmospheric resources. Due largely to our use of fossil fuel resources, the climatic system itself now moves toward a less stable state that is much less conducive to human life. How can psychoanalysis shed light on this process of unrelenting ecosystemic destruction? How can we learn from other branches of psychology, sociology, and the earth sciences to contribute to finding a way out of this impending and unfolding disaster? What is the interaction of the legal system of environmental protections with conscious and unconscious motivations and defenses?

In this brief chapter, I will introduce the concept of "the tragedy of the commons," a theory put forth by Hardin, a biologist, who explained the motivations of individuals overusing resources held in common with one's group (Hardin, 1968). The psychoanalytic concepts of vulnerability and interdependence, in relation to the nonhuman environment, and our manic, omnipotent strivings to be free of this interdependence, will be discussed, with an overview of Searles, Freud, Jung, and contemporary analysts' thoughts about this. The rights of today's children to a livable, stable future environment, as being brought to court in Juliana versus the United States, will be discussed.

The need to use both a hermeneutic approach and an action-oriented approach in response to the current climate crisis, as advised by Lifton and others, will be put forth.

The tragedy of the commons

The climate crisis can be understood as the end result of an initially rational choice made by many individuals holding resources in common. Hardin asks us to imagine a pasture which is available to a community of herders for grazing their animals. It is in each herder's best economic interest to graze as many animals as possible on the land, to eventually derive income from the sale or trade of one's animals. Due to typical drops in the populations of herders and animals from natural and human causes, the carrying capacity of the common land is maintained, even when a herder adds an additional animal. However, when the population of herders and animals grows to the land's carrying capacity, the addition of one more animal benefits the additional animal's owner, but detracts in a small measure from the health of all the other animals, and degrades the landscape, again in small measure. The herder who has added the one animal makes a gain of +1, but their loss is much less than -1, so it is in one's economic interest to continue adding animals to one's herd. Continuing to deplete the commons by adding additional animals is therefore the "rational" choice. The herder with a conscience, who sees the longer-term dilemma, and chooses to not add more animals, is actually worse off economically than the non-conscientious herder. However, the "rational" choice, to add another animal and therefore provide more economically for one's self and offspring, actually worsens living conditions for all offspring in the long run. Thus, the "tragedy of the commons," and the need to regulate the use of resources which were initially held in common, and unrestricted, by communities. Hardin also pointed out that human population growth greatly accelerates the malevolent effects of this tendency toward overuse.

The secondary tragedy, at this point in time, is that regulatory agencies are not adequately regulating the extraction and use of fossil fuel resources that are the primary drivers of climate change. This is termed the "pipeline problem," as opposed to the "tailpipe problem" of consumers using fossil fuels. Hardin would likely point to the economic gain of the fossil fuel companies, as well as the economic gain, and health, of individuals surviving longer in homes heated and cooled with fossil fuels. Added to these are the economic gains of individuals using air travel for business; and the economic gains of individuals driving or riding vehicles to work. But our government, and legal system, could have used the knowledge of science in overseeing a broad transition to a fossil-free future in the 1990s, when the science of global warming was unequivocal. Sustainable infrastructure could have been developed by now, safeguarding generations to come, as well as safeguarding innumerable plant and animal species on land and in the seas. The data about human-caused climate change was documented by the 1940s (Fleming, 2009), and became increasingly clear each decade thereafter. A recent article about the many missed, and dismissed, opportunities to take appropriate action to curb fossil fuel use in the United States (Rich, 2018) during the 1970s and 1980s paints a tragic picture of political and economic self-interest prevailing over the preservation of our ecosystem. Furthermore, the US government, in recently opting out of the Paris Agreements, and in failing to address this crisis in time to alleviate the current and coming climate tragedies, has abdicated its basic duty to protect life.

From an analytic perspective, we (in the USA, at least) are now in a similar position to an adolescent with a neglectful caretaker. One could use stronger terms by saying that rather than providing for the basic human rights to clean air, water, and a sustainable ecosystem, the caretaker/authority/federal government has, in important ways, abandoned the child/citizen, leaving them to a certainly darker future. This, while abdicating responsibility for doing so, and instead urging people to doubt the science of climate change.

The realization will gradually or suddenly dawn on people that we have been misled by the fossil fuel companies, who are currently proposing a carbon tax with the loophole that they cannot be sued for climate-related damages. The energy industry/Republican party has been engaged in an agnatology campaign, using psychological tactics to attempt to convince the public that the science of climate change is faulty (Carter and Woodworth, 2018; Mann and Toles, 2016). Or, at the least, that there is enough uncertainty that the entire theory can be thrown out. Failing that (and this can be expected as the climate situation worsens), the US government may lean on the human tendency to expect a return to normalcy after periods of upheaval: that there will be some weather extremes, but we can ignore the problem, and the environment will find a new but reliably good enough steady state afterwards. This is not what climate scientists know to be true.

In recent years, many individuals have come to understand the perilous, worsening situation we are in, with tipping points approaching or passed, and some have tried to speak up about it and influence legal, public policy (Intergovernmental Panel on Climate Change, 2014). There is an inherent trauma to this situation, as when Dora spoke up about her abuse, and her expectation of more, only to hear from a patriarchal Freud that she brought it on herself, and it's not so bad. DeMocker has described the situation as similar to parents of teenagers continuing to bring out more kegs to the drunken adolescents at a party in the family home (DeMocker, 2018). Would we blame the kids here?

Vulnerability and dependence

In "Civilization and Its Discontents," Freud noted that human suffering came from three sources: our bodies (which are subject to decay and infirmity); from interpersonal relations; and from the "outer" world, which may "rage against us with overwhelming and merciless forces of destruction" (Freud, 1930, p. 77). Freud believed that suffering that came from the "dreaded outer world" could be defended against by "becoming a member of the human community, and, with the help of a technique guided by science, going over to the attack against nature and subjecting her to the human will. Then one is working with all for the good of all" (Freud, 1930, p. 77). Vulnerability to the nonhuman was seen as a temporary societal state, on the way to scientific mastery of protections against objectified, nonhuman elements. Freud was grounded in Enlightenment principles, seeing the progress of civilization as the journey from "primitive"/indigenous ways of life; through agrarian modes of living, and a reliance on religious institutions; and culminating in a rational, science-based, atheistic society of nation-states. This was in line with the dominant anthropological theory of unilinear cultural evolution, which saw indigenous peoples as barbaric, and as mentally inferior to "civilized" individuals. Franz Boaz, in his studies of indigenous peoples on Vancouver Island, British Columbia, disproved this theory in the late nineteenth century (Rohner, 1969). However, many westerners carry unconscious shadows of this belief, if not conscious biases in line with it.

Despite his Cartesian leanings, Freud nonetheless was flexible enough in his thinking to bring therapy into the urban environment of Vienna on his walks with patients. The analytic frame could occur in a restaurant, or when Freud was away on summer vacation in the Semmering Mountains of Austria. His flexibility was not practiced by American "Freudian" analysts for decades. The idea of bringing the therapy out of the office and into the outdoors was written about by Stefano more recently in his work with children (Santostefano, 2004).

In contrast, Jung privileged indigenous peoples as holding an innate environment-suffused wisdom that was largely inaccessible to modern peoples. He saw "civilized" peoples as having little conscious or personal relationship with the nonhuman environment. Jung traveled to Taos, New Mexico, and to Tanzania and Uganda to live with and learn from indigenous peoples. Jung was ahead of his times when he wrote in his autobiography:

> What we from our point of view call colonization, missions to the heathen, spread of civilization, etc., has another face—the face of a bird of prey seeking with cruel intentness for distant quarry—a face worthy of a race of pirates and highwaymen.
>
> (Jung, 1962, p. 248)

This echoes the tragedy of the commons: the exploitation of resources (and the indigenous peoples dependent upon those resources) by those wanting economic power. This exploitation denies the interrelationship, and interdependence, of all aspects of our ecosystems. It objectifies nonhuman elements, and indigenous peoples, in a doer–done-to relation, playing out an I-It dynamic as opposed to Buber's I-Thou. It avoids feelings of vulnerability and interdependence with ecosystemic elements.

Orange has written about this in her recent text about the tragic suffering of indigenous peoples, from the days of chattel slavery in the USA, through current populations affected by the climate crisis (Orange, 2017). Those currently affected include residents of low-lying islands who are losing their lands; subsistence farmers who cannot subsist on land stressed from extreme weather events; and migrants fleeing wars related in part to dwindling natural resources. She sees climate change as a social justice issue of major proportions, requiring empathy with the suffering of those already impacted by both our use of fossil fuels, and our systematic disregard of the ecosystem.

Unlike indigenous peoples who consciously and intimately depend on the earth environment, and are therefore vulnerable to its changes, individuals living in post-modern cultures can ignore, deny, or minimize their awareness of, and dependence upon, the climate, water, air, plants, and animal life that sustain us. As Searles noted in 1960, more than 99 percent of what we interact with is nonhuman, yet our psychological theories ignore this aspect of interrelatedness (Allured, 2014; Searles, 1960). In his 1960 text, Searles wrote:

> It is my conviction that there is within the human individual a sense, whether at a conscious or unconscious level, of relatedness to his nonhuman environment, that this relatedness is one of the transcendentally important facts of human living, that –as with other very important circumstances in human existence – it is a source of ambivalent feelings to him, and that, finally, if he tries to ignore its importance to himself, he does so at peril to his psychological well-being.
>
> (Searles, 1960, p.6)

Much as we have a tendency to deny psychological dependence on those intimately involved with our care, we also deny our psychological dependence upon physical environments that set our circadian rhythms, develop aspects of reality testing, and provide relief from anxiety (Searles, 1960). Searles later theorized that the psychoanalytic community was under the sway of what would now be termed the social stigma bias, avoiding speaking about the environmental crisis due to fear of censure by our colleagues (Searles, 1972). When a colleague of mine recently spoke up about the dearth of conference presentations on the climate crisis at an open microphone portion of a plenary address (IARPP, New York City, 2018), one of the conference organizers responded, "Maybe we are all feeling overwhelmed." Maybe this is an understatement.

Searles boldly spoke up about the environmental crisis in 1972 because he saw the destructive forces inherent in society as potentially leading to ecocide, and suicide for humanity. He implored analysts to study the unconscious processes at work in this crisis, and theorized that extinguishing life for our children and future generations would make us victors in the Oedipal struggle: upcoming rivals for our spouse would be denied a full life and therefore a chance to replace us. Searles saw our apathy about the crisis as having depressive undercurrents, like "the psychotically depressed patient based on suicide by self-neglect (Searles, 1972, p. 366)." Searles suggested that up until recently, humanity lived in "meaningful kinship" with the nonhuman world, and each person found individual, unique ways to differentiate from the nonhuman on the journey from childhood to adulthood. In 1972, he saw the civilized populace as, instead, merged into a technological world that was powerful, complex, and overwhelming.

In Searles' view, omnipotent strivings are projected onto this techno-world, and the mature understandings of loss and inevitable death are not achieved. Rather than experiencing the human conflict between our vulnerabilities and our omnipotent, invulnerable longings, Searles saw us as projecting this conflict into the struggle between vulnerable ecosystems and technology's destructive impact. It seems clear that both are real conflicts needing awareness and thoughtful action.

Weintrobe saw our struggles with the environmental crisis in a similar way: we have two basic parts of the self, one that loves reality, is aware of our ability to harm, and wants to make reparation; and a second, narcissistic part that hates the limitations of reality, sees ourselves as "special," and is prone to magical thinking (Weintrobe, 2013). The more degraded the environment becomes, and the less predictable the climatic system becomes, the more difficult it is to face this very real aspect of interrelationship and dependency.

Dependence upon our ecosystem can be experienced as castrating, regressive, and overwhelming. The climate crisis developed in part because of a disavowed dependence on the ecosystem, and false dichotomies between the human and the nonhuman. It continued because fossil fuels promised both economic benefits and lifestyle pleasures, which together often led fossil fuel users to a less vulnerable societal position in relation to those not using them. The crisis is partly about a lack of imagination of the potentially mind-numbing implications of the catastrophe, especially in the USA. The USA by history was distant from New World threats, and had, until the Second World War, seen itself as invulnerable to catastrophic external threats. The current US administration belittles personal and national vulnerability. Scientists who can understand deep time, and are trained in envisioning vastly different geological ecosystems, cannot easily convey their larger perspective, which took years of training to hold in mind. Bureaucratic inertia, citizens' fears of confronting the dysfunctional authority/federal/regulatory system, and short-term economic self-interests compound defenses against knowing/feeling. Disavowal and manic invulnerability can become the standard defenses in holding fears at bay.

I have written before about our avoidance of our dependence upon the ecosystem, and our manic flight away from a psychological rootedness in the earth (Allured, 2018a). The ancient Greek myths of Pegasus and Icarus both convey the theme of the desire for an escape from ties to earthly struggles and connections. An exploration of our greatest fears related to our dependence upon the earth and its ecosystems seems most timely right now. It would be helpful to confront the fallacy of the individual self, a Cartesian error that can contribute to denying and dissociating our active participation in the whole ecosystem. An acceptance of our psychological and physical dependence upon the ecosystem can re-activate a yearning to re-connect with nonhuman landscapes, and listen to what is occurring in them. Metaphorically, if we are not paying attention to our mother, how can we know what she needs?

Winnicott was the first to propose that not only did the baby depend upon the mother, but that the baby was not an individual unit of being (Winnicott, 1975). Likewise, it is time to shift our analytic theories to reflect the fact that *there is no person without an ecosystem*.

This is as true *psychologically* as it is physically. To ignore the ecosystem in our analytic theories is to ignore some of the most profound and meaningful aspects of the psyche. Ignoring the ecosystem in our theories, at this point in time, is as dysfunctional as ignoring the blaring sirens Winnicott spoke up about in the "Controversial Discussions" in England during the Second World War. We are of the nonhuman, in our basic elemental chemical nature, our animal instincts to reproduce, and our ancient mammalian attachment system (founded on the mammary glandular system, with the suckling/let down reflexes in partners). We are constantly suffused with the inflow/outflow of nonhuman elements: food, breath, warmth, cold, light, musical vibration, vocal cords singing or crying our pain, the resonant vibration of a lover's voice, a thunderclap, excretion. In honoring Sullivan's humble, equalizing statement, "We are all, more simply, human than otherwise," I will elaborate, *We are all, more simply, nonhuman than otherwise.*

This enlarges our sense of self rather than denigrating it. Whether we see our uniquely human aspect as frosting on the cake, the fly in the ointment, or an aspect of divinity, it is not in a binary with our nonhuman aspects. Human and nonhuman interpenetrate, and co-create each other, especially at this time.

The one percent of our genetic makeup that distinguishes us from chimpanzees, which includes enlarged frontal cortexes, has brought us to the brink. Our human-with-human interactions (remember, these comprise less than 1 percent of what we are interacting with all of the time) are what psychoanalysis in the USA has traditionally focused upon. *Do we psychoanalysts want to continue to be "the one percenters"?* Or can we find a way to help our patients, and ourselves, engage with the joys, struggles, and fears of being in kinship with this earthly home? How can we hold in mind the needs and rights of those to come after us, who have had no part in altering, for the worse, the ecosystems they will be born into? What can we do, besides casting our votes, to stop the wholesale diminishing of their futures? And how will they feel towards us when they realize what post-modern generations have done?

Activism: confronting our disavowals

In 2015, 21 children, and their guardians, filed suit against the US government. They claimed that through governmental actions or inactions pertaining to climate change, their rights to life, liberty, and property have been violated (Juliana vs. the United States). The suit also claims that the US government "failed to protect essential public trust resources" (Ourchildrenstrust.org). Joining the plaintiffs were a nonprofit organization called "Earth Guardians," and, finally, climate scientist Dr James Hansen, who signed on as guardian of "Future Generations." Their lawsuit hopes to force the US government to put in place a national plan to phase out fossil fuel use, and draw down excessive levels of atmospheric carbon dioxide that threaten the lives of future generations.

The Trump administration and the US government filed to have the case dismissed. This was initially denied. In mid-July of 2018, a second attempt to dismiss this landmark case was rejected. Recently (July 30, 2018) the US Supreme Court unanimously voted to preserve the start date for this lawsuit against the federal government, to be held on October 29, 2018.

Our strongest human instinct is to protect the life of our vulnerable offspring. With these children coming to the courtroom, our protective instincts come before the law. If the legal system will not protect the future livable environment for these children, then, what is the point of the law? When is it time for the analytic community to actively oppose the foreshortening of our children's futures? And, based on our understanding of the psyche and defenses, what is the most effective method?

Randall sees the problem of effective action as located in our typical binary narratives about climate change (Randall, 2009). She writes that we experience two primary climate change narratives: 1) the narrative of future losses, or losses occurring in faraway environments, that are horrifying and dramatic; and 2) the narrative of solutions, which typically does not address the enormity of the changes that will be involved to effectively deal with the climate emergency. The narrative of solutions often exists independent of an awareness of losses. Randall offers that this splitting protects the public psyche from a current, emotional experience of the crisis (which, now in 2018, is more difficult to ignore, or locate elsewhere/in the future). She and Brown present an analytic model of the use of grief and mourning, in small groups, to raise awareness and to help individuals work through conflicts about relinquishing aspects of self, culture, and security that are obstacles to appropriate action (Randall and Brown, 2015). Splitting may be breaking down as the climate crisis worsens, but this "parallel narratives" framework can help analysts understand how the climate emergency is typically held in a semi-dissociated psychic state, when no therapeutic or interpersonal holding environment exists to contain anxiety, mourning, and fear. Actions which are relatively ineffective in reducing the climate emergency (though they may be useful in addressing other environmental problems), such as recycling plastic bottles, can be seen at times as a desperate defensive attempt to feel less guilty and helpless in regard to climate change.

Lifton begins a discussion of the concept of environmental guilt in his book *The Climate Swerve* (Lifton, 2017). Lifton described the great guilt felt by the scientist, Arthur Galston, whose research was crucial in the invention of the herbicide Agent Orange, which was used with devastating impacts on animal/human and plant life in the Vietnam War. Galston made many visits to Vietnam and China, and became an outspoken, dedicated antiwar activist arguing against the use of toxins such as Agent Orange. Lifton notes that Galston was "deeply troubled by the part his work played in extending war into environmental destruction," and that he spoke often about "his sense of guilt and responsibility" (p. 12). Lifton refers to this psychological development in Galston as "an animating relation to guilt."

Lifton, whose initial studies involved research into the survivors of the Hiroshima attack, sees a specific type of defensive operation at play in facing the twin crises of nuclear holocaust and climate destabilization, terming this "psychic numbing." It is presumed that this numbing must have occurred among scientists who developed the nuclear bomb in Los Alamos, New Mexico, and among fossil fuel executives of today who work to promote the extraction and use of fossil fuels. Fossil fuel executives did not join the oil companies to destroy humanity. The rationale of providing for a "better way of life" and lifting people and countries out of poverty may have underlay the motivations of many long-term leaders in that industry. Lifton notes the difficulty of "imagining the real" future scenarios of climate change, especially if one's livelihood currently depends upon fossil fuels. He compares "psychic numbing" to the practice of animals "freezing" in the face of likely imminent destruction. If we think about this, it becomes apparent that we clinicians need to provide a place to contemplate the unimaginable, to mourn the great losses, and to turn feelings of helplessness and paralysis into responsible, reparative actions.

The discipline of psychoanalysis was founded on the principles of hermeneutics, and analyzing rather than acting. However, if we cannot liberate our patients', and our own, efforts to save our lives and those of our children, we have missed a crucial opportunity. Lifton sees both personal action and political change in the face of ecocide as necessary. How do we inspire effective action in our patients without shaming, blaming, proselytizing, or moralizing?

Andrew Samuels tackles the tricky issue of psychoanalytic activism by expanding our view of the meaning of "active engagement" with the patient/client (Samuels, 2017). This includes an exploration of political and social systems that have helped and constricted individuals. Samuels offers that psychic wounds and constricted self-states can have their genesis in the darker sides of socio-political systems. These systems may involve racism, sexism, ageism, income inequality, all of these, or other factors, including climate denialism. Certainly, those who are appropriately terrified, anxious, or depressed as climate change unfolds have been affected by the darker side of politics. Finally finding one's voice with an abusive caretaker or spouse is often a crucial step away from fear and depression on the way to agency and empowerment. Likewise, becoming aware of ways that one engages in racist behaviors can lead to more effective functioning, and a greater ability to connect with those of different backgrounds than one's own. In a similar way, working towards personal or political engagement in work that mitigates environmental destruction can decrease dissociated, or conscious, feelings of helplessness, guilt, and fear.

Samuels sees a lived focus on social responsibility as contributing to individual "psychological vitality." He sees what may appear as apathy or depression regarding social issues to be, instead, failed activism. Likewise, Lertzman found that many individuals she interviewed regarding degraded local environments who initially seemed apathetic were actually experiencing an arrested mourning process. This "environmental melancholia" foreclosed more active engagement with the issue (Lertzman, 2015). And, Orange's concept of the "ungrievables," the individuals who have suffered and died to provide for our lifestyles, can be extended to refer to the nonhuman environments that we dare not think about for fear of feeling overwhelmed (Allured, 2018b). Psychoanalysis sees the relinquishment of narcissistic entitlement as a marker of psychological maturity, leading to the development of appropriate guilt, feelings of loss, and subsequent social responsibility to make reparation for those we or society have harmed. These reparative strivings conceivably exist within all of us in latent or unconscious ways concerning the environmental crisis. As analysts, we can work to develop these strivings in ourselves, as role models for our patients.

On my office waiting-room wall, across from framed diplomas and the "no smoking" sign, another sign reads, "This house is powered by the sun."

The photovoltaic panels that produce all the electricity for my home and office are not easily visible from the street. Lately I have been ready to "come out of the closet" about my love of the environment. The office sign is my coming out statement, part of my narrative about my ongoing dependence upon both the nonhuman environment and sustainable human permutations of that environment. It is a call to personal agency in moving toward a livable future: mine, my children's, and the future of all children alive today.

Conclusions

- Certainly, large-scale immediate legal regulation of carbon-emitting technologies is necessary to avoid ecocide and the extinction of our, and innumerable other, species. Governmental oversight of radical systemic industrial change, similar to that in the Second World War, is necessary. The more aware, on both emotional and cognitive levels, we are of this ourselves, the greater help we can offer our patients in this regard.
- We need to understand our own defensive strategies concerning this crisis, and begin to experience the great losses already occurring, in order to not project disowned affects onto patients who need clinical help to process their environmental concerns.
- We also need to be familiar with specific information and resources to help patients who are ready to take reparative action. Paul Hawkens' book *Drawdown: The Most Comprehensive Plan Ever Proposed to Reverse Global Warming* (2017) clearly lays out many

effective strategies to draw down atmospheric carbon and reverse the precarious path we are on. Whether our patients decide to compost, eat less meat, drive less, fly less, bicycle more, run for a political office, donate to a political campaign or environmental organization, grow vegetables, or all of the above, our analytic offices can provide a crucial holding environment on the way from psychic numbing to the ability to hold this crisis in mind, and actively respond.

The climate emergency is both a legal, regulatory problem and a personal, psychological problem. It was born within a socio-political structure that rewards the economic exploitation of the nonhuman environment, and "others" that environment. Psychoanalytic theory helps us understand the tragic mistakes of the past, the perilous point of the present, and can help in the psychic/societal task of developing a sustainable future.

References

Allured, E. (2014). Blind spot in the analytic lens: Our failure to address environmental uncertainty. In B. Willock & R. Curtis (Eds.), *Understanding and Coping with Failure: Psychoanalytic Perspectives*. New York: Routledge.

—— (2018a). Holding the un-grievable: A psychoanalytic approach to the environmental crisis. *Contemporary Psychoanalysis, 54*(1), 239–246. Review of Climate Crisis, Psychoanalysis, and Radical Ethics (2017) by Donna M. Orange. New York: Routledge.

—— (2018b). Becoming Pegasus: Hope and the manic dream. Paper presented at IARPP annual conference, New York City.

Carter, P., & Woodworth, E. (2018). *Unprecedented Crime: Climate Science Denial and Game Changers for Survival*. Atlanta, GA: Clarity Press.

DeMocker, M. (2018). *Climate Revolution: A Parent's Guide*. Novato, CA: New World Library.

Fleming, R. (2009). *The Callendar Effect*. Chicago, IL: University of Chicago Press.

Freud, S. (1930). Civilization and its Discontents. *The Standard Edition of the Complete Psychological Works of Sigmund Freud, Volume XXI (1927–1931): The Future of an Illusion, Civilization and its Discontents, and Other Works*, 57–146.

Hardin, G. (1968). The tragedy of the commons. *Science, 162*, 1243–1248.

Hawkens, P. (2017). *Drawdown: The Most Comprehensive Plan Ever Proposed To Reverse Global Warming*. New York: Penguin Books.

Intergovernmental Panel on Climate Change (2014) *Climate Change 2014: Impacts, Adaptation, and Vulnerability*. Cambridge: Cambridge University Press.

Jung, C. (1962). *Memories, Dreams, and Reflections*. New York: Random House.

Lertzman, R. (2015). *Environmental Melancholia: Psychoanalytic Dimensions of Engagement*. New York: Routledge.

Lifton, R. (2017). *The Climate Swerve: Reflections on Mind, Hope, and Survival*. New York: The New Press

Mann, M., & Toles, T. (2016). *The Madhouse Effect*. New York: Columbia University Press.

Orange, D. (2017). *Climate Crisis, Psychoanalysis, and Radical Ethics*. New York: Routledge Press.

Randall, R. (2009). Loss and climate change: The cost of parallel narratives. *Ecopsychology*, September 2009, 118–129.

Randall, R., & Brown, A. (2015). *In Time for Tomorrow? The Carbon Conversations Handbook*. Sitrling: The Surefoot Effect.

Rich, N. (2018). Losing Earth: The decade we almost stopped climate change. *New York Times Magazine*, August 1, 2018.

Rohner, R. (1969). *The Ethnography of Franz Boaz*. Chicago, IL: University of Chicago Press.

Samuels, A. (2017). The 'Activist Client': Social responsibility, the political self, and clinical practice in psychotherapy and psychoanalysis. *Psychoanalytic Dialogues*, 27(6), 678–693.

Santostefano, S. (2004). *Child Therapy in the Great Outdoors*. New Jersey: The Analytic Press.

Searles, H. (1960). *The Nonhuman Environment*. New York: International Universities Press.

——— (1972). Unconscious processes in relation to the environmental crisis. *Psychoanalytic Review*, 59(3), 361–374.

Weintrobe, S. (Ed.) (2013). *Engaging with Climate Change: Psychoanalytic and Interdisciplinary Perspectives*. Sussex: Routledge Press.

Winnicott, D. (1975). *Through Paediatrics To Psychoanalysis*. New York: Basic Books.

Chapter 4

The International Psychoanalytical Association at the United Nations

Vivian B. Pender

Introduction

In 1945, the Second World War ended leaving many countries of the world destroyed. People wanted peace and an end to conflict. Later that year representatives of 50 countries met in San Francisco and drew up the United Nations Charter. The mission of the United Nations (UN) would be to maintain international peace and security, protect human rights, deliver humanitarian aid, promote sustainable development, and uphold international law.

The UN currently consists of 193 Member States and its main bodies – the General Assembly, Security Council, Economic and Social Council, International Court of Justice, Trusteeship Council, and the Secretariat. Each Member State is a member of the General Assembly. The Secretary-General (SG) is the chief executive officer of the UN. The current and ninth SG is Mr. António Guterres of Portugal who started his 5-year term on January 1, 2017. There are also funds, programs, and specialized agencies such as the United Nations Children's Fund (UNICEF) and the World Health Organization (WHO). It also partners with approximately 4500 non-governmental organizations, such as the International Psychoanalytical Association (IPA), that represent civil society. In order to implement its goals the UN uses treaties, conventions, and resolutions that are in effect voluntary. Its success depends on good relationships, good will and cooperation. Because of its status with the UN, the IPA can use its expertise to educate and advocate.

The IPA was founded in 1910 to act as an accrediting organization for its professional psychoanalyst members. Its aim would be to advance psychoanalysis worldwide through education, participation and development of the science of psychoanalysis. Although founded much earlier than the UN, the IPA had no significant presence at the UN until 1997. With thousands of members in tens of countries, the IPA's UN Committee was formed to address this need. The charter mission of the UN Committee was to bring psychoanalysis to the UN and to bring the global concerns of the UN to members of the IPA. (As of June 2018 the IPA has 12,770 members with a formal presence in approximately 50 countries.)

In order to further this goal, in 1997 the IPA applied for accreditation by the UN Economic and Social Council (ECOSOC). Later that same year the International Psychoanalytical Association became accredited as a non-governmental organization (NGO) of the United Nations with Special Consultative Status. This accreditation allowed the IPA to work within the entire UN system in New York, Geneva, and Vienna as well as other cities that have a significant UN presence, such as Paris, Nairobi, and Brasilia.

The IPA's UN committee began a trajectory of raising awareness of psychoanalytic theory and psychoanalytically informed individual and group behavior in the international community and likewise raising awareness of international and global concerns amongst IPA members. It was the beginning of an increasing and necessary trend to move psychoanalysis outside of the office and into the community and the world. It was decided that scientific and professional knowledge could transcend political-ideological limitations to enhance humanity and human development. Psychoanalysts could collaborate, provide expertise and leadership as well as benefit from the UN's tools. This chapter will give some examples of the IPA at the UN and how it is able to further psychoanalysis.

IPA collaboration with UN staff

In the first ten years after the IPA UN Committee was formed, reception of psychoanalytic ideas amongst UN personnel was positive. There were a few key senior UN staff members familiar with psychoanalysis. The Secretary-General Kofi Annan, a Ghanaian diplomat and co-recipient of the 2001 Nobel Peace Prize, was a progressive in consideration of mental health. Under his ten-year administration he released statistics on the incidence of depression, anxiety disorders, substance abuse and suicide in UN staff. From that willingness to be open, a task force was formed with members of the IPA's UN Committee and representatives from various levels of UN entities. The charge of the task force focused on providing a model for pre-mission screening, intra-mission therapeutic support, and post-mission evaluation. The understanding of the task force was that previously there was no extensive protocol to address the needs of UN staff in this context. In order to do a needs assessment the task force sent a notice to UN staff and invited them to meet with a few members of the task force. Several focus groups met over the first year to exchange information about their field mission experiences.

In one such group that was well attended, UN staff members explained their circumstances. An example was provided by a man who had a "desk job," researching and writing on his computer, but was asked to fly to a country with a briefcase of cash for a warlord to broker a peace deal. An armed security guard accompanied him. Nevertheless, they were kidnapped, held without knowing what their fate would be, but ultimately released. His distress from this near-death experience was not so much from being kidnapped, but rather when he returned to his desk no one asked him how he was feeling or doing. No one checked with him. Another example was a man who spoke of going on a training mission to help local people complement their security measures. His team was attacked with rocket fire. He saw body parts of his colleagues lying next to him. Fortunately he escaped but he reported persistent nightmares and considered suicide. A third example was a woman with mental health training who was sent on a mission to an earthquake and tsunami area to help disaster victims. Infrastructure had sustained extensive damage and she had to drink contaminated water and eat spoiled food. She developed malaria and had to end her mission early. She felt guilty. She did not complain about her unhealthy circumstances or that she contracted malaria because of her poor health. In fact, she returned to the mission as soon as possible because she thought the UN could have done more for the people who were devastated by the disaster.

The UN staff members who spoke at these focus group meetings were visibly distressed, their voices and bodies shaking, some with tears and red faces. They were re-experiencing their traumatic experiences, that is, they were having post-traumatic stress symptoms. They uniformly complained that they felt alone, isolated and uncared for. They reported that they were given a chest x-ray but not a mental status exam. Specifically, they were not asked about their psychic symptoms. They also reported that they were not in any treatment or therapy and none had been encouraged or offered.

The IPA psychoanalysts and UN members of the task force met approximately every two weeks, sometimes monthly, for three years. Protocols were established that incorporated psychoanalytically informed interventions. One of the findings was the need for more UN staff trained in mental health. A grant was submitted to the Center for Disease Control by another NGO named Disaster Psychiatry Outreach that joined the task force. We learned from meeting with Doctors Without Borders that they usually apply a team approach to their missions, never sending individuals to work alone. This "buddy" system could be understood using attachment theory and relational psychoanalysis. The protocols and findings were submitted to the UN medical staff and the Secretariat. One result was an increase in the number of psychiatrists and psychologists who act as first responders to critical incidents. They also instituted some of the suggested methods of screening, support, and intervening.

Crucial to this project was a psychoanalytic understanding of human development, specifically attachment theory and institutional transference. The existing method of sending UN staff on individual missions or without adequate safety was identified as a critical problem. A suggestion was made to use at a minimum the buddy system so that no one person would feel isolated and alone. Also, a simple post-mission inquiry consisting of "How are you feeling?" was debated and ultimately accepted. The myth of making things worse by asking how a person was feeling was essentially debunked. A UN Committee member led discussion groups of UN staff on the risks and benefits of debriefing methods.

It was also clear that the UN as a whole deals every day with traumatic situations and traumatized individuals. Large numbers of people live with violence, wars, disasters, poverty, famines, unhealthy conditions, poor health and lack of healthcare, human rights abuses, and lack of education. These are a few of the constant concerns of the UN. The concept of secondary or vicarious trauma was brought to the attention of UN agencies. Post-traumatic stress symptoms such as dissociation, anxiety, depression, substance abuse, suicide, and violence could potentially be identified and treated. In addition, under the pressure of such events and issues, regression to childlike affects and behavior is inevitable. Although the UN can offer a holding container-like environment, individual relief from stress and trauma is crucial.

IPA expertise and the UN

The IPA has had multiple opportunities to be in leadership positions at the UN. IPA members have organized and participated in numerous UN conferences. The IPA also has provided expert consultations to various UN agencies and Mission States on group psychodynamics.

A consultation-liaison model is one method of providing psychoanalytic expertise to the United Nations. This involves appraisal of a situation combined with ongoing participation in its management. The UN Committee organized a day-long conference at the UN Headquarters in New York entitled "Approaches to Prevention of Intergenerational Transmission of Hate, War and Violence." In collaboration with the UN Department of Public Information, it provided an opportunity to speak directly to an international audience using psychoanalytic concepts such as projection, projective identification, and superego. The relationship between the individual and society was explored. The origins and vicissitudes of aggression and hatred were discussed in terms of intolerance of difference and the Other. A UN Under Secretary-General noted the need to understand human psychology and the need to inoculate children against the mental damage caused by violence. In severely traumatized individuals psychoanalysis reveals unresolved mourning and a deficit in symbolization. This involves un-metabolized concrete psychic structures organized into a conscious family narrative that is transmitted from one generation to the next (Pender, 2007).

One participant, Dr Claudio Laks Eizirik, President of the IPA, 2007–2011, noted the influence of cultural factors on personality development. Concluding his remarks with some thoughts about prevention, Eizirik remarked:

Informed by analytic knowledge, we know that establishing ways of reducing social division and the projection of hatred are also important mechanisms for social cohesion. This requires finding ways to implement the difficult task of listening to others, be it the stranger, or even the enemy. It was Freud who discussed how this 'stranger' is in fact someone who represents a hidden and unwanted part of ourselves. A good example of listening to the other was recently established at the Barenboim–Said Foundation, where, through music, Israeli and Palestinian children learn how to listen to each other and to play together.

(Pender, 2007, p. 508)

Emergency Sex and Other Desperate Measures (Postlewait, Cain, & Thomson, 2004) was written by three UN relief workers and recounts the loneliness and isolation they felt while on mission in distant war-torn countries. Their experiences are derived from the 1990s in places such as Somalia, Bosnia, and Rwanda that were facing genocides. The three authors describe their stories of desperation and comfort with drugs, alcohol, and sex. They illustrate extreme examples of the stress on workers under such conditions. The local citizens were being massacred and the UN was tasked with peacekeeping. The book's value lies in conveying an inside view of an institution that is otherwise closed. There is a hierarchical chain of authority at the UN where everyone has a superior. The stories in the book were corroborated by the in-person stories heard in the UN peacekeeping focus groups. Implicitly, "emergency sex" is a metaphor for the solution that human beings devise to deal with such inhumane conditions. Psychoanalysts understand this to be regression in the service of the ego. One of the authors, Andrew Thomson, worked as a physician on such projects as exhuming and identifying bodies from mass graves in Srebrenica, the site of a massacre in 1995. Although the book has been criticized for making serious allegations against the UN for corruption, negligence and ineffectiveness, the authors consider the work to be of value in that it brings to light aspects of their work that were hitherto unacknowledged.

Information from *Emergency Sex* corroborated what the IPA members understood about the emotional risks of working in a dangerous profession. The task of the United Nations is greatly affected by the sentience of its work and an understanding of psychoanalytically informed theory is necessary. One psychoanalytic conceptual model is based on the Tavistock study of large groups (Miller & Rice, 1973). The UN can be conceived of as an organism, with input, processing, and output. It is important in studying a system of organization to examine the task and sentient boundaries. The input of the UN system consists of the global public concerns of the world, such as human rights, conflict, mental health, and wellbeing. These come to the attention of the UN directly or indirectly, formally or informally, and the UN is obligated to respond – to crises, to monitor stabilization and progress, to re-constitute and promote development. The group mentality is based on humanitarian goals. In this endeavor its task is always subject to sentient goals. Human suffering, and the alleviation of it, is not only a coincident goal but it can become superordinate. Safety, security, and regression to infantile human needs can overwhelm the work of the UN as illustrated by *Emergency Sex*. There are several ways that the UN seeks to control its boundaries and its narcissistic integrity; however, it is frequently at risk of failing to achieve its work task due to sentient goals.

In addition, an institutional transference to the UN could be identified amongst UN staff as well as in the general public (Gage & Gillins, 1991). For individual and group motivations, an idealized transference to the UN overestimates its power to supply resources and security. Although this image of the UN can bind a community, as a useful phenomenon it can also belie a sign that individual transferences are not working. The fantasied power may also be a sign that a greater source of protection and comfort is necessary in the face of global and potentially life-threatening events. In the example of psychoanalytic work with UN staff, they seemed to have an institutional transference to the UN as if it were an all-providing mother and protecting father. The UN must constantly manage such expectations. The IPA met with leaders such as Under Secretaries-General to provide consultation on the vicissitudes of the relationship with their staff as well as their interface with the public.

IPA leadership at the UN

The IPA's accreditation as an NGO has enabled UN Committee members to be active in large coalitions of NGOs. One such coalition of approximately 100 NGOs (including the IPA) is the NGO Committee on the Status of Women (NGO CSW), established in 1972. Each of the 100 NGOs represented numbers of their members ranging from thousands to millions. The author of this chapter joined the NGO CSW and became Chair from 2007–2011. In that role she presided over events at the UN Commission on the Status of Women, a functional commission established in 1948 and mandated by the UN to meet yearly. The commission's two-week meeting, usually the first two weeks in March, is composed of a delegation of Member States charged with reviewing all aspects of the status of women. At the end of the two-week meeting an outcome document of agreed conclusions is produced. The various NGOs have the opportunity to contribute language or ask a government to include language in the document of approximately 10 to 20 pages. This document goes to the General Assembly where it is voted on by all 193 Member States and becomes recorded as a UN resolution. Such UN resolutions can be binding and enforced by the International Criminal Court in The Hague.

The history of the women's movement at the UN

As evidence began to accumulate in the 1960s that women were dispro-portionately affected by poverty, the work of the Commission began to focus on women's needs in community and rural development, agricultural work, family planning, and scientific and technological advances. The Commission encouraged the UN system to expand its technical assistance to further the advancement of women, especially in developing countries.

In 1972, to mark its 25th anniversary, the Commission recommended that 1975 be designated International Women's Year – an idea endorsed by the General Assembly to draw attention to women's equality with men and to their contributions to develop-ment and peace. The year was marked by holding the First World Conference on Women in Mexico City, followed by the 1976–1985 UN Decade for Women: Equality, Development and Peace. Additional world conferences took place in Copenhagen in 1980 and Nairobi in 1985. New UN offices dedicated to women were established, in par-ticular the UN Development Fund for Women (UNIFEM) and the

International Research and Training Institute for the Advancement of Women (INSTRAW).

The Commission served as the preparatory body for the 1995 Fourth World Conference on Women that adopted the Beijing Declaration and Platform for Action. Forty thousand women attended the 1995 conference. Hillary Rodham Clinton as First Lady of the United States spoke and said famously: "Women's rights are human rights." After the conference, the Commission was mandated by the General Assembly to play a central role in monitoring the implementation of the Beijing Declaration and Platform for Action and advising the UN Economic and Social Council (ECOSOC) accordingly. As called for in the Platform for Action, an additional UN office for the promotion of gender equality was established: the Office of the Special Adviser on Gender Issues and Advancement of Women (OSAGI).

In 2011, the four parts of the UN system – DAW, INSTRAW, OSAGI and UNIFEM – merged to become UN Women, later renamed as Secretariat of the Commission on the Status of Women. As Chair of the NGO Committee on the Status of Women from 2007–2011, the author was instrumental to the establishment of UN Women. Working with health and finance ministers, and Ambassadors of key governments the NGO Committee on the Status of Women on behalf of 100 NGOs the author of this chapter advocated for one UN entity to focus on the status of women and girls.

As an example, at the end of 2011 the only female psychoanalyst in Syria was arrested at the airport as she was leaving to see her daughter in France. It was widely publicized in the media. Rafah Nashed's health was not good. She was reported to suffer from high blood pressure, heart problems, and cancer. Her family was only allowed to see her for an hour each week. Nashed, a French-speaking Syrian psychoanalyst, had obtained her degree in clinical psychology from the University of Paris-Diderot, and was the first female psychoanalyst to practice in Syria (Aboujaoude, 2011). Working with UN Women and the Secretary General, the NGO Committee on the Status of Women used every avenue to monitor her safety while in captivity and demanded her prompt release. The IPA and other psychoanalytic organizations also advocated for her release. She was held for two months and arrived home in reasonably good health.

IPA–UN collaboration benefits

The United Nations provides a great public service by collecting social and economic data documenting best practices and monitoring conditions worldwide. It does this through the World Health Organization, UN Women and the Office of the High Commissioner for Human Rights. Such information is of great importance to the IPA in their assessment of human behavior and needs on a world scale.

World Health Organization

The World Health Organization (WHO) designated as non-communicable certain chronic diseases of long duration and generally slow progression. The four main types of non-communicable diseases are cardiovascular diseases, cancer, chronic respiratory diseases, and diabetes. Many cases are considered preventable by lifestyle modification, such as cigarette smoking cessation and healthier eating habits (World Health Organization, 2016).

Consideration of mental disorders as non-communicable diseases has historically been a difficult topic to advance at the United Nations. Pervasive cultural stigma has contributed to this. The designation "mental illness" is not often mentioned. For the past few years, the term "mental disability" has started appearing in the yearly conference on disabilities. One difficulty is that there are NGOs that complain about "over-medicalization." As an illustration of the tolerance and inclusivity of the UN, an accredited NGO named the World Network of Users and Survivors of Psychiatry has successfully advocated for an absolute prohibition of forced commitment and treatment. This is now an amendment to the UN Convention on the Rights of Persons with Disabilities. Theoretically, a clinician who participates in forced psychiatric commitment and treatment can be brought before the International Criminal Court in The Hague. Only recently in order to focus on the positive, the term "wellness" is supplanting "mental health." The IPA UN Committee members successfully advocated that mental disorders and substance abuse disorders be included in discussions of non-communicable diseases (Pender, 2015).

The World Health Organization initiated a Mental Health Action Plan spanning 2013–2020 to review and implement strategies to improve mental health worldwide. In the Mental Health Atlas 2017, 177 out of 194 (91 percent) of WHO's Member States reported on the progress of implementation of the Comprehensive Mental Health Action Plan 2013–2020 (World Health Organization, 2013). Progress values for 2016 indicate that the global targets can be reached, only if there is a collective global commitment that leads to substantial investment and expanded efforts at country level for mental health policies, laws, programs and services across all Member States.

IPA projects and programs in partnership with other nongovernmental organizations, UN agencies and governments, include topics such as human rights; all forms of violence against women; child protection and abuse; human trafficking; integrated care of mental health with primary care physicians; mental illness; substance abuse; female genital mutilation; and other forms of torture, prejudice, and racism.

UN Women

As Chair of the NGO CSW in addition to representing the IPA at the UN, the author had access to the resources of UN entities (Pender, 2016). These include rich sources of data and statistics on health, including mental health as well as best practices and evidence-based protocols for helping individuals and groups. One such tool is the UN Women's Communications Procedure, which states:

> Any individual, non-governmental organization, group or network may submit communications (complaints/appeals/petitions) to the Commission on the Status of Women containing information relating to alleged violations of human rights that affect the status of women in any country in the world.
>
> (UN Women, 2011)

Benefits of the Communications Procedure

In 2010, six women approached the author, requested to meet and asked for assistance. They lived in a country governed by a totalitarian regime. They had broken the rules of the regime, but not those of the

UN by addressing gender inequality and attending a women's conference in New York. They reported that they had been photographed by what they assumed were agents of the regime and that they would most likely be arrested and tortured upon returning home. They were distressed and anxious. The author as Chair of the NGO Committee on the Status of Women arranged for a meeting with senior UN officials who followed the Communications Procedure. That is, they documented their concern for their physical safety and anticipated human rights violation. The document was sent to the Secretary General who sent it to the government in question which was asked for a reply. In addition, through the networks of the NGO Committee on the status of Women, hundreds of NGOs were alerted.

The following are additional examples of categories of communications received and trends and patterns identified in recent years:

- arbitrary arrests of women
- deaths and torture of women in custody
- forced disappearances or abductions of women
- discriminatory application of punishments in law based on sex, including corporal and capital punishment
- violation of the rights of women human rights defenders to freedom of expression and assembly
- threats or pressure exerted on women not to complain or to withdraw complaints
- impunity for violations of the human rights of women
- stereotypical attitudes towards the role and responsibilities of women
- domestic violence
- forced marriage and marital rape
- virginity testing
- contemporary forms of slavery, including trafficking in women and girls
- sexual harassment of women in the workplace
- unfair employment practices based on sex, including unequal pay
- lack of due diligence by States to adequately investigate, prosecute and punish perpetrators of violence against women

- discrimination against women under immigration and nationality laws
- violations of the rights of women to own and inherit property
- discrimination against women in accessing international humanitarian aid
- forcible evictions of women in conflict situations

(UN Women, 2011)

Office of the High Commissioner for Human Rights (OHCHR)

As the OHCHR is mandated to promote and protect human rights for all, it leads global human rights efforts to speak objectively in the face of human rights violations worldwide. It provides a forum for identifying, highlighting, and developing responses and acts as the principal focal point of human rights education, public information, research, and advocacy activities at the UN. Although recently the global citizen is morphing into the isolationist citizen, the UN continues its global compacts and multilateral agreements. Diplomacy is the mainstay of UN operations. Relationships are important and are based on trust and goodwill. The UN Universal Declaration of Human Rights reads like an optimal primer for the needs of human development – *recognition of the inherent dignity and of the equal and inalienable rights of all members of the human family is the foundation of freedom, justice and peace in the world.*

There are reportedly corrupt governments that are regularly accused by the High Commissioner for Human Rights. The High Commissioner's work entails on-the-ground monitoring of abuses on an almost daily basis. Psychoanalysis can be effective in understanding the effect of a paranoid leader and regression in large groups under totalitarian ideologies. (Simmel, 1969; Volkan, 2014). Psychoanalysis can also understand a group when it behaves like a mass (Le Bon, 1960).

An example of the current High Commissioner's daily news release reads as follows:

Given the scale and gravity of reported violations in the Democratic People's Republic of Korea, I remain convinced that the situation should be referred to the International Criminal Court. Pursuant to this Council's resolution 34/24, my Office is moving forward with an Accountability Project to document human rights violations, particularly those which may amount to crimes against humanity.

Turning to China, President Xi has called for "people-centred development for win-win outcomes as part of a community of shared future for mankind," a commendable ambition. Sadly, China's global ambitions on human rights are seemingly not mirrored by its record at home. My Office continues to receive urgent appeals regarding arbitrary detentions, enforced disappearances, ill-treatment and discrimination, emanating from human rights defenders, lawyers, legislators, booksellers, and members of communities such as Tibetans and Uyghurs.

In Ecuador, I commend the Government for conducting a very broad dialogue, including with media and human rights defenders, as a first step towards overcoming the country's polarization. In Saudi Arabia, I note with great interest the royal directive stipulating that all government services must from now on be provided to women without prior approval from male guardians. I commend The Gambia for its announcement of a moratorium on the death penalty last month. In Somalia, I welcome a number of positive developments, including the establishment of a national human rights commission with a diverse composition, and I encourage the Government to continue its efforts to build institutions and bring peace.

(UNOHCHR, 2014)

When working with religions psychoanalysts must have a deep understanding of how religions are structured and how they function. They are also accused sometimes of human rights violations (Davies, 2014). For example, the Holy See, representing the Vatican, repeatedly accused NGOs of being too "ideological" in supporting women's reproductive rights, while at the same time the Vatican was accused of facilitating sexual abuse of children. The Main Representative for the Holy See read a statement at UN Headquarters, Conference Room 4, on March 19, 2018 during the 62nd UN Commission on the Status of Women that illustrates their position:

Condoms, contraceptives, sex education programs fabricated elsewhere, … so-called 'safe abortions,' have become commodities that are more accessible to Africans than the way of delivering integral development, of which we have such a vital need. It can no longer be denied that under the euphemism of 'sexual and reproductive health and rights,' such programs are plainly imposed as a condition for development assistance. Such is also the case of the so-called 'gender perspective,' according to which motherhood, the filial and nuptial identity of the human being and the family based on marriage between a man and a woman would be 'discriminatory stereotypes.'

This process of ideological colonization needs to be called out. The development system should never be used as a Trojan Horse to attack the cultural and religious values of developing nations. We would never intend to criticize development assistance, but when it becomes an instrument of imposition and control over poorer peoples' and nations' ways of life and values systems, we have to call it out.

(Holy See Mission, 2018)

It should be noted that the Holy See has Observer status at the United Nations. They cannot vote or propose resolutions; however, they have a privileged role in speaking to UN audiences. They are recognized as a sovereign state.

United Nations Development Program (UNDP)

In 1990 the UN Development Program produced a report (Human Development Index, 1990) that introduced a new approach for advancing human wellbeing. In 2016 it was updated. Human development – or the human development approach – is about expanding the richness of human life, rather than simply the richness of the economy in which human beings live. It is an approach that is focused on people and their opportunities and choices.

Human development focuses on improving the lives people lead rather than assuming that economic growth will lead, automatically, to greater wellbeing for all. Income growth is seen as a means to development, rather than an end in itself. It is also about giving people more freedom to live lives they value. In effect this means developing people's abilities and giving them a chance to use them. For example, educating a girl would build her skills, but it is of little use if she is denied access to jobs, or does not have the right skills for the local labor market. Three foundations for human development are to live a long, healthy and creative life, to be knowledgeable, and to have access to resources needed for a decent standard of living. Many other things are important too, especially in helping to create the right conditions for human development. Once the basics of human development are achieved, they open up opportunities for progress in other aspects of life.

In addition, human development is, fundamentally, about more choice. It is about providing people with opportunities. No one can guarantee human happiness, and the choices people make may or may not increase their happiness. The process of development – human development – should at least create an environment for people, individually and collectively, to develop to their full potential and to have a reasonable chance of leading productive and creative lives that they value.

As the international community moves toward implementing and monitoring the 2030 agenda of the WHO Mental Health Action Plan, the human development approach remains useful to articulating the objectives of development and improving people's well-being by ensuring equitable, sustainable, and stable environments.

Summary

The United Nations is a system of governments, administrative bodies, and civil society activists that work to achieve agreements, resolutions, treaties, conventions, and protocols for the benefit and progress of humanity. It focuses on peaceful resolution of disagreements and seeks to ensure human rights. Much of the participation in the UN system is voluntary. The IPA partners, collaborates, provides expertise and leadership at the United Nations. Psychoanalytic theory has been and continues to be a useful tool to educate and advocate for the benefit of humanity. In order to carry out these activities psychoanalysts are mindful of the complex global nature of the United Nations.

Global mental health is a burgeoning field that will benefit greatly from the input of psychoanalytic understanding of psychic processes. Such examination can include ego development, identity formation, integration of environmental values and proscriptions, as well as the effect of mental illness on an individual. Likewise, psychoanalysts can benefit from the global programs that the United Nations constructs and implements.

In the last twenty years the IPA has progressed in increasing awareness of and advancing psychoanalysis at the UN. Other NGOs and the IPA are currently advocating that each Member State Mission to the UN designate a specific representative to focus on issues of mental health. Such an arrangement will contribute to an expanded focus on the importance of psychoanalytically informed approaches to the problems faced by the UN. The IPA will surely have a large role to contribute to future UN mandates.

References

Aboujaoude, E. (2011). Muting a therapist: The case of Dr Rafah Nashed. *Psychology Today.* www.psychologytoday.com/us/blog/compulsive-acts/201109/muting-therapist-the-case-dr-rafah-nashed. Accessed June 2018.

Davies, L. (2014). Catholic church leaders prepare for grilling by UN human rights panel. *The Guardian.* www.theguardian.com/world/2014/may/05/catholic-church-un-human-rights-torture-sex-abuse. Accessed June 2018.

Gage, K., & Gillins, L. (1991). Institutional transference: A new look at an old concept. *Journal of Psychosocial Nursing and Mental Health Services 29*(4), 24–26.

Human Development Index (1990). United Nations Development Program (UNDP). http://hdr.undp.org/en/content/human-development-index-hdi www.wnusp.net/. Accessed June 2018.

Le Bon, G. (1960). *The Crowd.* New York: Viking Press.

Miller, E.J., & Rice, A.K. (1973). *Systems of Organization.* London: Tavistock Publications.

Pender, V.B. (2007). Approaches to prevention of intergenerational transmission of hate, war and violence. *International Journal of Psychoanalysis 88,* 507–514.

——— (2015). "Invisible Disabilities" at the 9th Conference of States Parties of the Convention on the Rights of Persons with Disabilities, United Nations Headquarters, December 3, 2015. http://i.unu.edu/media/iigh.unu.edu/news/4685/Making-Invisible-Visible.pdf. Accessed June 2018.

——— (Ed.) (2016). *The Status of Women: Violence, Identity and Activism.* London: Karnac.

Simmel, G. (1969). *Conflict and The Web of Group-Affiliations.* New York: Free Press.

The Permanent Observer Mission of the Holy See to the United Nations (2018). https://holyseemission.org/contents//statements/5ab038668965c.php. Accessed June 2018.

United Nations Office of the High Commissioner for Human Rights (2014). www.ohchr.org/EN/pages/home.aspx. Accessed June 2018.

UN Women (2011). Brief History. www.unwomen.org/en/csw/brief-history. Accessed June 2018.

———— (2011). Communications Procedure. www.unwomen.org/en/csw/communications-procedure. Accessed June 2018.

Volkan, V.D. (2014). *Psychoanalysis, International Relations, and Diplomacy: A Sourcebook on Large-Group Psychology.* London: Karnac.

World Health Organization (2013). WHO Comprehensive Mental Health Action Plan 2013–2020. www.who.int/mental_health/action_plan_2013/en/. Accessed June 2018.

———— (2016). Noncommunicable Diseases and Mental Health. www.who.int/about/structure/organigram/nmh/en/. Accessed June 2018.

Chapter 5

The politics of evil

The American Psychological Association, psychoanalysis, and the law[1]

Ghislaine Boulanger

In November 2014, the American Psychological Association (APA) appointed David Hoffman, Esq., of the Chicago law firm Sidley Austin, to assess whether there was any factual support for the assertion that the APA engaged in covert activities that would constitute collusion with the Bush administration to promote, support, and/or facilitate the use of enhanced interrogation techniques by the United States in the war on terror.

This is an astonishing accusation to be leveled against a professional organization charged with establishing and enforcing an ethical code for its members and, furthermore, with representing the public face of that profession to America, indeed, to the world. For close to a decade, psychologists, both members of the APA and those who had resigned in the face of growing evidence that this charge was correct, had been requesting such an investigation. Nonetheless, and true to the APA's practice of ignoring or denouncing critics from within its ranks, the appointment of the independent reviewer was made not in response to members' protests and resignations, but after the publication of *New York Times* Pulitzer prize-winning author James Risen's 2014 book, *Pay Any Price: Greed, Power and Endless War*. Risen offered detailed evidence about a conspiracy between the APA and the Department of Defense (DoD). Originally, Risen's book had been met with the usual skepticism with which the APA greeted detractors, but, in a sudden turnabout, then APA President Nadine Kaslow announced that the association had engaged a special investigator to look into these charges. She instructed APA staff and all psychologists with information to share to be in touch with Mr. Hoffman.

When it was made available by the *New York Times* on July 11, 2015,[2] the 542-page report (Hoffman, 2015) concluded that prominent psychologists worked closely with the DoD to blunt dissent within the APA over an interrogation program that is now known to have included torture. It also found that APA staff colluded with the Pentagon to ensure that the association's ethics policies did not hinder the ability of psychologists to be involved in the interrogations in Guantanamo Bay and the CIA black sites. The APA is revealed to be an organization that, while insisting on its impeccable human rights record and repeatedly arguing that its ethics code had prohibited participation in torture since 1987, continually revised the ethical guidelines in such a way that they did not depart in substance from DoD policies. In this way, the organization simultaneously made it possible for members to engage in coercive interrogations while actively shielding them from ethics complaints.

In many ways the Hoffman report reveals as much about the duplicitous culture that has been rife throughout the organization for many years as it does about APA's stance on torture. For over ten years by lying, denying, and deceit, the Ethics Director, Chief Executive Officer, vice Chief Executive Officer, Director of Communications, General Counsel, and various elected presidents of the association worked to keep the special relationship with DoD secret in the face of mounting protests from the membership. Many of those implicated in the cover-up have now left the organization; some were dismissed, most took early retirement with generous packages and public expressions of gratitude for their years of service!

Coming as it did, a month before the APA's annual August convention in 2015, the report gave the Board of Directors (BOD) an opportunity to entertain new motions that would address the most obvious ethical loopholes, for example by voting to enforce a referendum against the presence of psychologists in Guantanamo Bay. The referendum had, in fact, been adopted by the membership in 2008, but its implementation was consistently undermined by the Ethics Director in consultation with the DoD, as the Hoffman Report reveals (Aalbers and Teo, 2017).

In *Torture and Democracy* (2009), Darius Rejali points out that when the state begins to torture, many decent professionals leave their posts while those who remain create a "culture of impunity." The APA functioned as a culture of impunity for 15 years and more. This chapter offers a summary of those years as ethical loopholes were created to bypass gross violations of human rights and to provide a legal cover for the conduct of APA military psychologists in Guantanamo Bay; all the while, the APA dismissed protests from its members, claiming a strict policy against torture.

In 2002, shortly after the terrorist attacks in New York and Washington, the APA altered its ethics code and created its own "culture of impunity." To a clause that read: "If psychologists' ethical responsibilities conflict with law, regulations, or other governing legal authority, psychologists make known their commitment to the Ethics Code and take steps to resolve the conflict," the following sentence was added: "If the conflict is unresolvable via such means, *psychologists may adhere to the requirements of the law, regulations, or other governing legal authority*" (emphasis added). As former chair of the APA's Ethics Committee, Kenneth Pope, who resigned from the APA in protest over these changes and other ethical breaches, commented, the APA's ethics code "now runs counter to the Nuremberg Ethic" (Pope & Gutheil, 2009, p. 162). In other words, if American psychologists were charged with unethical conduct, they could claim that they were merely following orders, just as healthcare professionals in Nazi Germany did when they were prosecuted at Nuremberg.

The APA maintains that this change, officially known as Ethical Standard 1.02, had been under consideration for several years (Puente, Evans, & Boulanger, 2017), but the timing was fortuitous, and the change ran counter to medical ethics worldwide. In fact, the World Medical Association's International Code of Ethics states that a doctor's conscience and duty of care must transcend national laws, but the United States government never signed on to this global agreement.[3]

Not only did the APA stake out a position that was in direct opposition to the International Code of Ethics, clearly the organization also felt no pressure to align itself with American health professional organizations that had withdrawn support from members working in Guantanamo Bay. For example, when, in 2006, the American Psychiatric Association overwhelmingly voted to discourage its members from participating in the interrogation process in Guantanamo Bay, Steven Behnke, the Director of Ethics for the APA, emphasized the "unique competencies" that psychologists brought to their role in interrogations, and claimed that psychologists who help military interrogators made a valuable contribution by safeguarding the welfare of detainees (Lewis, 2006). In a mantra that was to become familiar, repeated hypnotically on every occasion when psychologists' role in Guantanamo Bay was challenged, Behnke stated that the presence of psychologists kept interrogations "safe, legal, ethical, and effective."

Human rights organizations and congressional oversight committees took a very different view of the close ties between psychologists and the Bush administration's war on terror. Physicians for Human Rights, the International Committee of the Red Cross, the UN Commission on Human Rights, and the Senate Armed Services Committee documented cases of psychologists advising, and, in some cases, directing the interrogation of detainees in enhanced interrogation techniques that constitute torture under international law.

Waterboarding was the benchmark used to measure the depths to which the Bush administration was prepared to sink in its wrongheaded assertion that inducing terror is the best way to wrest accurate information from uncooperative informants. Waterboarding also became a litmus test for what was considered torture; however, in 2004 the International Committee of the Red Cross maintained that the conditions of detention in Guantanamo Bay in and of themselves were "tantamount to torture." Metin Basoglu, an internationally renowned authority on war, torture, and the treatment of survivors, concurred.

In a 2009 paper, Basoglu argues that considerations of what constitutes torture must take into account the setting in which those behaviors occur. By their presence in the chain of command, psychologists were implicitly and explicitly complicit in these particular violations of human rights. At Guantanamo Bay, psychologists shared responsibility for designing and implementing the "softening up" process by which prisoners were prepared for interrogation. Psychologists played a role in determining which detainees would be placed in solitary confinement and for how long. To foster dependency and compliance, they designed a system in which detainees were regularly deprived of sleep, exposed to temperature extremes and incessant loud music, and their religious practices frequently violated. In this system personal items, such as mail, pens, books, soap, and even toilet paper, were considered "comfort items," and were thus under the control of the mental health staff who distributed them in a system of rewards and punishment.

While some psychologists were assigned to the Behavioral Science Consultation Teams (BSCTs) that were responsible for the conditions described above, and purportedly for guaranteeing that interrogations were safe, legal, ethical, and effective, others functioned as counselors, working with detainees who were referred for psychiatric treatment. These counselors routinely made highly questionable diagnoses. For example, naval psychologists Kennedy, Malone, and Franks (2009) wrote that of approximately 50 individuals in treatment in Guantanamo, 43–45 percent were diagnosed with a personality disorder; 17–19 percent were diagnosed with a mood disorder; and 15–17 percent with an anxiety disorder. Bearing in mind that some of these men had been in combat prior to their detention, all of them had been summarily parted from their families and held virtually incommunicado for six years when this data was collected, all had been subjected to humiliation and to random acts of violence, most of them faced the terror of interrogation and – at the time these diagnoses were made – had no idea how long they would be detained, it is clinically improbable that less than 20 percent of them should be exhibiting symptoms of anxiety or depression. How were these diagnostic decisions made? Legal arguments developed by the Bush administration (Bybee 2002) claimed that harsh interrogation strategies could only be considered torture if the perpetrator *intended* to cause prolonged mental harm. Psychologists whose diagnoses emphasized pre-existing personality disorders and overlooked acute symptoms clearly permitted the DoD to argue that torture had not taken place.

Iacopino and Xenakis (2011) questioned not only these diagnostic practices but also the clinical treatment detainees received. After reviewing declassified documents, they concluded that psychological assessments of detainees indicate that these evaluations were conducted to identify psychological vulnerabilities, not evidence of intentional harm. The authors elaborate: although seven detainees had symptoms supporting the diagnosis of Post Traumatic Stress

Disorder, clinicians did not inquire about or document the possible causes of these symptoms. In this way, the authors argue, medical and mental health providers failed to document physical and/or psychological evidence of intentional harm. Iacopino and Xenakis conclude that the evidence of severe physical and severe and prolonged psychological pain suggests that such pain had to be the interrogator's precise objective and therefore constitutes torture according to the Bush administration's definition of torture and was, furthermore, in violation of the United Nations' Convention against Torture and the Geneva Conventions.

In 2007 I was invited to speak during a series of panels on Ethics and Interrogation at the APA Convention in San Francisco. In order to prepare for my presentation, I interviewed one of the pro-bono lawyers who regularly visited Guantanamo to prepare detainees' *habeas corpus* briefs. The six Algerian detainees this attorney represented had been arrested in Bosnia in 2001. They were diapered, hooded, put on a plane with earmuffs to prevent them communicating with one another, shackled to the floor, their hands manacled, and flown – with several stops in which more detainees were picked up – until, after 30 hours without food or bathroom facilities, they disembarked among the first 500 prisoners to arrive in Cuba in January 2002. When the attorney I interviewed arrived at the prison camp nearly three years later, no one had spoken to these men except interrogators since their arrival. All of them had been subjected to the various softening-up treatments described above in addition to different forms of interrogation. "It was as if there was a series of interrogation consultants passing through," the attorney told me. "Either that or we were training interrogators. Each one was pushing his own techniques." But solitary confinement appears to have been a staple.[4]

The insidious effects of sensory deprivation and isolation have been well documented. The literature consistently points to the fact that even those individuals who do not have predisposing psychological disorders may develop paranoid delusions and schizophrenic symptoms in solitary confinement. Basoglu (2009) found that mean distress ratings for physical torture were comparable to several non-physical stressors including isolation and sensory deprivation in causing traumatic reactions.

Being the object of another's malevolence leaves an indelible mark on the psyche. Even if that malevolence does not involve lasting physical damage, it can, and frequently does, lead to the collapse of the self; a kind of psychic disenfranchisement that makes the survivor question whether he did, in fact, survive. For many, during the actual persecution, there is a temporary respite from terror when what I call catastrophic dissociation (Boulanger, 2007b), and Krystal (1978) describes as a catatanoid reaction, sets in to protect the victims from feelings of utter helplessness, terror, and fear of sudden death. The Army Field Manual's (2006) guidelines for how much sensory deprivation and isolation a prisoner may be subjected to are clear: "Physical separation of an individual may only last for an initial period of 30 days. Any extension of that initial period must be reviewed by the Staff Judge Advocate and approved by the General Officer who initially approved the use of separation" (para. M-29). However, extensions were routine in Guantanamo.

The attorney I interviewed witnessed the progressive deterioration of one client's mind when he was kept in isolation for far longer than the Army Field manual prescribed. An Arabic scholar and schoolteacher, this detainee was arrested, along with the five other Algerians who had moved to Bosnia to work with the Red Crescent, because he was married to the daughter of the janitor at the US embassy in Sarajevo and therefore theoretically had access to the embassy. By June 2006, this man had spent more than half his five-plus years in Guantanamo in varying degrees of forced isolation. In June 2006, he was once again put into isolation.

On August 17, 2006, the detainee swore in an affidavit recorded by his attorney: "I have suffered being totally alone, not seeing the sun and not having anyone to speak with in a language I understand. I feel hopeless being here in isolation with no reason."

He was held in an 8ft x 6ft cell. A fluorescent light was kept on 24 hours a day; the only window had been painted over, limiting the natural light, so there was no distinction between day and night. He received no family mail, was not allowed to keep the legal mail he did receive, and was denied a pen to write his counsel. Several months after his affidavit was recorded, in November 2006, when his attorneys next visited him, the detainee had lost approximately 38 pounds. He was talking to himself, bursting into spontaneous laughter and shouting apparently in response to hallucinations. In the moments when he could communicate clearly, he told his counsel that he thought of killing himself every day.

At his attorney's next visit several months later, he would not respond to the invitation to visit with him. "When he was informed we were there, we were told that he was lying listlessly on his bunk staring at the wall," his attorney told me. "He has been unresponsive for some time. I think he has given up."

This is what Krystal (1978) describes as a lethal surrender pattern. "The physical immobilization observable in this state is accompanied by a massive blocking of virtually all mental activity, not just affects, but all initiative" (p. 94). Sudden outbursts of activity, such as suicide attempts or self-mutilation, or shouting represent life-saving attempts at mastery, a bid to interrupt the state of helplessness and the process of surrender. These behaviors grow out of the need to create some kind of stimulation, any sensation that distinguishes inside from outside. But for this detainee, these last-minute psychic protests appear to have ended by the time his lawyers returned in March 2008. The surrender had become lethal.[5]

Emphasizing to the APA's insistence that psychologists were present in Guantanamo Bay to protect the welfare of the detainees, I concluded my address to the panel on Ethics and Interrogation with the question: "Where are the psychologists when they are needed?" (Boulanger, 2007a). It would be safe to assume that despite the APA Director of Ethics' claims to the contrary, the protection of human subjects was not foremost in the minds of the psychologists present in Guantanamo Bay.

Pope (2016) makes a distinction between professional ethics designed to "protect the public against abuse of professional power, expertise, and practice" and guild ethics that "place members' interests above public interest, edge away from accountability, and tend to masquerade as professional ethics." The APA's Code of Ethics did not fail; it served exactly the purpose for which it was continually revised in the years between 2002 and 2009. It placed the association's interests in maintaining a special relationship with the DoD above the public interest, and protected military psychologists from charges of professional misconduct, as the Hoffman report documents. "In some ways," Hoffman writes, "DoD is like a rich, powerful uncle to APA, helping it in important ways throughout APA's life. Acting independently of a benefactor like this is difficult" (p. 72).[6]

What does this deplorable account of a professional association losing faith with its members and losing sight of its original purpose have to do with psychoanalysis? Many, but not all, of those who originally led the opposition to the APA were psychoanalysts.[7] Ours is a seditious practice, an investigative discipline that seeks the truth even if that truth could be a threat to the social order (see also Reisner, 2010), even as that truth runs counter to ethical codes. We encourage our patients to look beneath the surface, not to accept easy explanations. Using our psychoanalytic skills to interrogate the APA's rationalizations and frequent revisions to its ethical guidelines proved critical in uncovering the depth of duplicity that the Hoffman Report laid bare. Deconstructing APA practices exposed the stark differences between our psychoanalytic tools and the law, particularly as the APA used the law to mislead the public and its own members.

The APA employs a rhetorical style that pays careful attention to detail, to *the letter of the law*, but nonetheless ignores, indeed denies, the substance of an argument. For example, in 2009 the APA website gave details of the changes in APA policy brought about by the passage of the referendum banning psychologists from working in settings that violate international human rights law. APA officials frequently mentioned this policy in conversation with other professional groups. Yet, at that point, the policy had never been implemented, and would not be for six years. Military psychologists continued to work in Guantanamo Bay until 2015. (Aalbers & Teo, 2017; Puente et al., 2017)

Bollas (1995) argues that a state, like a family, must be founded on the presumption that its citizens are governed by leaders who have their best interests at heart. Knowing our leaders are ill-intentioned undermines our most profound assumptions about human safety. I extend Bollas' analogy to professional organizations where choosing to belong is surely predicated on the belief that the leaders represent the members' best interests. Yet, Bollas holds, the politics of evil trade off this need for much of the time we are complicit in overlooking our leaders' moral failures. With its facile rhetoric, constantly evolving ethical standards, and cynical manipulation of the facts, APA's policies devolved into a politics of evil. The majority of rank-and-file members were lulled by the leaders' reassurances and by their wish to believe that the organization was representing their best interests; indeed, many members turned viciously against the dissenting psychologists for questioning their leaders' integrity (Boulanger, 2017). The members' inaction made them complicit in overlooking the erosion of the association's moral standing. In the end, however, the actions of those who were determined not to overlook this ethical breakdown but rather to confront it finally bore fruit.

After the Hoffman Report was published, reforms appeared to be underway. In August 2015, less than a month after the report became public, a policy (35B), making good on the promise to ban military psychologists from sites that are in violation of international human rights, was enthusiastically adopted by the Council of Representatives (COR) with only one dissenting vote. Finally, seven years after the passage of the referendum, military psychologists were withdrawn from Guantanamo Bay.

Yet, I found myself repeating the old joke about how many psychologists it takes to change a lightbulb. The answer, of course, is one; "but the light bulb must want to be changed." I wondered, does the APA really want to change? Can it? As psychoanalysts we know that traumatic roots run deep; they can be dissociated, passed from one generation and enacted in the next. What about on an institutional level? Institutional memory is short. Does the malignant organizational structure Welch describes (2017) remain buried in the fibers of APA governance?

My skepticism was not misplaced. At the APA Convention in August 2018, it was resolved to remove the link to the Hoffman Report from its prominent position on the APA website, a mark of transparency carried proudly for three years. Whether the link's removal was in response to a defamation lawsuit brought by two former employees of the APA and three retired military psychologists against Mr. Hoffman, the APA, and several of the dissident psychologists who, along with the plaintiffs, had provided information to Mr. Hoffman and his team is a matter of speculation. The plaintiffs claim that the report was biased and that after they lost their jobs they have been unable to find comparable employment.

Far more challenging, however, was a bill to return military psychologists to Guantanamo Bay proposed by two military psychologists and fully supported by the BOD. In response to this attempt to reverse the policy that had been accepted enthusiastically three years earlier, a loose alliance of psychologists from many different branches of the discipline organized several weeks ahead of the 2018 APA Convention to discuss individually with each member of the Council of Representatives the possible ramifications of passing the proposed bill (APA Watch, 2018). Simultaneously, more than a dozen human rights organizations and the UN Special Rapporteur on Torture and other Cruel, Inhuman and Degrading Treatment or Punishment wrote letters to the COR "protesting the proposal to roll back protections instituted to safeguard psychologists from complicity in torture and abuse and to facilitate ethical and independent mental health care for detainees at the Guantanamo Bay Detention Center" (APA Watch, 2018). The bill was defeated with 60 percent voting against.

It is unusual, if not unprecedented, that a bill to which the BOD has lent its full support is not carried. Within six weeks of this legislative upset, however, Jessica Daniel, then President of the Association, in a letter to the DoD published on the APA website, reassured the DoD that "APA Council resolutions are *aspirational* statements and are not *enforceable*," unlike the requirements of the Ethics Code (Daniel, 2018) (italics mine). It is worth noting that APA Bylaws give the COR "full power and authority over the affairs and funds of the Association … including the power to review, upon its own initiative, the actions of any board, committee, Division or affiliated organization" (American Psychological Association Bylaws, 2018a). Nonetheless, in her statement to the DoD, the APA president is publicly challenging the authority of the COR and the viability of the landmark 2018 vote.

In her letter, Daniel is exploiting a loophole that was initially introduced in the Ethics Code of 1992 when the distinction between enforceable and aspirational codes was first made. At the time it referred specifically to the "general Principles of Psychology that are aspirational goals to guide psychologists toward the highest ideals of the profession," whereas the Ethical Standards are enforceable rules for conduct. But in the 25 years since it was first made, the APA has come to rely on this distinction as if it were a dead letter drop into which inconvenient policies, such as this one that challenges the APA's special relationship with DoD, remain trapped in a no man's land between aspiration and enforcement.

In theory, any attempt to turn an aspirational goal into an enforceable standard would have to go through the Ethics Committee, all the members of which are nominated by the BOD, and voted for by the COR. This ostensibly democratic process however leads to carefully selected APA members, known to support the APA directors' agenda, being nominated. In effect, there is no conversion mechanism in place that would reliably change aspirational policies than run counter to the BOD's interest into enforceable ones.

As if this were not reason enough to question the APA's good faith, the association has built in a further check against assuming responsibility for an ethics policy that appears to reflect the will of the majority of its members when it comes to the ban on APA psychologists in Guantanamo Bay, while simultaneously maintaining a relationship with the DoD. In a seismic policy shift, the APA recently announced that it will only adjudicate ethical complaints if there is no alternative forum in which to hear the complaints (APA, 2018b). Putting aside the effect of this decision on the majority of psychologists, be they in private practice or employed by corporations or agencies, in the context of this chapter it is clear that the APA has once again abdicated responsibility for overseeing the conduct of psychologists in Guantanamo Bay should they return to work there. We have come full circle. Once again, as with ethical standard 1.02, psychologists will not be called upon to answer to their own profession's Code of Ethics (which has become considerably more forceful as a result of the battles waged between psychologist dissidents and the APA in the first decade of this century) but rather to "an Inspector General, the military chain of command, or other government grievance channels" (Pope, 2018). And once again, if they are challenged about their treatment of detainees, the psychologists will have recourse to the Nuremberg defense. Their professional association has publicly declared that it will not hold them to either the profession's aspirational goals or enforceable standards.

Notes

1 This chapter is adapted from the introduction to a special issue of *The International Journal of Applied Psychoanalytic Studies 14*(2) on the APA and the War on Terror (Guest Editor: Ghislaine Boulanger). Reused by kind permission of the journal. Many thanks to Brad Olson, PhD, and Bryant Walsh, PhD, whose reliable grasp of some of these elusive facts is always welcome.

2 Originally the APA had claimed that it would release the report after the BOD had had an opportunity to review it, but when it was not forthcoming it was leaked to and released by the *New York Times*.

3 In 2009, after years of pressure from dissident members and human rights organizations, the APA amended Ethical Standard 1.02 to read: "If psychologists' ethical responsibilities conflict with law, regulations or other governing legal authority, psychologists clarify the nature of the conflict, make known their commitment to the Ethics Code and take reasonable steps to resolve the conflict consistent with the General Principles and Ethical Standards of the Ethics Code. Under no circumstances may this standard be used to justify or defend violating human rights."

4 The description of these events is based on the notes I took when I interviewed the attorney and on the letters and personal notes he showed me while I was in his office.

5 In September 2008, in ruling on this detainee's *habeas corpus* petition, the court found that there was no evidence to support classifying him as an "enemy combatant," and that he should be released. He was transferred to French territory on November 30, 2009, where the French foreign ministry pledged to help reintegrate him into society.

6 Summers 2008 offers a detailed history of this relationship which began benignly enough with funding for research and opportunities for training in the 1940s.

7 Dan Aalbers, a psychologist dissident, who is not a psychoanalyst but an expert in the history of psychology, is a notable exception. Together with clinical psychologist Ruth Fallenbaum and community psychologist Brad Olson, he crafted the 2008 referendum which became the basis for current APA policy banning psychologists from working in sites that are in violation of international human rights law.

References

Aalbers, D., & Teo, T. (2017). The American Psychological Association and the torture complex. *Journal fur pychologie, 25*, 179–204.

American Psychological Association (2018a). ByLaws and Association Rules. www.apa.org/about/governance/council/index.aspx, retrieved October 28, 2018.

———— (2018b). Filing an Ethics Complaint, www.apa.org/ethics/complaint/index.aspx, retrieved October 30, 2018.

APA Watch (2018). Alliance for an Ethical APA website: http://allianceforanethicalapa.com/, retrieved September 25, 2018.

Basoglu, M. (2009). A multivariate contextual analysis of torture and cruel, inhuman, and degrading treatments: Implications for an evidence-based definition of torture. *American Journal of Orthopsychiatry*, *79*(2), 135–145.

Bollas, C. (1995). *Cracking Up: The Work of Unconscious Material*. New York: Hill and Wang.

Boulanger, G. (2007a). Where are the psychologists when they are needed? Paper presented at mini conference on Ethics and Interrogation, APA Annual Conference, San Francisco, 2007.

———— (2007b). *Wounded by Reality: Understanding and Treating Adult Onset Trauma*. Mahwah, NJ: The Analytic Press.

———— (2017). What can reality television teach us about psychoanalytic politics. *Contemporary Psychoanalysis*, *53*(4), 533–546.

Bybee, J. (2002). Memorandum for Alberto R. Gonzales, Counsel to the President. Available: https://nsarchive.gwu.edu/NSAEBB/NSAEBB127/02.08.01.pdf accessed 2/14/2019, retrieved February 14, 2019.

Daniel, J. (2018). Letter to the Secretary of Defense for Health Affairs, www.apa.org/news/press/statements/interrogations.aspx, retrieved October 28, 2018.

Dept of the Army (2006). Army Field Manual N0 2–22.3, Human Intelligence Collector Operations.

Hoffman, D. (2015). The Hoffman Report Revised, 9/04/2015 www.apa.org/independent-review/revised-report.pdf, retrieved September 12, 2018.

Iacopino, V., & Xenakis, S.N. (2011). Neglect of medical evidence of torture in Guantanamo Bay. A Case Series. PloS Medicine April 2011, *8*(4).

Kennedy, C., Malone, R., & Franks, M. (2009). Provision of mental health services at the detention hospital in Guantanamo Bay. *Psychological Services*, *6*(1), 1–10.

Krystal, H. (1978). Trauma and affects. *The Psychoanalytic Study of the Child*, *33*, 81–116.

Lewis, N.A. (2006, June 7). Military alters the makeup of interrogation advisers. New York Times. www.nytimes.com/2006/06/07/washington/07detain.html, retrieved June 8, 2006.

Pope, K.S. (2016). The code not taken: The path from guild ethics to torture and our continuing choices. *Canadian Psychology/Psychologie canadienne*, *57*(1), Feb 2016, 51–59.

——— (2018). The American Psychological Association Outsources Adjudication of Ethics Complaints: 5 Far-Reaching Consequences.

Pope, K.S., & Gutheil, T. (2009). Psychologists abandon the Nuremberg ethic: Concerns for detainee interrogations. *International Journal of Law and Psychiatry*. *32*(3), 162–166.

Puente, A.E., Evans, A.C., & Boulanger, G. (2017). Correspondence. *Int. J. Appl. Psychoanal. Studies*, *14*, 163–164.

Reisner, S. (2010). From resistance to *resistance:* A narrative of psychoanalytic activism. In A. Harris & S. Botticelli (Eds.), *First Do No Harm: The Paradoxical Encounters of Psychoanalysis, Warmaking, and Resistance.* New York and London: Routledge.

Rejali, D. (2009). *Torture and Democracy*. Princeton, NJ: Princeton University Press.

Risen, J. (2014). *Pay Any Price: Greed, Power and Endless War*. New York: Houghton, Mifflin, Harcourt.

Summers, F. (2008). Making sense of the APA: A history of the relationship between psychology and the military. *Psychoanalytic Dialogues*, *18*(5), 614 – 637.

Welch, B. (2017). The American Psychological Association and torture: How could it happen? *International Journal of Applied Psychoanalytic Studies*, *14*(2), 116–124.

Part II

Problems of diversity and identity

Social violence and social control

Introduction

Plinio Montagna and Adrienne Harris

In this part, we take up problems where the legal and the psycho-analytic/psychodynamic forces are in tight and often uncomfortable tension.

These matters are much in our awareness in this period, in the wake of an international set of movements about harassment, power, consent, and freedom in relational configurations where equality is sometimes difficult, sometimes impossible. #MeToo is a variable set of experiences sometimes within the law, sometimes yielding to punishments or action outside the law. It is perhaps one of the unique contemporary problems where the psychodynamic and the legal are in such exquisite tension. Whether thought of as boundary problems, or the contesting of identities as legal and psychological structures, or the particular form that criminality takes when it can be said to be gendered, the chapters in this part bring the discomfort and agony of these legal/psychological matters right into our consciousness.

Adrienne Harris and Katie Gentile push the focus on boundaries problems and abuses of power into our own psychoanalytic institutes and traditions, though it is clear that many structures – legal, educational, and cultural – contain, mask, and often explode over these issues of right action and respect across varieties of differences (status, power, gender, sexual identities, race, and class). The human subject as a matter of law and dynamic formation sits at the heart of all the chapters in this section.

In addressing the problems and challenges of supporting diversity, we have been particularly interested in representing different communities. Each culture addresses diversity from its own history and value structure. The struggle for basic rights is one of the underlying themes of this volume and the question of subjectivity and difference is taken up by a number of our authors across all the parts of this book (Laura Orsi and Alicia Beatriz Iacuzzi regarding women's rights develop this perspective in this part of the book, while Rakesh Shukla discusses it in Part 4 with regard to caste in India).

In Chapter 8 Gley Costa (from the situation and experiences of diversity in Brazil) and Ann Pellegrini, in Chapter 9 (from the perspective of North America) unpack both the cost of phobic practices and the long struggle for rights and status and respect for difference. Costa's focus is on the gains within the clinical situation and the social to developing a perspective on gender's complexity and diversity, a necessary escape from the pathologizing force of heteronormativity. Pellegrini is looking at the contradictions that arise in the encounter of law, politics, and complex models of gender and sexuality, often underwritten by psychoanalysis. She is attentive to the contradiction in legal rights for gay citizens and the constriction of abortion rights for women in the United States. The law is still the disciplinarian of sexuality and many forms of identification.

Chapter 6

Femicide-feminicide

Laura Orsi and Alicia Beatriz Iacuzzi

Violence and femicides in the media, networks, and their impact

Laura Orsi

Violence against women, in particular its most serious form (femicide/feminicide), responds to many factors, such as social constructions and the symbolic violence that exists around what it means to be a man and to be a woman in different societies.

Mass media have a fundamental role in these constructions, because of the contents, languages and narratives that they use, as well as for the consumption by the audiences. What effects, if any, can be covered and spread in cases of murders of women among victims and criminals? What role can or must journalism and media play in violence against women?

Women's homicides have gained more social and media attention in recent decades. Although there is more information on the serious problem of gender violence and the growing number of feminicides is covered as never before by the media, the number of cases does not decrease; on the contrary, it increases alarmingly.

Many women have used Twitter and Facebook to organize and speak publicly about gender violence. The virtual exchange transcended the networks and the media, and took manifestation in the streets: the march of #Niunamenos, which was replicated in other places of Latin America and also in Europe.

According to a report published by "La Casa del Encuentro,"[1] between January 1 and December 31, 2016 there were 290 femicides in Argentina and, as a result, 401 children lost their mothers (242 of them were minors). The survey reports a growth in the number of murders of women (in 2015 there were 286). Statistics are maintained: every 30 hours a woman is killed in the country because of her gender.

Among the hard data in the report, another statistic stands out in the matter of femicides: most of the women (102) were murdered by their husband, partner or boyfriend. Of the total number of murdered women, 10 were pregnant and 31 suffered signs of sexual abuse before their death. The majority were aged between 19 and 30 (102 cases), and between 31 and 50 (103).

As for the criminals, 49 of them committed suicide after committing the murder, 19 belong or belonged to the security forces, and 18 had a restraining order from the home. Out of the 290 cases, only 28 reported previous cases of gender violence, which shows a low tendency (approximately 1 in 10 cases) of women to report these cases, which deserves to be taken into account. Another interesting fact – and one that persists with previous reports – is that in 62 percent of the cases women were murdered in the place where they should have felt protected – their home.

Crimes are increasingly violent and women are still being killed despite many acts of violence being reported. In only 28 cases, the victims had reported gender violence. One in 10 femicides could have been avoided if the victims had received the necessary protection from the state.

The situation in relation to the assistance of women is the same. There are complaints, but what protection do women receive after the reports? Are the precautionary measures fulfilled? After reporting, the woman and the children are exposed.

Intimate femicides are often the corollary of prior violence applied on women by their partners or ex-partners, that is, they do not constitute isolated violent incidents. This highlights the role of gender-based violence policies in the prevention of femicides and the protection of women. Therefore, it seems that more effective action is needed. There is a gap between the action and what is written in the laws. There are deficiencies in campaigns that are dedicated to prevention.

It is interesting to analyze the connections between the murders of women on grounds of gender and the media coverage of these, particularly in Latin American countries. Different television cultures can offer different narratives and propose other visions of society through them. Thus, the narratives of the news varies according to the countries and their cultures: in some, they do not allow narrative resources of the fiction (music, close-ups, reiterations, melodramatic constructions), that are central in the narrative construction of the media in Latin America, which is more sensationalist.

The role of the media in the production and reproduction of gender stereotypes and, in particular, gender violence has been a concern of feminist studies for decades.

In the case of news production, it is important to consider the low participation of women in newsrooms and editorial positions, as in society as a whole.

In the media coverage of femicide/feminicide and violence against women, various approaches have been identified: the police's or "just the facts"; the one that considers that these events involve people different from "us"; the one who blames the victims and/or excuses the criminal; and the approach from the impact because the criminal is identified as "normal." These approaches maintain a critical disconnection between femicides/feminicides, presented as isolated and individual cases, and domestic violence as a broader social problem.

A recent study in Sweden shows how most of the news stories describe violence as the result of imbalances in the family system, putting the focus of the problem at the individual level, which prevents violence from being understood as a social problem.

Of course, there are some exceptions: journalists, radio and TV programs, certain media and (a few) advertisements that are unmarked from this type of approach. Since 2000, for example, the General Directorate for Women of the Autonomous City of Buenos Aires has awarded the "Lola Mora"[2] awards, a recognition given to those who, from different media, transmit a positive image of women, breaking with gender stereotypes and promoting equal opportunities and women's rights.

Closer in time, in July 2016, the International Network of Journalists with a Gender Vision of the Americas was formed in order to make women aware of and promote communication with a gender perspective throughout the region (Argentina, Brazil, Chile, Colombia, Paraguay, Peru, and Uruguay).

Can the communication generate a copycat effect? The copycat effect is mentioned in various reports in the case of acid-burned women. It allows us to identify a certain imitation effect when comparing the days when the news involves cases of femicides and the days when this type of news is not presented, concluding that the presence of intimate femicides in television news seems to increase the possibility of death because of this.

According to the reports of the organization "La Casa del Encuentro," in recent years there has been an increase in femicides in Argentina, with a peak in 2011. Likewise, cases of "burning" have begun to have a greater presence since 2010, the year in which Wanda Taddei's femicide occurred, from 2.6 percent of total femicides in 2009 (6 women burned), to represent 10.28 percent of the cases in 2011 (29 women burned). Since the death of Wanda Taddei and until the first half of 2013, 66 women were killed in this way in Argentina.

However, beyond the cases of consummated femicides, numerous cases of women attacked with fire have also been detected: in the three years after the death of Wanda Taddei, 132 women were burned by men in Argentina, of which almost half died. Women's organizations and some media as early as September 2010 warned about the repetition of the pattern in attacks on women, as well as the not-so-high media impact of those other cases.

The allusion to the "Wanda Taddei effect" is currently widespread at the media level in Argentina to allude to the multiplication of femicides committed by burning after that case. For this reason, the fear of being victims of violence, often fueled by the press, also constitutes a mechanism that contributes to ensuring the subordination of women. Media coverage of violence against women and femicide/feminicide adds to the multiplicity of social factors that influence these phenomena.

There has also been a protective effect of the news, when they are more focused on measures against violence against women and femicides than on crimes (regarding laws, statements and interviews with politicians and key figures in the field of violence against women or public acts condemning such crimes).

At the international level, different agencies have developed minimum standards to face content production and the development of cultural industries from a gender perspective. Along these lines, national and international manuals have been developed, with suggestions for producing content with a gender perspective, avoiding stereotypes and expanding the type and number of specialized information sources which the media usually takes into account.

While it is difficult to conclusively establish the magnitude of their effects or how they impact on the media in relation to other factors, it is also not possible to ignore that they have an impact. From the perspective of the mass media, good practices should be promoted that contribute to improving quality standards in the coverage of violence against women, which is consistent with the company social responsibility (CSR) policies that have been consolidated little by little.

It is necessary to admit that "violence against women and girls is an extreme manifestation of gender inequality and discrimination and it's also a tool, sometimes mortal, to maintain their subordinate situation" (UN Women, 2011).

As Charlotte Bunch says, "sexual, racial, gender, and other forms of discrimination in culture cannot be eliminated without changing culture."

Interstitials of feminicidal violence and its excesses. Femicides
Alicia Beatriz Iacuzzi

The environment that I am making reference to is composed by the fact of serving a sentence of liberty deprivation and its consequences. The psychoanalytic conceptual scheme offers metapsychological supports for problems with other representations, offering new work fields. Those field surveys and researches need a further doxa – episteme integration.

In the twenty-first century violence has been installed in the culture. Linking relations are increasingly being brought to court in search of answers to growing conflict. In most cases of feminicide violence or femicides the aggressor/killer is a partner. "Connected" femicides or feminicides have also increased (those are cases when the children are taken as hostages to harm the woman). Each victim's deadly silence is questioning us. That is why I considered it extremely current to focus on feminicidal violence, focusing on the other side, as there are few discussions about it.

Feminicide or femicide are often used as homologous categories. Although the suffix "cide" means particularly killing, I choose the word "femicide" to make reference to the homicide of a woman. And the broad meaning of the suffix "cide" (to eliminate, to exterminate) is used when I say feminicide to refer to the many ways of symbolically killing the subjectivity of women (both in omissions and episodic or permanent actions).

Femicides and feminicides reveal social pathology, harming the fate of the new offspring. They lead to social decomposition, being indicators of a "not good enough" public health. It is our job to work with clinical thinking on violent subjects of violent acts with the aim of preventing recurrences that end up only in taking them to the courts. Femicide/feminicide are not conceptualized as a clinical entity. Field work in a prison is a privileged space for it.

Harsher sentences do not necessarily have a greater deterrent effect. The law settles goals and aims in those sentences. The punishment looks simultaneously towards the future and the prevention. The key is what happens to the subject during the serving of the sentence.

The prison is created as a public safety device to prevent dangerous individuals from living in the community. But it is turned into a place only for punishing people. In order to legitimize our participation in the criminal execution, it is essential for us to be authorized voices that account for some type of process in the subjects that are subject to judicially indicated institutionalization. As mental health workers we could not ignore the importance that has falling into the precariousness of clinical offers.

The therapist is in great helplessness in these situations, this is also a declaration in order to give them the suitable tools when they are formed as psychoanalysts according to the different social spaces. I had to create my own way to reach the unconscious in any situation. After having spent more than 25 years in a penitentiary institution with my psychoanalytical toolbox, I believe that it is difficult to meet the complex intimacy that is established with prisoners in general and femicides and feminicides in particular. The motto is that custodial sentences have subjective meaning.

Although I can speak about the misfortunes that arise in the forensic field because of dealing with the effusiveness of the criminal's unconscious, who lost control over his miseries (impulses and passions, lacks, etc.), it is reassuring that psychoanalysts are not skeptical. Being part of the prison system generates visceral countertransference. As the interventions are in transfer we train ourselves in recognizing the textures of the corporal sensations that we experience. So many years of thought and clinical work with these distinctive subjective sufferings have left traces, as a person and as a psychoanalyst. But I attest that the clinical dynamics in this extraterritoriality are possible.

From the proper locus of enunciation one is competent to give account of a knowledge by virtue of transferring inter-transferring inter-games. Freud invited us not to impoverish the clinical offerings in the diverse social spaces, conferring validation to a task enriched by vivid practices.

Derivatives of clinical dynamics with femicides and feminicides who are imprisoned

My purpose of sharing interstices of practice with feminicides and femicides in a prison setting is to invite us to continue making paths by walking.

The inclination to these criminal modalities has been growing. The author of a criminal act is not a legal abstraction. As a social fact these actions merit clinical interventions even to put an end to the repetition compulsion. Addressing these cases is also to prevent.

The committer of a crime is not only a subject of security and criminal policy. As they are not thought about and treated within the scope of public health, it is a symptomatic issue while the community continues to attend women's funerals.

Although the conception of subject for criminal law and for an analyst differ, there is a guiding connection concerning the subject in question. The work in the psycho-socio-legal interface is a new practice and there is also a lot that remains to be investigated.

I stated that the psychoanalysts had to get involved, and to get "psychoanalytically" involved with these questions. I would agree that the time of deprivation of liberty is instituted as an opportunity for joint work with the prisoner. That time is sufficiently transcendent to establish a work contract to initiate and eventually move towards adherence to some type of treatment with all the impasses that qualify any clinical process. The demand for listening makes it necessary to co-create – along with these particular patients – an intersubjectivity with clinical edges as the position of the analyst is far from being that of an expert in these delineations. It is clear that in the difficult task of "attending" clinically a prisoner, he is not always "psychoanalyzed," we cannot even speak of healing, rather of subjects who manage to be transformed (and not transformed) through renewed life pacts from the activation of other psychic currents.

My inquiries were based on the optimization of proposals for approaches, individual and group clinical offers. It is the clinical attitude that makes the attempt to find the balance on the passage from "convicted subject" to an "analyzed subject," to "build" a patient. This is a hard point but the question changes when the subject can see the difference between expert intervention and analytical intervention. In my experience receptivity and acceptance is significant in this microcosm, it generally occurs the transference with clinical space and intersubjectivity because of the non-indifference to people with their own circumstances. Regarding results: it is sometimes hopeful and in others, adverse.

Regarding clinical field research with people deprived of liberty by femicide and feminicide – in order to give them more magnitude – we could refer to "Femicidal Spectrum Disorders" as a range of such disorders that include a deficit in the exchange and the circulation of the corresponding link (in different edges) with the woman that affects in different ways to each man and they can be from mild to serious (homicide). I make reference to Spectrum to represent and give a wide range of the different variants regarding context, background, and excesses of the group of "feminicides" forming a whole group with all of them together.

Testimony of an analyst in the exercise of her profession

I would particularly understand "treatment" with prisoners as a transformative linking experience. To operate in this way we need insight. In many cases reaching unfathomable low bottoms, they can approach the destination neuroses by characterological fixations.

The so-called criminal is instructed not to "reveal" his inner world. Introducing strategies of "encounter between powerlessness" (that of the analyst and the one of the subject) the change is notorious, bearing an intimate clinical nexus.

As we enter into the psychic reality of each case, there is a mobilizer déjà vu: as if the same language is not spoken, the language of action predominates, its transference expressions specify archaic binding modalities, etc. In a prison we must admit a clinical universe where what cannot be captured by language reaches its maximum expression. Many languages circulate in a whirlwind that are not compatible with ours. The analysts are forced to develop some form of figuration by the feelings of strangeness that go through them so as not to be annihilated in their specific function. In general, most people find it hard to look into their eyes. I realized by chance that when interventions are done looking into their eyes, the drifts are different. With this, and without alluding to the suggestion, I emphasize the importance of the look and eventually the fruitful work that together with the subject we can do around this sensitive part of his humanity that favors an integrated image with a human face of himself and of the other person. It is not taken for granted that it is always effective. Following the line of argument, the femicides' hands – having been the instrument with which they have committed the action, enabling the frenzy of killing – fill the analyst with a special creepy feeling.

The subjective impact produced by unconscious communication makes a gap. A tense face, a choppy tone of voice, reinsurance behaviors through subtle avoidance (others do not notice their gesture, the babbling, or the choppy tone of voice), that which deregulates the individual, are equations that concern us from the point of view of reliable analytical revelations since language cannot absorb everything. Another variation is revealed by unyielding faces, with no expressiveness. They are referred to as icy "people," when listening to them we can see how their complex histories appear disassembled or absolutely simplified. Silence is also heard (in gestures, intense breathing). In others, the thickness of silence works with effects of violence directed at the analyst (they try to disrupt the interlocutor with it).

It is not unknown that many subjects can serve a sentence and not assume responsibility for the crime committed with any possible internal reproach. At this point, remorse (which differs qualitatively from repentance when the latter refers only to the correlate of having lost the freedom by the act), is a clinical indicator that can give rise to reparatory mechanisms by recognizing with some dose of pain the damage caused.

There are times when no psychoanalytic act can be exercised. It is indispensable to probe what possibility the individual has to accommodate the analyst, in what place, etc. It is vital for the analyst to dive inside if he/she can accept it. In particular the influence of the look, the exchange of glances, are circumstances that imply an exposition of the analyst. It also requires cleverness to avoid becoming involved in the power game that they intend to impose. It must be admitted that no one can remain unaware to the disrespectful power they seek to obtain.

Listening to them it would be inferred that an exalted pleasure seemed to be located in the face of the victim who reflects alienation. The human face terrified, being crushed and depersonalized by the subjugation, or the face of the victim, who having succumbed to seduction through manipulations, is blindly "surrendered" to the domineering master, would promote satisfaction and concupiscence. That joy would establish a need for repetition. The pleasure in this aggression game is generated by controlling and cynically dominating the woman, who becomes an object with a terrified human face, depersonalized and underestimated. As the pleasure of loving has been replaced and overinvested by surrendering, the passage to the act becomes the way by which harassment and power over women would be attached to a "madness of control." Consequently, what happens around attachment patterns? Attachment seeks to maintain closeness at any price with someone who is meaningful to them. Exasperation, anger, fury, and aggression would be the correlate of an attachment-disorder perturbation matrix in its insecure and disorganized slopes. The degrading and destructive hostility towards the partner erupt when security is threatened or put at risk (loss). The traumatic affliction, the feeling of lack of protection and annihilation by the dissipation of the availability of the other to the codependency is transmitted irascibly to the act. The extremely deranged reaction is the predatory attack directed at the body of the other to hurt or injure her, to the extreme of sometimes not stopping to the point of criminal violence. Paying with life is the price to pay off the offense of having deserted a relationship. But is it only fear of separation and abandonment? In violent discharges there would be a quantum of endogenous excitation flowing hemorrhagic ally Feminicidal behaviors do not always bring pleasure, but the search for relief from internal tension by a high sensitivity of these individuals to the signals that predict abandonment.

Regarding the psychological approach *a posteriori* to the dictation of the judicial sentence by femicide, it is substantial to explore and deal with the psychological autopsy of the criminal, the quality and function of the object and its new place. Briefly, I conceive a "psychological autopsy" to reconstruct the conditions that led to the murderous crime of women; and the intention, fantasies, thoughts before her death some time after the moment of the mournful event. It would strictly suppose the process of subjective decoding with the femicide of the psychological traces of thoughts and feelings that the victim had towards the victimizer (and vice versa); of the conflict areas in the type of established relationship and the implications of the deadliness (guilt, pain, shame, resentment, etc.). I would put stress on: How does he hold the victim? Is there pity during the execution of the sentence? What did he lose with the loss? This would emphasize three aspects: 1) subjectivation of the crime scene; 2) where and how the victim remains within the internal world of the criminal; and 3) if a mourning process is done (can the mourning of an object that was not prepared to be lost be made?), and what modalities it adopts. Regarding the quality of the anguish before the loss of the significant other, what singularity does it take? Is the victim's disturbance present; or insists on her dishonor or accusations and reproaches?

They transmit that there would be no room for two, showing their discomfort.

The moment you make eye contact with somebody (as frightened as I am) leaves a mark forever. Anyway, empty looks are astonishing. The body of the analyst is the first to record the impact of the representational emptiness and the indomitable division of the revelation.

For the transferential experience would optimize its therapeutic role; the point is that the clinical function is not closed (or not seen as closed), that insanity would not dominate and oppress the clinical space. It is undeniable that the ace in the sleeve is that the preconscious comes to our aid.

It is not feasible to find prototypical clinical prints. The analyst throws herself into (without metaphors) her work, recreating procedures, reshaping and innovating them to establish intersubjective limits to reveal the funds of intolerable representations. The catharsis – which the patient expels, evacuates, throws away from him without significance – occurs in the least expected moments.

In spite of the montage that makes the subject understandable, the analyst has to make very clear what is not negotiated: the law, the verdict of judgments of the judicatures, their application and service as stipulated. This is a turning point. In this way, the discourse of psychoanalysis is situated, thus making evident the support to the law.

How can we reach these subjects to make them subjects subject to civilization? In the twenty-first century to remain being a psychoanalyst without succumbing requires the adaptation of our instruments to offer each one a sign of subjective investment, taking care that it does not become another violent act. In order to build bridges, it is appreciated some meetings, light dialogues that are creating some kind of "partnership." I insist: it counts the thought of the clinician regarding the assistance experience, proving crucial the vitality of the encounter between the subject and the analyst.

Forming groups as spaces for the exchange of experiences is a non-wasteful link since it sponsors pre-transferring to a personalized therapeutic space. It is true that being with others can strengthen unconscious alliances, persecutory aspects, etc., and so this window favors that the indifference is directed toward differentiation – personalization; the boundary and demarcation of interstitial zones with the other and acceptance of object relations. The group background supports each member of the feared helplessness and abandonment. It is important to note that the dangers of violence arising out of the group can take place outside the group, and therefore outside the clinical setting. This is very serious institutionally since these acts (retaliations, fights) – being conceived as misconducts – deserve sanctions. Although they are necessary to control as possible chaos, from another perspective they can go to the detriment of the convict and the process in progress. Hence the pre-eminence of the consistent daily presence so that the word could be more at hand than the action (of those who are on one side and the other of the bars).I will not extend here but it is very important the work that the analyst does with the authorities and the guards of the institution in relation to the nature of our work. The prisoner is obsessed by a dominant worry: what he will have to face when he regains his freedom. In the "Pre-Release Programs" it must be foreseen that the eviction to the extraterritoriality of the prison in its internal and external meanings carries no less clinical relevance.

I have accumulated satisfactions and frustrations but what I have learned – in Winnicottean expression – is good enough and precious enough to continue. I have been through many situations. Instead of resigning, I tried to restate our function not to resign. If an analyst is there, it does not have to be in vain. When the pact with Thanatos is very strong, even knowing the existence of utopias, I would pronounce in favor of the presence of mental health professionals in these spaces vitiated by denigratory patterns, in order not to fall into functional omissions.

Corollary: the presence of a psychoanalyst in a prison is a matter of Human Rights and a work in favor of Public Health. Crime is a human action of a subject that is framed as a psycho-social fact and as such deserves clinical interventions. Treating femicides and feminicides is another way of dealing with victims. From this statement I point out – do not silence them with psychoanalysis.

Notes

1 The report was released in February 2017. It was the first time that the Adriana Marisel Zambrano Femicide Observatory (named after a young woman from Jujuy beaten to death by her partner and father of her daughter), dedicates to the publication of the statistics. The act was carried out in the Senate of the Nation.

2 Named in tribute to the important Argentine sculptor, born on November 17, 1866 in El Tala, province of Salta. The recognition was born in 1999, when the Legislature of the City of Buenos Aires enacted Law No. 188, but the award was first given in 2000.

References

Aulagnier, P. (1979). *The Destinations of Pleasure*. Barcelona: Editorial Petrel.

———— (1980). *The Lost Meaning*. Barcelona: Editorial Trieb.

———— (1982). Condemned to invest. *APA Magazine* 2–3.

———— (1994). *An Interpreter Looking for Meaning*. Mexico: E. Siglo XXI.

———— (1997). *The Violence of Interpretation*. As. A.E. Buenos Aires: Amorrortu Editores.

Foucault, M. (1976). *Discipline and Punish*. Mexico: E. Siglo XXI.

Green, A. (1990). *Life Narcissism, Death Narcissism*. Buenos Aires: Amorrortu Editores.

———— (1993). *The New Psychoanalytic Clinic and Freud's Theory*. Buenos Aires: Amorrortu Editores.

———— (1993). *The Work of the Negative*. Buenos Aires: Amorrortu Editores.

———— (1994). *On Private Madness*. Buenos Aires: Amorrortu Editores.

———— (1997). *The Chains of Eros*. Buenos Aires: Amorrortu Editores.

———— (1998). Live speech. Ed. Promolibro. Valencia.

———— (2005). *Key Ideas for a Contemporary Psychoanalysis*. Buenos Aires: Amorrortu Editores.

———— (2010). *Clinical Thinking*. Buenos Aires: Amorrortu Editores.

Iacuzzi, A. (2004). Setting psychoanalysis in motion at a penal institution. 2004 FEPAL Award. Guadalajara, Mexico.

———— (2005). Psychoanalytical work in a penal institution. *APU Magazine* 101. Uruguay.

———— (2006). Concerning the mental health unit in a penal institution. 1st Argentine Congress of Mental Health.. 2006 and 2007 Award. Buenos Aires, Argentina.

———— (2007). "Psychoanalysis and work in prison." Presentation at the Research Training Programme of the IPA (International Psychoanalytic Association) at University College of London. London (England).

———— (2007). Co-writer of "Psychoanalysis inside. Inside the psychoanalysis." Printer Topia, Buenos Aires, Argentina.

———— (2009). The enigmatic prison labyrinths. A psychoanalytic itinerary. Ediciones de las Tres Lagunas. Argentina.

———— (2010). Crimes against sexual integrity. Psychoanalytic link from the shadows of being in prison. Ediciones de las Tres Lagunas. Argentina.

———— (2012). The psychoanalytical clinic with prisoners convicted for sexual crimes. *Magazine of Psychoanalysis of Guadalajara*, 6. Guadalajara, Mexico.

———— (2016). "Relational violence against women and their excesses" published in book COWAP: Parental issues and Gender. Its impact on subjectivity. Buenos Aires: Editorial Letra Viva.

Kancyper, L. (1992). *Resentment and Remorse*. Buenos Aires: Editorial Paidós.

Welldon, E. (2014). *Playing with Dynamite: A Personal Approach to the Psychoanalytic Understanding of Perversions, Violence, and Criminality*. Madrid: Psimática Editorial.

Winnicott, D. (1990). *Deprivation and Delinquency*. Buenos Aires: Editorial Paidós.

Chapter 7

Boundary violations, consent, the law, and the lawless

Adrienne Harris and Katie Gentile

In this chapter, we consider the matter of boundary violations, sometimes but not always in forms of sexual assault, as they occur, are addressed or ignored, or, more rarely, handled with due process and sometimes with immediate action and sanction. We look at this process in institutes of education and in the institutions of psychoanalysis and clinical psychology. We also broaden this inquiry to think about the boundary violations that occur in the workplace, in cultural institutions in the form of sexual harassment and exploitation.

We write this in a particular social/historical moment. Heightened awareness of the force and scale of sexual harassment, accusations of prominent individuals in business and in cultural institutions (which included complaints about our current sitting US President), give a quite different backdrop to the atmosphere of silence, amnesia, and dissociation that probably most women (the primary but not sole victims of such assaults) have lived with and in.

So the law and lawlessness interact in unpredictable ways. In this chapter, we look, as psychoanalysts, at this uneven and unstable social ground, first in psychoanalytic institutions and then in the broader culture. Most recently we see this process appearing in the world of the academy and inevitably perhaps cases in which women are being charged with such harassment or assault. In one prominently discussed instance, discussions have been fraught with conflict, including questions as to how gender and harassment are engaged, including how identified female victims of male violence might themselves also be accused as perpetrators. Clearly the current climate goes far beyond traditional ideas of do'er–done to, perpetrator–victim. As these binaries are challenged, we find ourselves in the midst of continuing accusations and affect-laden responses, where the neo-liberal individual takes the fall (or not) while the systems of oppression underlying these actions are left untouched. Thus we find ourselves in a temporal space that calls for a more complex analysis of power and the ways it functions within not just dyads, but within institutional and cultural bodies.

Boundary violations in the history and practice of psychoanalysis

It is now (finally) axiomatic in writing about and conceptualizing boundary violations to notice the severity of the damage and the scope and range of who is damaged and how. The violation of trust; the attack on linking of past, present, and future; the self-critical worry that it is the analysand's judgment that was impaired; the huge and seeming unending costs of splitting; and the death of goodness very widely conceived: these outcomes occur at the individual and at the collective level.

A boundary violation is certainly an attack on the analysand who is victimized. It is also an attack on the community that has supported and often deeply esteemed the person committing the boundary violation (Pinsky, 2011). As persons in a community in which boundary violations have occurred, we think often that these acts were made out of a hatred of psychoanalysis, of its disciplines and demands, and of its practitioners. Whether this is the perpetrator's intention, one cannot say definitively, but it is one hypothesis to explore as engaged members of psychoanalytic communities large and small.

The irony and the ghastly truth, of course, is that there is no analytic community immune from boundary violations. Boundary violations were present in the earliest periods of our psychoanalytic history, both as the acts of serial offenders and single instances that appear to have been driven by some particular set of circumstances. The history of institutional response to boundary violations has been more silencing than confronting. The work of Gabbard (2017) and Celenza (2007) and the recent courageous writing of Muriel Dimen (2011, 2016) mark a more determined effort to confront boundary violations.

So whatever conclusions or themes and processes one discerns in the current situation one can assume that the effects of silencing and amnesia have leaked through a number of generations. This global and totalizing aspect of boundary violations adds to the terrible difficulties for community members in managing such events as they intrude into collective consciousness. We swim in poisoned waters.

Incest and primal scene

In 35 years of practice, I (AH) have had experiences with boundary violations in my communities, most of which follow a familiar path. I have had colleagues – some close, some more distant, all revered and admired – accused of boundary violations. All took some steps to move away from the community, leave posts in institutions and community projects; in some cases they retired medical licenses. All these practices were believed to be acknowledgments of culpability. And strategies to avoid official censure. None of these individuals made any acknowledgment publicly of what had happened. I have no experience of someone expressing remorse and in most cases there is simply a disappearance, in fact and in discourse, of the person who is believed or known to have committed a boundary violation. The imposition of silence is ubiquitous.

Perhaps paradoxically, silence in the communities and their subgroups are often fear-driven, built on the worries about lawsuits and a punishment of the community member who speaks out. Perhaps this is paradoxical because it is the bystander who is fearing punishment, often from the accused person who will sue on the basis of harm to his/her reputation. Also, we are all very familiar with the social antagonism towards the whistle blower, the person who breaks silence. Dimen (2011) has written about this in the context of her ongoing experience of having spoken out and written about a boundary violation which she experienced.

Many of us, therefore, speak as part of the collateral damage, practitioners who may feel that the practice, and the community of practitioners, and the theory itself are damaged by boundary violations. This damage has been with us from the beginning of psychoanalysis and we are just beginning to be able to see and assess its intergenerational effects. While we know many of the details and incidents that appear very frequently among the reports and accounts of early days in analysis, we don't always think about the long shadow of intergenerational effects that these early transgressions may have initiated. The long-term effects of boundary violations are part of the unspeakable history of this field, a history that threatens always to erupt and reinjure all of us.

The problems of silence and speech in the communities (micro and macro) are not merely a fear about litigation. When we reflect on the experience of discovering and assimilating an instance of a suspected boundary violation, I have always in some form or other had an experience of quite extreme cognitive and affective destabilization. It has taken different forms. Being upset itself becomes a problem, a symptom of something wrong with me. In extended discussions and conversations one can feel crazier and crazier. Who was the violator here? This worry surfaces in our fear of lawsuits. However real such fears are, they must also be driven by the unconscious guilt and terrors that the criminal is oneself.

As we all engage in more conversations and discussions about boundary violations, one can see that these symptoms of free-floating anxiety and distress are ubiquitous. A colleague requesting some public forum for discussion and continuing to make the request when the initial query was ignored, was finally asked by a more senior colleague why she was so anxious by this. The problem had migrated from perpetrator to bystander. Guilt was so contagious it could be acquired simply by a show of interest or concern.

Here, we must pursue a psychoanalytic answer. Among other matters, a boundary violation breaks our western, First World version of the incest taboo, a taboo of near universality. Given transference and countertransference, we must experience the breaking of an absolutely indissolvable boundary between parent and child to be at the heart of a boundary violation in an analytic treatment. To the degree that a taboo always entails and even privileges anxiety about its breaking, the violence of incest within a community must destabilize everyone. Through processes of identification or projection, the surrounding people, close or far from the center of the crisis, must feel implicated. Every element or instance of erotic countertransference that has arisen in our practices or supervisions rises to haunt us.

We should not forget that we have unconscious elements that remain untamed and always partially unmanageable. How can we practice psychoanalysis without this understanding of everyone's vulnerability? It is not that anyone can commit a boundary violation but that with the alignment of various forces and circumstances, a risk, never entirely absent, may reach impossible levels. And most importantly, the vulnerability to anxieties about taboo breaches, even if such breaches never occur in an analyst's life and practice, create, in him or her, heightened levels of anxiety when something does occur in the community. This vulnerability is the byproduct of the necessary agreement analysts make to work with uncertainty and to be able to notice and tolerate the ongoing mysteries of elements in the unconscious, particularly the erotic.

In communities, the silences and the silencing create the worst conditions for healing splits and sometimes fatal alienations. Institutes and communities have actually been destroyed by the appearance and mismanagement of boundary violations. Here I believe we find the potency and terror evoked by the primal scene.

When a boundary violation is uncovered, in print, or through communications within a community, a private door is thrown open, something unsavory and dangerous revealed. We feel excluded. We feel sick. We feel grateful if our analyst has been steady and containing. We fear that everything will be destroyed: reputations, livelihoods, communities. A tsunami threatens. In this mix there is both perception and fantasy.

The primal scene has been of interest in some theoretical endeavors more than others. Bionian and Kleinian, classical and modern, anchor development with a mature genital couple as a kind of structuring background. The system is potentiated by barriers, hierarchy, and exclusion, with its humiliating but also relieving features for the child.

It must be that the revelation of a boundary violation invokes both a breaking of the incest taboo and a dramatic even violent plunge of all surrounding persons into the sight and reality of the primal scene. Guilt, but a guilt also linked to excitement, is at least one of the inevitable outcomes of simply being a bystander. Many people in analytic institutes have experiences and knowledge of boundary violations as an intergenerational problem. Whether carried as rumor or factual history, these phenomena make institutes unsafe. And unsafety is one of the derailers of thinking. Because legal issues often seem to force a collective silence, the mix of fantasy and reality in regard to the health or weakness of one's institutional home remains unanalyzable. We are often enjoined not to use the most important tools in our professional lives: introspection and relatedness.

Violations and harassment occur in particular social conditions. There is subjugation and the exercise of domination, but I also think that there may be subtle forms of envy and anxiety in some of these scenes/situations. As Gabbard observed, while perpetrators might be cast out, exiled in an attempt to purify the community, there can also be a simultaneous envy of the violating analyst who is also seen as having gotten away with it. Thus there are conflicting responses to these incestuous boundary crossings, all of which indicate the need for different, more integrated responses that include the communal body.

Institutional betrayal and restorative justice

In the handling of boundary violations and harassment we see the failure of legal process, the fear and intimidation and in some more recent instances, the swift retribution of public sanction, firing and criminal process initiated. Within psychoanalysis historically, boundary violations were either hidden, or when visible led to swift and fatal exile. Is there a place in these phenomena of violation, for restorative justice? What would it look like? Who would it serve?

In her recent book *Ethical Loneliness* (2015) the philosopher Jill Stauffer, drawing on Levinas and the post-Holocaust writer Jean Amery, speaks of the collective or individual failure to witness and attend to the suffering of others as a moral lapse, grave at the level of the individual and the culture. Some of her examples are in the realms of legal institutions like war tribunals and truth commissions where massive social crimes are addressed. But this argument works on many levels.

As the current incidents of harassment and assault unfold, some have asked what we should we do with "the men." This conundrum is pointing not just to the men who have been accused but to the well-meaning men who are floundering around in this new sea of potential male accountability, as well as the men who have chosen to double down, buttress their misogyny, like those of Incel and those crying "witch hunt" foul (see Gentile, 2018d). While colleges and univer-sities are not perfect in their approach to dealing with sexual violence, and under the current Department of Education are rapidly losing any social justice ground, they have been more apt to engage some community-based interventions. As I have written elsewhere (Gentile, 2017, 2018b), although this ground was explored as a result of Title IX lawsuits, thus they were motivated by potential financial cuts, psy-choanalysis could still learn from the lessons colleges have provided as they have developed community-based programs in bystander inter-vention (see Gentile, in press a) and restorative justice (see Gentile, 2017, 2018b). Both of these approaches, however, make the most sense through the overarching understanding of institutional betrayal (see Gentile, 2018b).

Smith and Freyd define institutional betrayal as "when an institu-tion causes harm to an individual who trusts or depends upon that institution" (Smith & Freyd, 2014, p. 578) and this is an additional component of trauma for most survivors of boundary violations. Institutional betrayal as a concept incorporates the multiple layers of violence felt by victims, such as the social networks that promote victim-blaming and that protect and prop up perpetrators, reinfor-cing abusive behaviors and interactions. This includes the professional structures that reward accused analysts who sue accusing patients (see Celenza, 2007; Blechner, 2014).

Shifting to institutions expands the focus beyond that of individual men to the systems of racialized, heteropatriarchal sexual violence that are operationalized within institutional practices. This expanded focus deconstructs the splitting of perpetrator–victim, do'er–done to dyads, and "witch hunt" scenarios (Gentile, 2016; 2017, 2018b, 2018d), enabling more potential spaces for resistance and transformation,

While we in psychoanalysis have a list of factors that put individuals at risk for committing boundary violations, Smith and Freyd (2014) have identified characteristics of institutions that are most likely to engage in betraying behaviors. Such at-risk institutions typically have membership requirements, are hierarchical in structure, and have a cer-tain prestige. We can easily see how Hollywood systems, the Catholic Church, and psychoanalysis itself, fit into this pattern. While these traits are common to many organizations, the risk of institutional betrayal mounts in those that see themselves as being outside of the common law.

In a recent article responding to the damning report on the sexual abuse in the Pennsylvania Catholic Church, the *New York Times* ran a commentary describing their organizational "playbook" for cover up (Dodd, 2018). This list was chilling for many reasons, not the least of which was how many similarities it shared with tactics used by the psychoanalytic community. For instance, at the very top is language: never describe what happened or use the terms "rape" or "sexual abuse." Instead the church advised euphemisms such as "inappropriate contact" or "boundary issues." This is not a far stretch from psychoanalysis' choice of "boundary violations" that obscures the action, the perpetrator, and the victim. The boundary, not the patient, was violated. (In this part I (KG) will use the term "sexual misconduct" as per Koss, Wilgus, & Williamsen, 2014, see Gentile, 2017, 2018b). At least three "plays" for the church involved controlling the information by keeping all investigations internal, or "in house." How many institutes keep investigations internal, often calling on the idea that external people might not understand the complexities of transference (Gentile, 2018b)? Certainly this has been the standard tactic by colleges who have pressured victims to avoid local police in favor of campus security. Controlling information hits its peak when stories are spun to make meaning of someone's sudden departure. Certainly communities talk, but rarely is information accurate and flowing to the health of the communal body. Instead it is hidden away and leaked perhaps, with the threat of lawsuits always present. While the church was told to transfer troublesome priests, psychoanalysis just kicks them out of institutes, not always reporting them to state boards, again, for fear of retribution or a reluctance to turn in one of our own, especially when that person is one with professional prestige (Dodd, 2018).

Of course this exceptionalism circles back to breed institutional betrayal. As psychoanalysts know, such a narcissistic structure and a fantasy of omnipotence are installed in the face of intolerable frustration, rage, and helplessness, such that limits and accountability become kryptonite for any narcissistic structure (Novick & Novick, 1994).

We know that betrayal that occurs within a trusted relationship (i.e. parents, romantic partners or friends, psychoanalysts, college administrators, bosses or colleagues) is associated with more severe psychological consequences than other forms of betrayal in part because, as Smith and Freyd (2014) observe, it requires one to remain blind to the trauma, to their own realities, in order to maintain the relationship. Thus institutional interactions require the accumulation of responsibility and accountability in the victim, while perpetrators, in perfect symmetry, emerge through disavowal. So we see that women speaking out, breaking these "rules," are seen both as disruptive heroes, and malignant dangers to the institutional body. By refusing to hold the secret, they actually refuse to protect the institution from its helplessness and shame.

The anti-"playbook" – restorative justice

Having mentioned the malignant use of euphemism, it is important to note that the term restorative justice is a misnomer. After all, when applied to racialized gender-based sexual violence, there is no past time of justice to restore. However, this term includes reconciliation-based justice practices, most of which emerged from First Nation and other communities of color, and religious organizations. Restorative justice is a communal form of justice that by definition situates all action, including the offending violence, within the communal body, which is seen as a co-participant. Sexual misconduct in restorative justice is seen as an aggressive act against the community/institutional body. However, in this form of justice it is also assumed that the misconduct was in some way enabled by the community. Thus restoration needs to come from the communal body/institution as well as from the perpetrator. This form of justice can mitigate institutional betrayal and ideally restore dignity to all participants.

Restorative justice, as a process-centered endeavor, seeks to ensure that victims have multiple avenues to report an incident, are guaranteed a timely, competent, and transparent process of investigation (i.e. if it is kept "in house," there is still transparent accountability to the community as a whole), and an assurance of appropriate accountability by the perpetrator and the community (Koss et. al., 2014). Unlike other forms of justice, however, both the perpetrator and the victim as well as the community have to be actively engaged in defining, navigating, and enacting validation and repair, what Koss et. al. call "circles of support and accountability" (2014, p. 247). Because the entire community is actively engaged, neither the offender nor the victim are left alone or isolated. This is important, as it means neither are left alone to build resentment or defensive layers of shame. Indeed, shame is held by the institutional body as a whole, ideally. Sentencing and transformation are communal processes where the victim has a central role. This communal focus, ideally, helps limit victim blaming and retaliation, and spreads the accountability and responsibility. The offender is the primary focus, but the community is responsible for the rehabilitation and reparation, thus the "bad apple" (Dimen, 2011, 2016) cannot simply be split off, and with them, the shame of the institution.

Shame is a key generative component of restorative justice, much like it is in other cultures where it becomes a recognition of a mistake and an opportunity for compassion and transformation (see Watkins, 2016). When held communally, shame can be processed into guilt, resulting in forms of reparations, remorse, reflection, and empathetic connection. So instead of being an isolating affect or one that is assumed to collapse space and reflection, shame is situated as the link to the capacity for meaningful connection. Narcissism, not shame, can collapse the process. By rendering institutions as well as individuals accountable, the narcissistic exceptionalism that breeds grievance and entitlement is directly challenged.

As a process, restorative justice itself also functions as a form of community-based harm reduction, as the restoration necessarily involves institutionalizing community engagement in ways that can interrupt and/or interrogate social norms and behaviors that support and fuel racialized gender-based violence and oppressive attitudes.

Of course, this is easier to write than to enact. Restorative justice requires psychological reflection as the perpetrator has to have or be able to develop the capacity to reflect on one's behavior and sustain empathy for the victim. Taking Gabbard's (2017) observations, some perpetrators might not be capable of engaging in these forms of reparation, rendering this intervention impossible. Also, if one has been raised with the privilege and stresses of white, heterosexual masculinity, and if one has watched others get away with, and perhaps have their status enhanced through forms of sexual misconduct, then the institutional response insisting on accountability for male sexual violence could feel not just like a form of aggrieved entitlement, but an active form of betrayal; a punitive change in the rules. Restorative justice ideally addresses this by involving the institutional body, thus actively shifting the rules of engagement for participants towards more just interactions.

#MeToo

This phenomenon, as it has emerged in North America and Western Europe, both demands the law and overturns it. It must be said that the power of this movement, first emergent and driven by social media, would not have appeared predictable. All that we have described in the complex management and amnesia within psychoanalysis is characteristic of the larger business, social, and political worlds. Due process has been served and overturned. Retribution or accountability, so long absent and despaired of by discriminations victims has been swift, often outside the law and driven by intense public opinion. Finding some way to work collectively and judiciously in this matter is proving difficult. There are generational differences, gender differences which effect public and institutional responses.

We take just one term to unpack to indicate something of the demanding times we find ourselves in. "Witch hunt' has been a term deployed in this movement, appearing often in the discourse around #MeToo and the matter of sexual harassment (Gentile, in press b, 2018c, 2018d). Most significantly it appeared in the essay signed by Catherine Deneuve (see Keslassy, 2018) and in an essay Daphne Merkin (2018) wrote for the *New York Times* opinion section.

As it is occurring in these texts and many others, the implications are clear. The objects of the hunting are men, the assault for which we see many versions of backlash (small and large) is upon men and often by extension Eros in general and male sexuality in particular. And in this current discourse, the witches are quite clearly the witchy women calling out men regarding sexual overtures.

But notice that something odd has happened to this term. Historically, in witch hunts women were the witches under pursuit and likely to be drowned or burned at the stake when apprehended. The attack usually undertaken under religious orthodoxy and usually by men.

Curiously, or not so curiously, we have flipped the genders and here the contemporary 2018 witchcraft is nasty women coming after men. Traditionally, witch hunts, the act of exposing a witch, typically brought status to the accuser who emerged through the action as the pious truth-teller, embraced by the hypocritical Puritanical social body. Female accusers in this suddenly upside-down, manic world, rarely gain status for any truth-telling. Indeed, few if any of us even know the names of most of the accusers (Gentile, in press b, 2018c).

If we pursue that quirky object, the 2018 "witch hunt," and if indeed men and women have switched places and men are now the helpless prey, does that not unconsciously or pre-consciously turn the men into vulnerable women? Isn't castration the great fear, whether in the form of economic ruin or disgrace and assault (Harris, 2018)?

Deneuve and Merkin articulate this mad idea – men the witches, men the hunted – but we all carry its traces. This massive sea change in the management of sexual exploitation causes all of us to fear the destruction of men, of sexuality, of the group Eros, to say nothing of the individual. We fear the collapse of some libidinal tie even as we struggle to differentiate predation from overture, and pursue the complex matter of consent.

But this hysteria relies on the cultural trope that Eros is masculine, that "pestering women" (quoting Deneuve in Keslassy, 2018) is flirting, and harassment is an expression of sexuality and not (also?) about power, control, and narcissistic rage.

Like any witch hunt, the hysteria is not fueled by the accusations (after all, they are not sudden as many had accumulated for decades, hidden away in corporate files), but by the responses of institutions, invested much more in avoiding litigation than protecting employees or changing corporate culture. Our Puritanical culture enjoys nothing better than to simultaneously patrol and stoke violence as sexuality, policing, and sexualizing violence. In this context individuals, not institutions, must be excised, buoying the very social systems that created the conditions for their emergence and continuity.

Digging deeper into this moral panic one can see its animating roots in heteropatriarchal anxiety. Claims of oppressive sexual morality or castration are the tropes designed to hide the vulnerability and shame of heteropatriarchal masculinity when it faces any challenge. This is akin to the fragility of whiteness when confronted with its own racism. It is a telling indication of the defensive use of the moral panic to deflect the vulnerability of patriarchal systems – "give a woman an inch, she'll take a penis" (Gentile, in press b, 2018a, 2018c).

In the end, the potential for this moment to swing towards increased Purtianism, punishment, misogynous backlash, or reflection and institutional change, hinges on those who defend the racist and classist heteropatriarchal institutions, and those who collude without solidarity. Take the structure of restorative justice as a guide, individual accusers and those who are accused need to be situated within institutional structures and systems of power. Only then can we all begin to differentiate playful, generative flirtation from harassment. But calling upon the age-old trope of witch hunts is just code for castration anxiety – the anxiety of a desperately disavowed vulnerability.

References

Blechner, M. (2014). Dissociation among psychoanalysts about sexual boundary violations. *Contemporary Psychoanalysis, 50*(1): 1–11.

Celenza, A. (2007). *Sexual Boundary Violations: Therapeutic, Supervisory, and Academic Contexts.* Lanham, MD: Aronson.

Dimen, M. (2011). *Lapsus linguae,* or a slip of the tongue? A sexual violation in an analytic treatment and its personal and theoretical aftermath. *Contemporary Psychoanalysis, 47,* 35–79.

——— (2016). Rotten apples and ambivalence: Sexual boundary violations through a psychocultural lens. *Journal of the American Psychoanalytic Association, 64,* 361–373.

Dodd, S. (2018). Pennsylvania grand jury says church had a 'Playbook for concealing the truth.' *New York Times.* August 14. www.nytimes.com/2018/08/14/us/pennsylvania-child-abuse-catholic-church.html

Gabbard, G.O. (2017). Sexual boundary violations in psychoanalysis: A 30-year retrospective. *Psychoanalytic Psychology, 34*(2): 151–156.

Gentile, K. (ed.) (2016). *The Business of Being Made: The Temporalities of Reproductive Technologies, in Psychoanalysis and Culture.* New York: Routledge.

———— (2017). Chasing justice: Bystander intervention and restorative justice in the contexts of college campuses and psychoanalytic institutes. In K. Davisson & E. Toronto (Eds.), *A Womb of Her Own*. Section III of Division 39. London: Karnac.

———— (2018a). Give a woman an inch, she'll take a penis: Backlash and the fragility of privilege. Public Seminar www.publicseminar.org/2018/01/give-a-woman-an-inch-shell-take-a-penis/

———— (2018b). Assembling justice: Reviving nonhuman subjectivities to address institutional betrayal around sexual misconduct. *Journal of the American Psychoanalytic Association, 66*(4), 647–678.

———— (2018c). Give her an inch, she'll take a penis. *Studies in Gender and Sexuality, 19*(4), 241–245.

———— (2018d). From the "Ontology of the rape joke" to #metoo – "witch hunts" and reckonings. *19*(4), 233–234.

———— (in press a). When the cat guards the canary – A new look at sexual boundary violations in psychoanalysis. In C. Levin (Ed.), *Boundary Trouble: The Ethics of Psychoanalytic Intimacy in Relational Perspective*. New York: Routledge.

———— (in press b). Give her an inch, she'll take a penis: The expanded version. *Contemporary Psychoanalysis*.

Harris, A. (2018). Witch-hunt. Publicseminar. The New School www.publicseminar.org/2018/01/

Keslassy, E. (2018). Catherine Deneuve signs letter blaming #metoo for spurring 'Puritanism,' unfair punishment of men. *Variety*, January 9, 2018. http://variety.com/2018/film/news/catherine-deneuve-letter-blaming-metoo-puritanism-unfair-punishment-of-men-1202658163/

Koss, M.P., Wilgus, J.K., & Williamsen, K.M. (2014). Campus sexual misconduct: Restorative justice approaches to enhance compliance with Title IX guidance. *Trauma, Violence, & Abuse, 15*(3), 42–257.

Merkin, D. (2018). Publicly, we say #MeToo. Privately, we have misgivings. Op-Ed, *New York Times*, January 5, 2018. www.nytimes.com/2018/01/05/opinion/golden-globes-metoo.html?_r=0

Novick, J., & Novick, K.K. (1994). Externalization as a pathological form of relating: The dynamic underpinnings of abuse. In A. Sugarman (Ed.), *Victims of Abuse: The Emotional Impact of Child and Adult Trauma* (pp. 45–68). Madison, CT: International Universities Press.

Pinsky, E. (2011). The Olympian Delusion. *J. Amer. Psychoanal. Assn., 59*(2), 351–375.

Smith, C.P., & Freyd, J.J. (2014). Institutional betrayal. *American Psychologist, 69* (6), 575–587.

Stauffer, J. (2015). *Ethical Loneliness*. New York: Columbia University Press.

Watkins, M. (2016). The social and political life of shame in the US presidential election 2016. Presented at "Shame and the experience of class in the US conference," co-sponsored by the Massachusetts Institute for Psychoanalysis and the Psychosocial Work Group of the Psychology and the Other Institute. Cambridge, MA. October 19, 2016.

Chapter 8

The diversity is the destiny

Gley P. Costa

> The requirement that there shall be a single kind of sexual life
> for everyone, disregards the dissimilarities, whether innate or
> acquired, in the sexual constitution of human beings; it cuts off a
> fair number of them from sexual enjoyment, and so becomes the
> source of serious injustice.
>
> (Sigmund Freud, 1930[1929], p.125)

Introduction

Part of what constitutes an analyst's unravelling task nowadays is
studying new presentations of sexuality and parenting, keeping in mind
that reviewing the psychoanalysis foundations in the area of this topic
implies debating and questioning the consensus about the different
theorizations about sexual difference, Oedipus complex, envy of penis
in the woman and castration complex, as well as about the conceptions
of sexual and gender identities.[1] For this reason, it is necessary for
the psychoanalysis to be opened to new ideas, which take into consideration the changes in the contemporary world and which present
enough porousness and mobility of their limits to enhance revisions
and exchanges with other knowledge fields.

Aware of this reality, in this chapter we intend to study the concept
of gender as a way of rethinking the processes of subjectivization in
the actual world within the psychoanalytical frame.

Brief revision of the psychoanalytical theory

Freud wrote 30 articles about sexuality, that go from 1898, with
"Sexuality in the aetiology of the neuroses," up to 1931, with

"Feminine sexuality," besides two chapters of the "New introductory lectures of psychoanalysis," of 1933, and of the posthumous publications: "Psychoanalysis schema" and "The splitting of the ego in the process of defense," both from 1938. This production not only reveals the importance given by Freud to the topic, but also its complexity, responsible for some contradictions in his statements. In spite of that, in a reference to what today we relate to gender, he highlighted that the connections of libidinal feelings towards the same-sex people do not perform as factors of a normal psychic life, a much smaller role than those which are addressed to the opposite sex: they do represent the freedom to openly and indifferently dispose of masculine and feminine objects in their love relationships.

This point of view is emphasized in the following three passages:

> A person's final sexual attitude is not decided until after puberty and it is the result of a number of factors, not all of which are yet known; some are of constitutional nature, but others are accidental. No doubt a few of these factors may happen to carry so much weight that they influence the result in their sense. But in general the multiplicity of determining factors is reflected in the variety of manifested sexual attitudes in which they find their issue in mankind.
>
> (Freud, 1905. Added note in 1915, p. 146)

> All human individuals, as a result of their bisexual disposition and their cross- inheritance, combine in themselves both masculine and feminine characteristics, so that pure masculinity and femininity remain theorical constructions of uncertain content.
>
> (Freud, 1925, p. 320)

> It is well known that at all periods there have been, as there still are, people who can take as their sexual objects members of their own sex, as well as of the opposite one, without the one trend interfering with the other. [...] Every human being is bisexual in this sense and that his libido is distributed, either in a manifested or a latent fashion, over objects of both sexes. [...] A man's heterosexuality will not put up with any homosexuality and vice-versa. If the former is the stronger it succeeds in keeping the other in hand. [...]

Each individual only has a certain quota of libido at his disposal, for which the two rival trends have to struggle. But it is not clear why the rivals do not always divide up the available quota of libido between them according to their relative strength, since they are able to do so in a number of cases.

(Freud, 1937, pp. 277–278)

Actually, Freud always believed in the strength of the sexual dispositions, masculine and feminine in both men and women, characterizing an innate bissexuality. In *The Ego and the Id* (1923), he attributes to this strength the outcome of the Oedipal situation, which is, if he will identify with the mother or the father, justifying the impression that Oedipus' complex is always complete: positive and negative. According to his own words,

it is to say, a boy has not merely an ambivalent attitude towards his father and a affectionate object-choice towards this mother, but at the same time he also behaves like a girl and displays an affectionate feminine attitude to his father and a corresponding jealousy and hostility towards his mother.

(Freud, 1923, pp. 47–48)

In spite of the fact that these texts show that Freud, throughout all his work, didn't keep away from his conviction about the existence of an innate bissexuality and the polimorphism of the infant sexuality, but apparently the psychoanalysts clung to the sentence "The anatomy is the destiny" (Freud, 1924, p. 222). Disagreeing with this tendency, we find in McDougall one of the most embracing psychoanalytical post-Freudian contributions in relation to the human sexuality. In *The Sexual Theory and Psychoanalysis* (1999), she highlights that, whatever value we could give to the different psychoanalytical theories, in the end all of them agree in placing sexuality in a somato-psychic universe created by the universal libidinal drives from the first contact of the baby with the mother's body. This already generates from the birth a series of psychic conflicts, aggravated by the inevitable shock between the internal impulses of the newborn and the restrictions of the external reality. For this reason he emphasizes: "The sexuality is inborn and inevitably traumatic, and this pushes the human being to an eternal questioning" (p. 12).

The most important part of this author's contribution is the approach she makes into the archaic sexuality, related to the findings about the Otherness and the difference between genders. According to this point of view, in the Oedipal stage, in their homo and hetero-sexual dimensions, children face multiple frustrations and impossible dreams: in particular, the wish to belong to both genders and possess either the mother's or the father's genitals. As a result of the universal bisexual desires, the primary homosexuality of the girl includes her desire of having her mother sexually, penetrating her vagina, entering her body and many times, devouring her, as a means of total possession of the maternal object and its magic powers, in a world where men are ruled out from.

But the little girl's imagination also includes the desire of being a man like her father, of having his genitals, and, thus, to possess all the world and qualities attributed to him, making in her mother's life the father's role. The little boy dreams of being his father's sexual partner, fantasizing of embodying orally or anally his father's penis so that he ends up possessing his father's genitals and his rights, thus becoming a man. However, this little boy is also taken by the dream of taking over his mother in the sexual intercourses and generating a little baby from his father. Likewise he dreams of being penetrated by his father as well as he imagines his mother has also gotten fantasies of penetrating his father. Actually there are countless potential ways through which this libidinous stream can find expression and so be integrated to the psychosexual organization. Although these impulses can originate neurotic or psychotic suffering, they can simply and readily become a reason for psychic enrichment. McDougall says in the cited article:

> The bisexual substractum of human beings is not only suitable to enrich and establish the loving and social relationships as well as it also provides one of the adequate elements to stimulate the creative activity – although it's important to admit that this very dimension can be the source of creative blocks if the bisexual unconscious desires are the source of conflicts or prohibitions.
>
> (1999, p. 17)

Therefore, any sexual preference should only be considered a clin-ical problem in search for a solution if it gets to such a level that the subject's sexuality creates conflict and psychic suffering, and should only be considered perverse if those subject's sexual activities that do not take into account the necessities and desires of his partner. Hence according to the author heterosexuality is just one of the traumatic and multifaceted possibilities of infants' sexuality.

About the concept of gender

The concept of gender became consolidated starting in the 1970s in several areas, such as sociology, anthropology, psychiatry, psychoanalysis and culture as a whole. It's possible that its origin had been the feminist movement starting in France, specially Simone de Beauvoir's book *The Second Sex* (1949), where we quote her: "one is not born, but rather becomes a woman."

The gender is constituted by behavior, preferences, interests and attitudes, including the dressing, walking and talking codes, historically and socioculturally settled, setting up the masculinity and femininity – not always in agreement with the gender identity established by the anatomy. For this reason, somehow, it is the other, working as a talking mirror, that grants the identity of gender to the person.

An important contribution to the difference between sex and gender is found in the pioneer studies of Money (1955, 1956, 1965) about hermaphroditism. The author and his collaborators pointed out that the first crucial step for the differentiation of gender was the self-designation of the child as being of the feminine or the masculine sex according to the sexual attribution and the education, resulting in the definitions of *identity of gender* (the private experience in the function of gender) and of *gender role* (the public expression of the identity of gender). It is pointed out in Money's works that the gender differentiation is defined around a year and a half of age and that, around four years old, it is already complete and irreversibly established.

In its relation with sex, gender, the product of a cultural construction, is neither the casual result of anatomic sex nor is it as steady as it is, establishing between both a radical discontinuity. Nevertheless, Butler asks (1990):

And what is sex, after all? Wouldn't it also be the 'natural' feature of the dualism of sex a product of the scientific discourse?

Maybe the very construct named 'sex' is as culturally produced as gender is; strictly speaking maybe sex has always been gender, so much so that the distinction between sex and gender is revealed as non-existent.

(p. 27)

As a matter of fact, in Person's and Ovesey's meaning (1999), gender precedes sexuality, when they state that, based on Baker (1981), "gender results from after-birth events, organizes the choice of the object and sexual fantasies" (p. 145).

In the field of psychoanalysis, the idea of gender, taken up until now with restrictions, has slowly developed since Stoller (1968, 1975, 1985), with the differentiation between *sexual identity*, given by the genitals, and *gender identity*, given to the child by the surrounding, because, as the author points out, when we are born we do not know what masculine or feminine is; it is the parents and the society that teach us. For Stoller, the terminology *gender identity* refers to the blending of masculinity and femininity inside the subject, meaning that both masculinity and femininity are found in everybody, but in different shapes and degrees. It corresponds to a conviction supported by the parents and by the culture, for which it suffers mutations in time and space. The *nuclear gender identity*, still according to Stoller, is a conviction that the designation of a person's sex is anatomically and psychologically correct and it is complete in an almost unalterable way at around three years of age. This author's works have offered a better understanding of transsexuals – people in whom the sexual identity and gender identity are in opposition, forcing in some cases the surgery for the anatomic sex change to correspond to the gender.

More recently, Lander (2010) published an interesting article, titled "The masculinity questioned," where he develops the concept of "gender essence," correspondent to the internal sexual structure, related to the Freudian unconscious starting from four differential registers: (1) sadism and masochism; (2) perversion and erotomania; (3) naivety and intrigue; and (4) murderous violence and hidden wickedness.[2] The unconscious sexual structure or, as Lander called it, the gender essence – masculine or feminine – does not depend on being born a man or a woman or on his/her orientation in the choice of the sexual object to be homo or heterosexual. Consequently, one subject can be born with the anatomic male organ, develop an unconscious feminine sexual structure and establish a heterosexual relationship, whether it is with a woman, or homosexual if it is with a man. Depending on the unconscious sexual structure of the partner, these relationships will be homosexual or heterosexual just externally.

Through readings about the topic, including the psychoanalytical writings mentioned above, one can have the impression that gender is something well defined. However, we can consider that it is not always so well defined. Its weakness as a concept comes exactly from the fact that it is based upon a definition. Butler (1990) says that, explicitly,

> gender is a continuous stylization of the body, a group of repeated actions, inside a regulatory extremely strict frame, that crystallizes as time goes by so that it produces the aspect of a natural way of being.
>
> (p. 69)

The author disproves the notion of an innate gender identity when she states that gender is not what we are but what we do, and as a result of doing so, we have our body designed as masculine or feminine. Thus gender is, for Butler, performative and it is constituted from a discourse.[3] She states that the breaking news to the parents that "it's a girl" or "it's a boy," given by the doctor looking at an ultrasound screen, triggers the process of making this body feminine or masculine. It deals with a performative act that starts a sequence of performative acts that will constitute a subject of sex/gender. Rather than a description of a body, Butler asserts, each piece of news designs and defines the body, setting up, and we quote her, a "founding interpellation" of gender from a heteronormative pattern imposed by means of cultural and political hegemonic devices.

Although the concept of "gender essence," of Lander, has as its basis psychoanalytical theory, Freud's implied ideas deserve consideration in light of the contemporary questions that influence the construction of subjectivity. According to Fiorini (2014), the changes in the feminine position and a bigger visibility and acceptance of the various presentations of sexuality set up the discussion of analytic theory as to what concerns and defines sexual difference, the concept of masculinity and femininity, the phallic priority, the penis envy in the girl and the notion of desire, enlarging the Oedipus far beyond the nuclear family model. The author's proposal is "to analyse the processes of sexual subjectivation far beyond the restricted binaries of the positive Oedipus" (p. 55), which is to say, in the limits of Oedipus' complete complex so that we are capable of historicizing what appears as an immutable axiom of the theory.

The analyst's position

Paraphrasing McDougall (1999),[4] maybe we might say that it is unwise to establish that a determined analyst be heterosexual or homosexual, let alone because either the heterosexuality or the homosexuality do not fit inside any singularity, always and irreparably set up in a plurality. By the way, it is possible that this does not matter: what does matter is for the analyst to be free to lose his/her identity in order to work in any necessary positions to the patient. Nevertheless we should keep in mind that the analyst, inside and outside his office, is irreparably found in the condition of a sexed individual, thus, subordinate to his own unconscious conflicts related to the hetero or the homosexuality begotten by the innate bisexuality and by the polymorph and traumatic infant sexuality. In Isay's perception (1996),

> if the psychoanalyst adopts the traditional psychoanalytical theory that a normal development leads just to the heterosexuality, it will be difficult for him, howsoever he tries, not to be prejudiced, but instead to act neutrally.

(p. 42)

The author goes even further suggesting that, on account of this theoretical position, not asking the necessary questions, he will block the possibility to help his patients feel less inhibited or have fewer conflicts with their homosexuality. Even if he does not intend to change the sexual orientation of his patients, he might show his prejudice through comments, suggestions, indifference towards certain topics, and even by the tone of voice adopted in his interventions. On the other hand, the analyst's homosexuality presents transferential and counter-transferential difficulties that should not be discounted in relation to either heterosexual or homosexual patients. The fact that is presented is whether they are the same when the analyst is heterosexual, in case we can rule out the influence of the dominant culture in both the analytical theory and practice. Having in mind Freud's warning (1937) that the analytical relationship is based on love for the truth, and that this rules out any sham or lie, we push ourselves into questioning Isay's observation that

> when a *gay* therapist chooses not to tell his patients that he is *gay*, for shame or fear to the exposition, he omits to offer the patient a personal model of integrity that is essential to the difficult self-exam of any well succeeded therapy.
>
> (p. 46)

Considering the mandatory neutrality of the psychologist, we might contemplate the issue as neither being exactly in the disclosure of the homosexuality nor in the heterosexuality, but in the fact that the analyst might be ashamed of his condition as *a gay person*, and the fear of the exposition, evidence of the difficulty of homosexuals in overcoming barriers imposed by prejudice deep-rooted in the culture.

Parenting

Related to sexuality, with equal importance we see the new presentations of parenting growing in the contemporary world, enlarging the possibilities in the familiar relationships and child rearing far beyond the traditional nuclear, patriarchal, hierarchical, vertical, monogamous, and heterosexual family model, which prevailed from the nineteenth century until the middle of the twentieth century. Focusing on the diversity and complexity of families in twenty-first-century families, Walsh (2012) mentions that "the definition of 'family' needs to be expanded to hold either a new spectrum or the fluid remodeling of the relational domestic pattern" (p. 3), recalling that "the normalizing theories were constructed by dominant groups, reified by religion or science and used to pathologize people who did not fit the prescribed standards" (p. 4). Nowadays, besides the traditional models, we find reconstructed families, with children from the present relationships and from previous marriages of the spouses, single-parent families[5] and, more and more frequently, families whose spouses have the same sex and the children are adopted or born through assisted fertilization and other means like "surrogate mother." At the moment, they also demand the recognition of a family couple formed by transgender partners and resulting from other presentations of sexual and gender diversity.

Even considering what is called the "traditional model" – namely that it does not have to do with the nature, but with the dominant culture – we cannot avoid asking ourselves if these new conformations do constitute a family, if they are able to adequately act in the education and moral formation of the children and, even more, if they are able to raise and maintain the longed for and valorized family feeling which, it seems, is rooted in the eighteenth century. In answer to these questions, Alizade (2016) highlights that the parenting couple stopped being a basic element in the children's education, allowing the capability of putting love in the foreground, as well as sacrifice and responsibility. The author emphasizes that the introduction of the concept of function – paternal and maternal – took the biological origin and the parents' sexes away from the necessary care with their children in the different stages of development and created instead the notion of "family function," extended as a net that surpasses the limits of the "nuclear conventional family" envisioning ways to provide the child with access to the symbolic universe.

A recurrent consideration nowadays concerns the question of the paternal function and the consequences of its decline in the new parenting combinations. Regarding this issue, Fiorini (2016) argues that the paternal function is an heiress of the *pater familie* from the Roman Law Rights, which supported itself throughout the centuries with the aid of a hierarchical sex division, where the dichotomy "mother-nature" on the one side and "father-culture" on the other side is correspondingly found, depriving the woman of symbolic capacities in her own right and not only when the paternal function is internalized, as it has been referred to many times. The author refutes calling this symbolic function "paternal" denomination, suggesting the terminology "third function," having in mind that this is a way to generalize what is in fact a symbolic operation, always to a certain type of society and ideology.

Final comments

In the context of the diversity in the contemporary society there is no doubt that gender occupies a central and paradigmatic position. Nevertheless, one criticism we make about this concept is that it maintains the binary character of sexuality, whose linearity with anatomic sex establishes a normality standard when the sexual identity and the gender identity are in accordance and a digression when they are not. In a certain way, medicine, including psychiatry, differently than happened in the past, seems to naturally accept this digression, up to the point that it offers the possibility to surgically change sex, which is free in large Brazilian hospitals. Nevertheless shouldn't we consider that, in this situation, even inadvertently in some cases, a new stage of prejudice opens up, represented by the idea of a pretentious real gender and the respective presumed sexuality? And still, wouldn't some of the subjects who undergo this surgical procedure be treated since then as patients, also be submitted to society's prejudice granted by the scientific community? One transsexual subject who had undergone this surgery said that he not only wanted to feel his body, but also to feel that it was his body, according to the compulsory order: sex, gender, and desire. A blunt criticism to this linearity is found in the feminist French writer Monique Wittig, to whom the very morphology would be a consequence of a conceptual hegemonic system. She therefore proposes a "disintegration" of the culturally constituted bodies (Butler, 1990).

The analysis of lesbian patients, whose sexual preference reflects, for many analysts, a desexualization of the feminine body, makes us focus on the consideration of Laura Mulvey (1975), British feminist and film scholar, that the pleasure of watching and the attraction for the feminine body in its possible poetical and erotic curves are not just a male privilege and neither does it follow the same voyeuristic logic. If this consideration represented an adequate criticism to the cinema at that time, 40 years ago, nowadays the "seventh art" has given evidence of a comprehension less committed with regulation and social prescriptions. As an example we mention the film of the young and talented Canadian director Xavier Dolan, *Laurence Anyways* (2012), where the main character, although feeling well in long hair, lipstick and beautiful earrings, loves and sexually desires his wife in an intense way. She also loves him, but succumbs to the social prejudice. This happens in the beginning, but later she succumbs to the diversity and singularity of the human sexuality. It is necessary to keep in mind Butler's (2016) warning that

> for Freud sexuality is not naturally connected to reproduction. It has objectives that many times are incompatible with the hetero-sexual reproduction, and this produces a permanent obstacle to those who want to confirm the existence of natural ways of mas-culine and feminine desire or heterosexuality itself.
>
> (p. 49)

In this line, the non-commitment of Freud's works with the strict frame of regulations and behavior prescriptions established by the concept of gender becomes evident. The naturalization of hetero-sexuality establishes a mimetic relationship of gender with the body's materialness. It creates the heteronormativity and makes it compul-sory for men and women. Even if Freud had highlighted throughout his work the inborn bisexuality and the polimorphism of children's sexuality, in the clinic, up until now, we look forward to finding a cause for homosexuality, in a paper that psychoanalyst Richard Isay, in the publication mentioned above, called, from his own experience as a patient, the "heterosexualization" of the patient.

Like Fiorini (2015) points out, it is the role of the contemporary psy-choanalysis to cover the broad spectrum of subjectivities that do not find place in the binary strict logic of sexual difference segregated in phallic-castrated and masculine-feminine dualisms, remembering that the statements "I am a man" and "I am a woman" do not correspond, necessarily and linearly, to the statements "I desire a woman" and "I desire a man." To this we add the questions related to transsexualities and to motherhood and fatherhood, especially the "desire of a child" which, for the author, transcends the limits of the biological father or mother. It becomes necessary, then, to review the oedipal narrative to explain the processes of the present subjectivation in the new ways of living love, sexuality and family setup.

Finally, we cannot forget to attribute importance to the identifications of the conflict and the symptoms in the expressions of the sexuality in the persons, far beyond the homo and heterosexualities, the vicissitudes of the difficult process of separation-individuation and, still, the genetics which, in the last years, has broadened the knowledge about the important field of human relations. According to such advances, where we highlight the phenomenon of the methylation with the formation of epigenetical marks anchored together to genes responsible for the sensitivity to testosterone capable of masculinizing the minds of girls or feminizing the boys' minds, the old vision of sex as binary conditioned by XX or XY chromosomes, as Varella (2015) suggests, should definitely be discharged. Actually, through recent studies about DNA, we can suggest that homosexuality is a phenomenon of nature as biological as heterosexuality, we are led to question the linearity sex-gender-sexual practice and to agree with Freud (1925) about the fact "that pure masculinity and femininity keep being the theoretical constructions of uncertain content" (p. 320). For many current authors, sexuality and gender need to be focused multidisciplinarily. In this line, we wonder if we could think, for example, of the *butterfly effect* of the chaos theory, the basis of the complex thinking, which allows us to conclude that "the unification and the homogenization are illusions that rule out the respect for the diversities and the heterogeneities" (Morin, Motta, & Ciurana, 1990, p. 63).

Consistently with this point of view we can read at Museu do Amanhã (Rio de Janeiro, Brazil) a short text that we copy below, to which, paraphrasing Freud (1924),[6] we could put the title to this paper:

> Love and affection happen in numberless ways. Marital relations, familiarity and kinship are the basic ingredients upon which our lives are built and they are present, in many ways, in our cultures. For this reason, the rites and habits related to the lives of couples and parenting, are essential components of every culture. Sexuality is one of the fundamental features of our experience. Love is also acknowledging and respecting the diversity of sexual orientations and the rights of men, women and children of our planet.

Thus, as a final issue, Walsh's (2012) words make sense:

> Beyond the acceptance of diversity, the cultivation of cultural pluralism, within mutual understanding and respect towards affinities and differences, might be a power that vitalizes a society.
>
> (p. 17)

Notes

1 This chapter first appeared in Portuguese as "A diversidade é o destino" in Psicanálise – *Jornal da Sociedade Brasileira de Psicanálise de Porto Alegre*, *19*(1), 2017, 54–68. Reprinted by kind permission of the journal.
2 Sadism here means active and penetrating, and masochism the desire to be penetrated passively, corresponding to the masculine and feminine structures, respectively. Perversion is related to the denial of castration of the masculine character; and the erotomania, of the feminine character, corresponds to transferring to the other the desire of being penetrated. The naivety corresponds to the masculine character and the intrigue (scheme), to the feminine character. Assassine violence sets up the internal masculine structure; and the hidden wickedness, the internal feminine structure.
3 Butler bases himself upon the theory of Austin's speech acts (which distinguish between the affirmative statements, that describe a fact, and the performative ones, which, once proclaimed, make happen what they proclaim) and in the notions of citation and reiteration of Derrida (Louro, 2016, p. 13).
4 "Maybe it is not precise to take for granted that a determined person is necessarily heterosexual or homosexual" (McDougall, 1999, p. 24).
5 According to Kreider and Elliott (2009), monoparental families, with a growing number of men, most of them homosexuals, represent more than a fourth of all North Americans with children aged below 18 (Walsh, 2012).
6 "The anatomy is the destiny" (Freud, 1924, p. 222).

References

Alizade, M. (2016). La liberación de la parentalidad em el siglo XXI. In P. Alkolombre & C.S. Holovko, *Parentalidades y género: su incidencia en la subjetividad.* Buenos Aires: Letra Viva.

Baker, S. (1981). *Biological Influences on Human Sex and Gender*. In C. Stimpson & E. Person, *Women: Sex and Sexuality*. Chicago, IL: University of Chicago Press.

Beauvoir, S. (1949). *The Second Sex*. New York: Vintage.

Butler, J. (1990). *Problemas de gênero: feminismo e subversão da identidade*. Rio de Janeiro: Civilização Brasileira.

────── (2016). Entrevista concedida à revista *CULT, 19*(6), 49.

Dolan, X. (2012) 'Laurence Anyways.' Film produced in France.

Fiorini, L. (2014). Repensando o complexo de Édipo. *Rev. Brasileira de Psicanálise. 48*(4), 47–55.

────── (2015). *La diferencia sexual en debate: cuerpos, deseos y ficciones*. Buenos Aires: Lugar.

────── (2016). La nostalgia del padre: función paterna o función tercera? In P. Alkolombre & C.S. Holovko, *Parentalidades y género: su incidencia en la subjetividad*. Buenos Aires: Letra Viva.

Freud, S. (1898). A sexualidade na etiologia das neuroses (Sexuality in the aetiology of the neuroses). *Ed. Standard Brasileira das Obras Completas de Sigmund Freud*. Vol. 3. Rio de Janeiro: Imago.

────── (1905). Três ensaios sobre a teoria da sexualidade. *Ed. Standard Brasileira das Obras Completas de Sigmund Freud*. Vol. 7. Rio de Janeiro: Imago.

────── (1923). O Ego e o Id. *Ed. Standard Brasileira das Obras Completas de Sigmund Freud*. Vol. 19. Rio de Janeiro: Imago, 1976.

────── (1924). A dissolução do complexo de Édipo. *Ed. Standard Brasileira das Obras Completas de Sigmund Freud*. Vol. 19. Rio de Janeiro: Imago.

────── (1925). Algumas consequências psíquicas da distinção anatômica dos sexos. *Ed. Standard Brasileira das Obras Completas de Sigmund Freud*. Vol. 19. Rio de Janeiro: Imago.

────── (1930[1929]). O mal-estar na civilização. *Ed. Standard Brasileira das Obras Completas de Sigmund Freud*. Vol. 21. Rio de Janeiro: Imago.

────── (1931). Sexualidade feminina (Feminine sexuality). *Ed. Standard Brasileira das Obras Completas de Sigmund Freud*. Vol. 21. Rio de Janeiro: Imago.

────── (1933[1932]). Novas conferências introdutórias sobre psicanálise (New introductory lectures of psychoanalysis). *Ed. Standard Brasileira das Obras Completas de Sigmund Freud*. Vol. 22. Rio de Janeiro: Imago.

──────(1937). Análise terminável e interminável. *Ed. Standard Brasileira das Obras Completas de Sigmund Freud*. Vol. 23. Rio de Janeiro: Imago.

────── (1940[1938]). Esquema de psicanálise (Psychoanalysis schema). *Ed. Standard Brasileira das Obras Completas de Sigmund Freud*. Vol. 23. Rio de Janeiro, RJ: Imago.

────── (1940[1938]). A divisão do ego no processo de defesa (The splitting of the ego in the process of defense). *Ed. Standard Brasileira das Obras Completas de Sigmund Freud*. Vol. 23. Rio de Janeiro: Imago.

Isay, R.A. (1996). *Tornar-se gay: O caminho da auto-aceitação*. São Paulo: Edições. GLS.

Kreider, R.M., & Elliot, D.B. (2009). *America's Families and Living Arrangements: 2007. (Current Population Reports 20-561)*. Washington, DC: US Bureau of the Census.

Lander, R. (2010). La masculinidade questionada. *Trópicos, 18*(1), 43–56.

Louro, L. (2016). Uma Sequência de Atos. *CULT, 19*(6), 12–15.

Mcdougall, J. (1999). Teoria sexual e psicanálise. In P.R. Ceccarelli, *Diferenças sexuais*. São Paulo, SP: Escuta, 1999.

Money, J. (Ed.) (1965). *Sex Research New Developments*. New York: Holt, Rinehart & Winston.

Money, J., Hampson, J., & Hampson, J.L. (1955). An examination of some basic sexual concepts: The evidence of human hermaphroditism. *Bull. Johns Hopkins Hosp, 97*, 301–310.

——— (1956). Sexual incongruities and psychopathology management. *Bull. Johns Hopkins Hosp, 98*, 43–57.

Morin, E., Motta, R., & Ciurana, E-R. (1990). *Educar para a era planetária: o pensamento complexo como método de aprendizagem no erro e na incerteza humanos*. Lisbon: Instituto Piaget.

Mulvey, L. (1975). Visual pleasure and narrative cinema. *Screen, 16*(3), 6–27.

Person, E., & Ovesey, L. (1999). Teorias Psicanalíticas da identidade de gênero. In P.R. Ceccarelli, *Diferenças sexuais*. São Paulo: Escuta.

Stoller, R. (1968). *Sex and gender*. New York: Janson Aronson.

——— (1975). *A experiência transexual*. Rio de Janeiro: Imago.

——— (1985). *Masculinidade e feminilidade: apresentações do gênero*. Porto Alegre: Artes Médicas.

Varella, D. (2015, November 14). Homossexualidade e DNA. Artigo publicado na *Folha de São Paulo*.

Walsh, F. (2012). *Processos normativos da família: diversidade e complexidade*. 4ed. Porto Alegre: Artmed.

Chapter 9

Responsibilization, same-sex marriage, and the end of queer sex

Ann Pellegrini

Why does the value placed on freedom in the United States – and it may well be the signal American value – come crashing to the floor when it comes to sex?[1] Not only that, why do US public debates about sex so often turn into public invocations of traditional moral values, values that speak a specifically Christian language? This conflation between values and a particular value system allows religion to float, sometimes appearing as "religion," at other instances just appearing as the kinds of universal values that an ordered society requires. These are issues I have pursued elsewhere with Janet Jakobsen (2004), in our co-written book, *Love the Sin: Sexual Regulation and the Limits of Religious Tolerance*.

Love the Sin inverts the usual relations between religion and sex: rather than allow that sex is a problem that religion must regulate and rehabilitate, we argue that sex, like religion, is a dense site for human activity, meaning-making, sensuous contact, and ethical relation. Both religion and sex, then, can be conceptualized as spaces of freedom and also of risk. These spaces are among the things that democratic freedom, including, prominently, the freedom of religion promised by the US constitution, should promote and protect. Religious freedom – which includes the freedom to be religiously different and the freedom not to be religious at all – is a structural condition for meaningful sexual freedom in the United States. As things now stand, however, American commonsense conflates particular religious values with morality, leaving little space to practice either religion *or* sex differently from a particular Christian norm. Nor does the growing cultural acceptance and legalization of same-sex marriage demonstrate otherwise. This last assertion may seem surprising and requires further elaboration.

But, first, how and why did sex, and homosexuality in particular, which is always imagined as out of control – even when it is clamoring for the restraints of state-recognized marriage – become the focus of this need for order? What accounts for the persistent public framing of religion and sex – and of religious liberty and "equal rights" for LBGT people and women – as opposed and antagonistic? In the main, *Love the Sin* pursues these questions historically and with an eye to reshaping legal and extra-legal debates over homosexuality, the meanings of freedom, and the "causes" of hate-motivated violence. In this chapter, I want to consider what resources psychoanalysis might bring to the table.

The opposition religion "versus" sex is not a new one. In many ways, this opposition is a legacy of a longer history of the ways "religion" and "sex" – that fleshy signifier of troublesome bodily difference – are constituted by secular modernity. Both sex and religion are sites of excess in modernity, but they are figured in very different ways. One, "sexuality," is the mark of modernity and the modern (western) subject. The other, "religion," is what modernity was supposed to have left behind, and yet religion has been remarkably persistent – and not just as some atavistic hangover or vestigial body part that has no ongoing function. These different relations to time – modern "versus" anti-modern, advanced "versus" primitive – contribute to the public framing of religion and sexuality as mutually opposed "identity positions" in the United States (but not just here).

Might this opposition, religion versus sex/uality, itself derive from a *psychic* desire to resolve and settle the contradictions and vulnerabilities of our dependence on others, human and non-human, for our very survival, the Enlightenment fantasy of the free-standing autonomous individual notwithstanding? Enfleshed subjectivity – and religion and sexuality are both incarnated and incarnating sites of human activity and becoming – exceeds such simple resolutions.

For many Americans, the scandal of homosexuality may well be the scandal of sex itself. If "sex is guilty until proven innocent," as anthropologist Gayle Rubin has famously quipped (1993, p. 11), homosexuality provides the perfect scapegoat. For all the ways in which American culture is saturated with representations of sex and sexuality, where sexiness is not simply used to sell various products but is the very commodity to be packaged and sold, we are nonetheless a culture in which it is difficult to talk about and affirm sexual pleasure as a good in and of itself – never mind homosexual sex. This hesitancy about sex and sexual pleasure, a moral hesitancy and even revulsion that get displaced (in psychoanalytic terms, "projected") onto non-normative, or dissident, sex and sexual subjects, is not simply the trace of specifically religious ideas about "good" sex versus "bad," bodily discipline versus anarchy. It is also evidence of the ways that sexual acts and sexed embodiment are overburdened psychic sites, testifying as they do to our vulnerability before the other, the ways our body-self comes to be only through the touch of another. Such traces of the other are formative for bodily life but can also be deeply deformative or destructive in the very act of bringing the "I" into shape and being.

The religious scaffolding that is continually rigged up around sex in the United States is constitutionally dubious, and it is certainly very bad for women – as the Supreme Court decision in *Burwell v. Hobby Lobby Stores, Inc.* (2014), eviscerating the birth control mandate of the Affordable Care Act, painfully shows. But this scaffolding makes a certain sense if we take seriously the way sex, because it is one of the places in which bodily boundaries become porous to others, can undo us, for better and for worse. To be clear, making psychic or emotional sense is not the same thing as making good law, let alone creating conditions for justice. Bodily vulnerability is one of the things humans share; it is a core aspect of our creaturely being. How individuals and societies respond to this vulnerability varies across time and place in ways that resist grand transhistorical or universal narratives or rules. We must rather look to the particular, which is a large enough task. For my own part, I am interested in considering both psychoanalysis and religion as historical discourses and practices that offer accounts of living with this creaturely vulnerability. These ways of living may be more or less systematized, more or less rule-bound.

In the contemporary United States, a particular religious account has been taken up into the state and systematized in ways that foreclose spaces for fantasy, change, and risk. In consequence, we are not able to be honest as a culture about what is hard and messy and risky in sex. Instead, we focus on sexual experiences that are understood to be irrefutably dangerous (such as sexual violence – though even here, as debates over #MeToo show, there can be profound disagreements as to what constitutes injury, legally or otherwise). Or anxieties cluster around sex that is held to be "morally suspect" because it is presumably unregulated and irresponsible (homosexuality, for example, or pre-marital sex). But these become smokescreens (to use a psychoanalytic term: displacements) behind which we deny the risks of our bodily life with others more generally. Policing sex and impugning other "wayward" bodily desires, as in the panic over obesity (Berlant, 2011), may become an alibi, a way to hold at bay more generalized but pressing insecurities. This need for an alibi may be even more acute due to the precarities introduced by the profound economic inequalities rationalized under neoliberal regimes in which corporations are people, capital moves with ease across national boundaries, but many actual people are stuck in place working for wages that do not sustain a livable life, let alone a flourishing one.

Freedom – that difficult keyword of US law and life – is about more than concrete social arrangements, though these matter deeply, intimately. Freedom is also crucially dependent on a capacity to *imagine* other ways of being in the world. Here I am thinking with Drucilla Cornell's argument for the value of the "imaginary domain" for feminist social possibilities. Cornell suggests that as a minimum requirement for equal participation in democratic social life (and she is arguing within the terms of liberal political theory), people must have "equivalent bases for [the] chance to transform ourselves into the individuated beings we think of as persons" (1995, p. 5). This capacity requires equal access to public life, yes, but public life also involves a domain or, better, domains plural of fantasy. This is what she means by invoking an imaginary domain, via Lacan. She is especially interested in the question, how can we produce the shared social conditions necessary to support "phantasmatic dimensions of bodily integrity" (p. 120), the ways in which we imagine ourselves into being. This is a crucial paradox: how to generate shared conditions in the social for the flourishing of what may be idiosyncratic, individual imaginations of the good life. Human being is a process, not a stable state, and the project of becoming and transforming "demands space for the renewal of the imagination," Cornell argues (p. 5).

One route to get at the way psychic life links up to social or collective possibility is to consider the surprisingly different fortunes (financial pun intended) of the contemporary politics of same-sex marriage and reproductive freedom, especially abortion, in the United States. Marriage is a three-way with the state, which uses marriage and the families defined through it as a way to privatize not just affective labor, but the manual labor of caring for children, elderly parents, and family members dealing with short- or long-term illnesses or disabilities. Legally recognized family members – the spouse, the child, the parent – do not exhaust the intimate relationships that make up a life, that make living possible, of course. But too often these other cherished intimacies – BFFs, for one example, or an army of exes who remain in each other's lives as queer kin, for another – cannot be comprehended by the cramped legal definitions of kinship as anchored in marriage and the conventionally coupled. As Lisa Duggan puts it (2004), "state regulation of households and partnerships does in fact affect the basic safety, prosperity, equality and welfare of all Americans – it determines who will make medical decisions for us in emergencies, who may share our pensions or Social Security benefits, who may legally co-parent our children and much more."

For the neoliberal state, marriage is a bargain; for individuals, in the diversity of ways they actually live their lives – building intimacies and kinship networks that exceed the couple form – the cost-benefit analysis is murkier. On the one hand, if the state is going to dispense 1000+ rights and benefits through marriage, then of course same-sex couples should have access to these benefits on an equal basis. Moreover, individuals marry for a variety of reasons, and it would be ludicrous to suggest that couples get married solely, or even primarily, in order to access the legal or economic goods of marriage. On the other hand, marriage comes in a cookie-cutter form. The economic goodies and cultural capital it dispenses do not actually tell us: what marriage is or could be for, why it is the vehicle through which so many rights and benefits are conferred at once, and what other ways individuals can and already do make intimate and sustaining lives with each other. The same-sex marriage movement in the United States ceded all these questions, and the issues of economic and social justice they implicate, when it focused on "marriage equality" as the end game of sexual liberation.

Marriage equality arrived with the Supreme Court's 5–4 decision in *Obergefell v. Hodges* (2015), but the equality it promised may be far less than freedom. And this shortfall is not simply nor even primarily due to the fact that many US states as well as the Supreme Court under Chief Justice Roberts, and the federal government under President Trump have moved to allow religious "objectors" to opt out of treating same-sex marriages as equivalent to heterosexual marriages. In an article whose title wittily and brilliantly encapsulates the problem at hand – "Sex + Freedom = Regulation. Why?" – Jakobsen argues that sexual regulation is internal to secular freedom, not an imposition upon it. She grounds this claim in an historical account of the Protestant Reformation and the specifically Protestant incitement to sexuality "over against the celibacy of priestly and monastic life idealized" by Catholicism (2005, p. 294). As Jakobsen explains, the understanding of freedom that emerged out of the Protestant Reformation turned sex and sexual relations into a pivot between Church and market: "The Reformation tie[d] the idea of individual freedom to the institution of marriage. The free individual is the individual whose sexual activity is regulated in marriage" (2005, p. 286). This willingness to self-regulate, a willingness enforced by zealous reformers and eventually internalized as the rule of gendered family life and of its members, became a marker of the male householder's ability freely to participate in the activities of market and of governance. This internalization – reform gets installed within the marital household and within its subjects – is a key site for the interpenetration of the psychic and the social. One of Jakobsen's key insights for contemporary debates over the meaning and scope of sexual freedom is that Protestant notions of *discipline as freedom* persist well into the secular state; indeed, the installation of religious norms of bodily life as internal to the good ordering of the state and of market relations is one of the hallmarks of secularism in its Protestant dominant form – and of secular subjects too.

I completed the first version of this chapter less than a month after the Supreme Court heard arguments in *Obergefell v Hodges* (2015), which challenged the constitutionality of individual state bans on same-sex marriage. A narrow majority of the Court (5–4) found such bans unconstitutional, thus mandating the recognition of same-sex marriage in every US state. In many respects, this result is remarkable; sodomy statutes were not found unconstitutional until 2003. For gay men and lesbians, the leap from being sexual outlaws to being state "in-laws" via civil marriage has happened at warp speed. What kinds of questions have LBGT people not had time to ask themselves about the pros and cons of same-sex marriage? As legal scholar Katherine Franke (2015) wryly observes in her book *Wed-Locked: How African Americans and Gay People Mistakenly Thought Marriage Would Set Them Free*, after 100 plus years of being regulated and punished by criminal law, "You'd think that we might have wanted a bit of break from the state. Leave us alone while we figure out what it means to be free." But what if, as Jakobsen points out, *regulation is what freedom feels like?*

It is not just state and federal laws and policies that have changed. Public attitudes toward homosexuality and same-sex marriage have also shifted at amazing speed – something even Chief Justice Roberts marveled at in the oral arguments in *Obergefell*, on April 28, 2015: "one of the things that's truly extraordinary about this whole issue is how quickly has been the acceptance of your position [for same-sex marriage] across broad elements of society. I don't know what the latest opinion polls show."

Here are some polling data that are indeed "extraordinary," albeit for reasons in excess of what Chief Justice Roberts might have meant. According to a 2010 poll conducted by the Public Religion Research Institute (PRRI, 2011), a strong plurality of Americans favor some sort of state recognition of same-sex couples, whether in the form of marriage (37 percent) or civil unions (27 percent). This is in comparison to 33 percent who opposed any form of state recognition. However, once age of respondents is factored in, the numbers get even more stark. As Robert Marus (2010) summarizes: "Among the youngest group surveyed (ages 18–29), a full three-quarters supported full same-sex marriage rights (52 percent) or civil unions (23 percent). But among those age 65 and over, only a small majority voiced support for same-sex marriage (22 percent) or civil unions (29 percent)."

Significantly, this generation gap holds even among white evangelicals, traditionally the group most vociferously opposed to same-sex marriage. An earlier 2008 PRRI study (published in 2009) found that:

> Support for same-sex marriage is significant among some young religious Americans. Among young (18–34) white mainline

> Protestants and Catholics, close to half (48% and 44% respectively)
> support same-sex marriage. Among young evangelicals (18–34),
> a majority favor either same-sex marriage (24%) or civil unions
> (28%), compared to a majority (58%) of evangelicals overall who
> favor no legal recognition of gay couples' relationships.

When it comes to winning the hearts, minds, and souls of the younger
generation on the question of same-sex marriage, religious and social
conservatives had lost even before *Obergefell* was heard by the Supreme
Court of the United States (This may be why they are now shifting
their own focus so intensely to passing laws at the statewide level to
protect the "religious liberty" of social conservatives who believe their
rights to be under attack by same-sex marriage, transgender equality
and, even, the very existence of transgender people.)

Women have lost, too. What do I mean by this? That same *Christian
Century* article contrasts the rising support for gay marriage, especially
among younger Americans, with public attitudes toward legalized
abortion. The survey found that support for abortion held steady
over the past five years, but so did opposition to it. More significantly,
there was no demonstrable generation gap, as there is on the same-sex
marriage issue. That is, both support for and opposition to legalized
abortion held steady across age groups. One clear implication of these
trends for younger evangelicals and, I would venture, for younger
Americans more generally, is a developing cleavage between legalizing
gay marriage, which they support, and legalized abortion, which they
continue to oppose. As PRRI researcher Robert Jones concludes: "The
survey reveals a decoupling of the social issues of same-sex marriage
and abortion, which have traditionally been mentioned in the same
breath in the public discourse" (cited in Marus, 2010).

Yes and no. Rather than see these two issues as "decoupled," I actually see a disturbing *connection* between rising support for same-sex
marriage and the continued and even hardened opposition to legalized
abortion, and, in the wake of the *Hobby Lobby* decision, to birth control. When rhetoric in favor of same-sex marriage equates marriage
with personal responsibility and psychological maturity – as many of
the advocates for same-sex marriage have argued – it promotes the
idea that gay people (and anyone else who does not want to buckle
down and marry) are childish, at best, and dangerously irresponsible

at worst. Such arguments for marriage equality turn into pleas for heterosexuals and the state to help homosexuals grow up and get on with the business of being responsible, disciplined adults. Now that same-sex couples are allowed to marry nationwide, we may even have to revise Rubin's formula and say that it is *unmarried* sex, "gay" or "straight," that is guilty until proven innocent.

This equation – marriage equals developmental maturity and the capacity to exercise responsibility – in turn contributes to a larger moral economy in US public life in which sex becomes the place where we measure whether an individual is "properly" self-disciplined or morally virtuous at all. Want to get married? You pass. Want or need an abortion? Not so fast. Abortion conjures raced and classed images of an out-of-control female sexuality. An unwanted or unplanned pregnancy, which can happen for so many reasons – including failed contraception or a failure to educate young people about contraception at all (as in: abstinence-only sex education) – is instead recast as a woman's failure in self-discipline and sexual morality.

The "responsibilization" of sexuality thus cuts both ways, towards a growing acceptance of and even promotion of same-sex marriage ("good" freedom) and the declining fortunes of abortion and contraceptive access ("bad" freedom) nationwide. This understanding of freedom's limits resonates powerfully across secular and religious boundaries, belying the separateness of the religious and the secular. Increasingly, the neoliberal state can make room for self-disciplined, "responsibilized" homosexual couples. This embrace of Adam and Steve alongside Adam and Eve can even go hand-in-hand with a diminution in reproductive freedom and a narrowing, as well, of public discourse concerning sexual ethics and social justice. The search for legitimation and this eager taking up of the tasks of "responsibilization" (*see, we're as upstanding and disciplined as you!*) are linked to psychic life – the psychic life of vulnerability – and are ghosted and propelled by motives and wishes not fully within our ken. Proponents of same-sex marriage are not to blame for the ratcheting up of laws aimed at limiting women's and girls' legal access to abortion. But they do contribute to a public political climate in which such laws make a kind of moral common sense and also promise a psychic defense against the disturbances of sex and bodily life more generally.

Note

1 This chapter was first published as "Responsibilization, Same-Sex Marriage, and the End of Queer Sex," *Psychoanalysis Culture & Society*, *20*(3) (2015), 237–245. Reprinted here by kind permission of the journal and Springer Nature.

References

Berlant, L. (2011). *Cruel Optimism*. Durham, NC: Duke University Press.

Burwell v Hobby Lobby Stores, Inc. (2014) 573 U.S. ___.

Cornell, D. (1995). *The Imaginary Domain: Abortion, Pornography and Sexual Harassment*. Ithaca, NY: Cornell University Press.

Duggan, L. (2004). Holy Matrimony! *The Nation*, February 26. www.thenation.com/article/holy-matrimony, accessed May 9, 2015.

Franke, K. (2015). *Wed-Locked: How African Americans and Gay People Mistakenly Thought Marriage Would Set Them Free*. New York: New York University Press.

Jakobsen, J.R. (2005). Sex + Freedom = Regulation: Why?, *Social Text 23* 84–85 Fall/Winter, 285–308.

Jakobsen, J.R., & Pellegrini, A. (2004). *Love the Sin: Sexual Regulation and the Limits of Religious Tolerance*. 2nd edition. Boston, MA: Beacon Press.

Marus, R. (2010). New polls show rising support for gay marriage, little change on abortion. *The Christian Century*, October 18. www.christiancentury.org/article/2010-10/new-polls-show-rising-support-gay-marriage-little-change-abortion, accessed May 9, 2015.

Obergefell v Hodges (2015). Argument transcripts, Supreme Court of the United States, April 28. www.supremecourt.gov/oral_arguments/argument_transcript.aspx, accessed May 9, 2015.

Public Religion Research Institute (2009). Report: American attitudes on marriage equality, February 18. http://publicreligion.org/site/wp-content/uploads/2011/06/American-Attitdues-on-same-sex-marriage-2008.pdf, accessed May 9, 2015.

Public Religion Research Institute (2011). Generations at odds: The millennial generation and the future of gay and lesbian rights. October 18. http://publicreligion.org/research/2011/08/generations-at-odds/, accessed May 9, 2015.

Rubin, G. (1993). Thinking sex: Notes for a radical theory of the politics of sexuality. In H. Abelove, M.A. Barale, & D.M. Halperin (Eds.), *The Lesbian and Gay Studies Reader* (pp. 3–44). New York: Routledge.

Part III

Family configurations and legal issues

Introduction

Plinio Montagna and Adrienne Harris

Both systems, the Family and the Laws, do not exist as closed systems remaining the same throughout human history. Their structures undergo many modifications according to the times and places where they are set.

"Totem and Taboo," a fanciful anthropological speculation of Freud published in 1913–14, proposes as the founding act of humanity the murder of the father of the primordial horde; from there the road would have been opened to what in the future would have resulted in legislation. In this sense it is postulated that the first human law will have its insertion as a Family Law.

This part presents chapters that deal with conceptual and defining issues within the scope of the Family Law in our times. But mainly it is composed of articles that also reveal possibilities for a practice involving the psychoanalyst in the judicial systems. All of these articles open paths for the discussion of the role of the psychoanalyst in questions related to the daily routine of dealing with family litigations, one of the main preoccupations in courts of justice all over the world.

In Chapter 10, Plinio Montagna and Luisa Branco Vicente discuss parenting in the context of family configuration changes originated in the second half of the twentieth century, with their current implications. As regards juridical issues, these encompass the inclusion of affect as a factor to be considered in legal decisions.

In Chapter 11, Louis Brunet discusses variables at stake for partners at divorce litigations involving children. He registers sensible psychic parameters to be considered when observation of the parental capacities to be guardian of the children come to the fore of the discussion.

In Chapter 12, Plinio Montagna examines the disturbingly frequent circumstance of parental alienation in litigations and divorces, including a psychoanalytical perspective about internal issues involved. It refers to a psychological manipulation of the child aiming to exclude a parent from the life of a child, observed mostly in litigious divorces, widely recognized in courts, accepted in some countries as a criminal offense, not so much considered in psychoanalytical or in medical literature.

In Chapter 13, Cynthia Ladvocat and Eliana Mello start with a compelling historical account of adoption, spotting its international importance and discussing the configuration of the adoptive family and adoptive bonds, offering examples of their clinical work experience in the area of adoption.

Finally, in Chapter 14, Adrian Besuschio brings specifically to the fore the litigious divorce, discusses their dynamics, the turbulences that arise, the tensions, and panoramas that have symptoms as possible consequences of disintegration.

Chapter 10

The context of socio-affective parenting

Plinio Montagna and Luísa Branco Vicente

Introduction

An effective dialogue between Psychoanalysis and Law requires more than a simple juxtaposition of knowledge from each field. It requires a real interpenetration between them. One which is at the same time unsettling and creative.

The first obstacle to be overcome refers to the fact that psychoanalysis searches the radical singularity of each individual, while law is concerned with external reality and the norms that govern human relations. Their interpenetration must take into account the cultural and historical contexts that exist as its substrate.

Several authors, originated in both areas, have attempted to find conceptual correlations and practical application between the fields. Freud himself (1906/1996) and jurists such as Thurmann Arnold (1935), Jerome Frank (1930, 1931, 1973), Albert Ehrenzweig (1971), Hans Kelsen (1986), and Pierre Legendre (1998) have brought relevant approximations.

Currently, Family Law is being swept away, in several countries, by this fruitful approach. The expression "We, family lawyers, we are also professionals of the listening" is significant.

We intend here to share reflections on pressing and current issues in our society, as well as timeless ones. Far from normativity, our perspective takes into account the anguish experienced in contemporary society as changes in traditional values challenge a traditional family model.

The increased number of divorces and the variations in family composition in recent years set common questions to the fields of psychology, psychoanalysis, and law, such as socio-affective parentality, multiparentality, etc.

In this context we wonder to what extent these new possibilities are opened up, conscious and unconscious, for individual and groups transformations, and if so, what new spaces will arise.

After all, we will have more and more data about questions such as what is it like to grow with the different references inherent in multiparentality and whether this "multi" favors the creation of a richer inner space or whether it poses more obstacles to naming and restraining children's anxieties.

We may suppose that the legalization of new configurations by the Society as a whole, influences the perception that each "new Family" has of itself as a legitimate component of the social order. This rises new questions about new forms of subjectivity of its components.

Psychoanalysis shows that a relevant element in personal identity construction is the internalization of the parental couple, of the father–mother link as regards their capacity to love or hate each other, their creativity as a couple (Vicente, 2017). These intrapsychic stories constitute a group of ideas about one's origin and insertion named by Freud as the "family romance" (Freud, 1959). It deals with the subject's internal experiences history, "with the mediation of ghosts created from an individual truth, which can not be superimposed on the historical reality" (Faure-Pragier, 2011, p. 1079). But new elements may be brought to scene, in the interplay between internal and external realities.

The psychoanalytical discussion of maternal and paternal roles, transcending gender, is at the core of the concept of parentality addressed here.

Let's take a clinical situation as a starting point in order to contextualize the notion of parentality. Some interrogations accompany the issues addressed in this work. Do new forms of family organization force psychoanalysis to review any basic concept of its theory? Do these new contexts favor the emergence of pathologies or, inversely, facilitate the elaboration of conflicts?

Rubens

"I have two fathers," was the first phrase uttered by Rubens at our initial contact (PM). This beginning was followed by an intriguing silence. Throughout our work, he dedicated a fair amount of time to internal sorting of his familial relations, fluctuating between what he felt as the intangible instability of his mother and the reliability of his adoptive father. His biological father, referred to with great ambivalence, had an almost marginal position. Part of Rubens's analysis was be dedicated to his assimilation of origins and operating them in his favor.

The initial phrase might have sounded like the confession of a "fault, a deficiency," or at least of certain exceptionality that he could not handle alone. But no, it was not so. More than his perception of exceptionality in personal history (compared to "ordinary people who only have one father"), he pointed to the importance of his identifying bonds with both parents, the biological and the "acquired." He was particularly grateful for what created him, after all, on an equal basis with his own biological children. He was capable of expressing authentic gratitude in his own way and, by rationalizing it or not, able to see some advantages in having two fathers.

But in general the inquiry about "what to do with the fact," was in the agenda, and it was up to the analyst to go along with him in his search.

Over time it became clear that this was a relevant question in the very structuring of his psyche, which went through an elaborate work of adequate responses to the questions he formulated about his essential condition. The adoptive father came to be a definitely good object sustaining his childhood since early age.

Intelligent and insightful, resilient, fresh out of the world of drugs, he struggled with conflicts of loyalty to both of them; although sometimes fancying to sack the distant one, the biological father, out of his life, he knew he wouldn't do that, for loyalty. He wondered how to deal with the new brotherhood, when his surname of origin plus the patronymic of his stepfather as a symbol that he was as dear to him as his true children, as dealing with jealousy and possession, where to put each of them within themselves after their mother's second divorce?

Rubens felt different for "having two parents"; both "unlucky" and "lucky." His ability to overcome frustrations led him to extract the possible advantages of this fact. And, indeed, some advantages he could find.

But for him, or as for any other person in similar circumstances, to be able to enjoy any benefit offered to him by the experience of multiparentality would require a good elaboration of his mourning for the separation of his parents, and in the background was one of the reasons, even if unconscious, for him to look for me and why it was so important to begin his analysis.

I will not dwell on clinical descriptions. But work through mourning on analysis about his parental separation was a fundamental step towards the use of resilient ability to turn his family on both sides into an extended family.

Extended family

One of the things I learned from working with "family emotions and the evolution of mental disorders" in the 1970s, developed from a research program at the University of London, "is that eventually psychotic patients inserted into so-called extended families may evolve more favorably than those in a nuclear family "(Montagna, 1982). This line of research has clearly shown that when emotional burdens in family relationships can be diluted by an environment in which more people live in key attachment positions, developments such as depression or schizophrenia are more favorable (Vaughn & Leff, 1976).

Over time, my clinical experience has been systematically suggesting that such favorable outcomes in extended families are not restricted to psychotic patients, not even to neurotic patients. An environment in which affective burdens are more diluted and diversified can also benefit individuals outside of any psychopathological classification. It is an environment in which strong affective bonds are distributed by several people, significant objects of attachment.

The French historian Phillipe Ariès (1975) shows that historical changes resulted from the differentiation between place of residence and work, with the industrial revolution and rising of the bourgeoisie, Family became, *par excellence*, the social locus for the expression of affect. It had other functions in the pre-industrial era (preservation of assets, daily mutual help, common practice of a trade), but no affective one; affect exchanges and social communications were carried out outside the family, in a medium composed of neighbors, friends, masters, servants, children, old people, in which affective communication could manifest itself freely. With industrialization, urbanization of society and family nuclearization, family affective exchanges should be carried out within the Family and not, for example, in the workplace, where such an event could disturb production and the consequent profit. Then, the nuclear composition can densify the affective charges directed to a member of the family.

Rubens went through separation and remarriage of the mother plus a second divorce from the latter. He was effectively raised by his mother's second husband, adopted by him as a son, thereby gaining a second father. To him, fate offered to experience multiparenting, in the context of a socio-affective parenting. In this case, only male parents were multiple, since their biological father remained single after their divorce.

Satisfactory elaboration of mourning for the separation of the biological parental couple was a condition for him to extract the possible positive aspects of new parenthood. So-called manic defenses could prevail, not favoring psychic integration.

Divorces and mourning

Any change requires elaboration of mourning for the loss of what is no longer. There is a need to work out the passage to the new. This is also true for individual life changes, groups, and societies.

This ability to mourn is essential for dealing with losses and separations one suffers during life. Mourning refers to losses and separations related to bonds, which naturally occur in the processes of change in life (Vicente, 2000).

When significant bonds break down suffering is inevitable. Separation implies pain. But new bonds are formed, succeeding to losses and pain (Kernberg et al., 1991).

The capacity to suppress the absence, the separation, to learn with the loss of the other, thus mourning, makes growth possible. These progressive movements favor, among other things, de-idealizations, thus the more realistic awareness of the relational world. Paradoxically, it is this ability to withstand separation that will enable emotional closeness and enrichment with the other, as being separate: similar and different (Vicente, 2000).

Pollock (1961), using Claude Bernard's concepts, suggested mourning as an internal adaptational process to external changes. He states:

> As the loss of a significant object causes a disturbance in object relationships that is seen as antiadaptational. In order to reestablish a state of ego equilibrium a mourning process is set in motion. The cathexis of a new object is not part of the mourning process alone but is an indicator of the degree of resolution of the object loss in terms of the adaptational process.

A separation can arouse the sentiment of abandon, of not being loved. In divorce, the spouses, when they have not sufficiently elaborated the losses, attack or violently confront themselves to limit situations, of which one example is parental alienation, or even the syndrome of parental alienation (Vicente, 2003; Montagna, 2019).

It should be noted, however, that there is not only one definition of violence, "there is a proliferation of meanings which must be included in a broader understanding, taking into account the practices, representations and relations of power" in each society (Lisboa, Vicente, & Barroso, 2005, pp. 7–8).

Debiologization of paternity

As a result of social malleability of the family system, beginning in the second half of the twentieth century, ties of paternity or maternity beyond biology become recognized. Affection becomes the paradigm of parenthood (Amarilla, 2014).

The new family configurations propitiate a debiologization of fatherhood and motherhood; "the affective relations seem to move forward in family projects, thus leading to the assumption of responsibility for the constitution of families" (Hironaka, 2000, p. 22). This "program" is also paradoxically due to the extraordinary advances in biology itself, which allows under certain conditions a baby to have up to five parents; the two who offered sperm and egg, two adoptive parents, eventually a woman who housed the egg in her womb. There is also the possibility that one egg may be genetically modified by the use of another, another donor woman – which leads to a possible number of six parents.

These configurations are based on changes boosted by the advent of the contraceptive pill. Women liberated from unavoidable motherhood, contributing to movements such as feminism, gender equality defense.

The new family configurations have favored the question (apart from intrinsic sex asymmetries) of the inexistence of biological, anthropological, or symbolic invariants, as Arantes (2014) ponders. The "inventive spirit of humanity" may bring considerable diversity. It might even be difficult to delineate the limits of the term "the family."

Etymologically the word family comes from famulus, "servant," with an economic connotation, indicating in Rome the quantity of the famuli, the slaves connected to the central house and then all who lived under the same roof, in authority of pater families, therefore linked to it.

In Brazil, until the last decades of the nineteenth century, family was instituted by indissoluble kinship. Mere parenthood dissociated from marriage did not constitute a family. This has changed on the way to the twenty-first century.

In Portugal, multiparentality is legally not yet premised, prevailing a traditional system that gives primacy to the biological; legal parents are only the biological parents.

Before the new configurations, the twentieth century brought about the primacy of the nuclear family, basically composed of father, mother, and children, without the presence of other members of the kinship in the dwelling. Often, by dissolution of the conjugal nucleus, a parent and child(ren) would remain in the residence.

Each historical moment, we know, has a socially constructed family model, often presented itself as a natural one. The twentieth century, in its first half, carried in its imaginary the fantasy of having achieved an ideal and definitive form of family, not assuming then the extraordinary sociological and psychological changes that were to come.

In this composition the man constituted the "head of the family," provider, owner of the final word, worked outside and drove the car. The mother was "from the home," to ease her situation called "queen of the home," and took care of household chores and children.

The following family configurations will "de-sexualize" and demystify family roles, "erase the difference between the sexes, and leave only the difference between generations" (Arantes, 2014, p. 125), making authority paternal and possibly maternal care give rise to parenting, or parental functions, which have undergone considerable changes. The couple of educators are valued. With parenting different functions are affirmed, but not hierarchical. The possibility of homoparentality and multiparentality is open.

Multiparentality is recognized as a multiple parent relationship, that is, when a child establishes a paternity/maternity relationship with more than one parent and/or more than one parent (Pereira, 2014).

With debiologization, the path to affective parenting is opened up, based on affective bonds, with or without a biological link. Reciprocally the socio-affective affiliation is the one that results not from biology, but from the affective bond.

Affectivity, which should not be confused with love alone, should not only play a relevant role in the juridical perspective of family composition, but may also support a relationship of kinship.

This positioning adopted by our legal system today has a close relationship with developments in psychoanalysis, as well as research and observations from psychology itself.

A pioneering body of work to inspire the psycho-juridical debate related to the appreciation of affect and psychological aspects in the parent–child relationship was Anna Freud's publications in conjunction with A. Solnit and Joseph Goldstein, a law professor at Yale University.

They stem from the growing acceptance of the thesis that the best interest of the child should prevail in the stipulation of his custody in litigious divorces of the parents, and it should not be taken for granted that mother should always be the best guardian. In the wake of these changes, and besides that, they formulate the concept of psychological parenthood, which is based on the idea that a child can establish close relations with an adult other than the biological parent. The adult becomes a psychological father through daily living and sharing with the child. An absent, inactive parent does not meet the child's needs for parenting (Goldstein, Solnit, & Freud, 1973).

Thus the concept of psychological parenthood refers to a person who has a parental relationship with a child, whether or not it is biologically linked. The term is primarily used in legal discourses, in litigation by guard. The authors suggest that, when discussing and judging custody, the importance of the child's established psychological paternity ties is important.

It is clear to them that close relationships are crucial to a child's development. They even question that the quality of the relationship between the child and the adult should be evaluated in this sense when the judicial separation of the child from the psychological father is questioned, which can be extremely painful and painful for the child.

Given these basic questions of paternality and maternality, we go to the concept of parenting, to reach that of multiparentality.

"Parentality" (*parentalidade*) is a neologism in Portuguese, as well as in Latin languages in general. It's derived from a neologism of the French language created by the psychiatrist and psychoanalyst Paul-Claude Racamier, who joined the words maternalité and paternalité; in English parenthood refers to the state of being a parent, but parenting is related to the *exercise* of motherhood, parenthood, and both together.

Racamier, working on puerperal psychoses (Racamier, de Sens, & Carretier, 1961) emphasized the dynamic aspects of the experience of becoming a mother, comparing it to adolescence, that is, a phase of existence in which the subject is confronted with profound identificatory transformations, reliving old conflicts in the passage to a new phase of life.

It should be noted that the father may also suffer psychophysiological processes related to the installation of paternality. Couvade's syndrome, conduct disorders, and paternity psychoneuroses are examples of this.

In French, "parent" can mean father or mother or have sense of family member, parentèle, set of relatives, parental, relative to parents (grandparents, in English and French). Apparenter means become a relative, ally by marriage, then have a similarity, from the seventeenth century (Baumgartner & Menard, 1996).

The word was exported to English parent, with the same meaning (Ayto, 2008), someone who gives life to another, including the words parturition and puerperal.

In Portuguese (Silveira Bueno, 1966), the term parent does not have the connotation of parents, it is restricted to the whole of the relative, meaning consanguineous, of the same family. When belonging to the family is by marriage and not by affinity, one is said to be related relative, and the term kinship, which belongs to the same family, has the connotation of consanguinity.

Parenting refers to parental function, be it parenthood, involvement with the children, and relationship with parents on common membership issues (Montagna, 2015).

Its etiological path begins in the Latin parens, father or mother, in turn related to the pario verb, parere, parir, to give birth, whose past participle is partum, calving, which also means the action of giving birth. Parens can figuratively mean: creator, author, inventor, founder. Also used in the plural as parents, ancestors, relatives.

Parenting is a psychic process, which starts with the desire to have the child, develops during pregnancy, and continues after the child is born (Solis-Ponton, 2004). It is a joint construction between parent and child.

It implies a psychic transformation, just as, *mutatis mutandis*, the child's birth transforms the mother's psyche creating the primary maternal concern. This is the denomination that Winnicott gives to the transformations undergone in the mother's psyche, at the birth of her baby, as an ingredient of her preparation for motherhood, a special phase in which she identifies herself closely and intuitively with the baby to supply her emotional needs, allowing the beginning of their integration and egoic development (Winnicott, 1987). The baby is the center of all attention of the mother's world (Vicente, 2005).

This is necessary for the installation of a "good enough environment," the good enough mother responds to the child allowing an illusion of omnipotence, realization of hallucinations, protection against the unthinkable anxieties that threaten the immature ego in a stage of absolute dependence.

Lebovici (2004) conceives parenting as the product of biological kinship plus parenting of the father and mother. It begins in the pregnancy and begins with the desire to have the child. It does not equate biological parenthood or maternity, but it develops by parenting, which implies in the child's action. In a sense, it is the child who parentifies the parents. There is an interaction, of action and feedback, that results in the care and development of the child who parentalizes the parents, who act stimulating the development of the child. The internal representation of the father and the mother is not exactly the father and the mother, but the parental care received. We are in the scope of functions, paternal and maternal. For Lebovici, it concerns intergenerational transmission and comprises an inner psychic work by the acceptance that we inherit something from our parents. Parental quality is in question. It understands the process by which the physical, emotional, intellectual, and social development of the child is promoted until reaching adulthood (Montagna, 2015, p. 776). It is a construction, in the minds of those involved.

This process is built within the relationship between parents and children and also intrapsychically, during the exercise of protection, education socialization, and integration of the younger generation. In the beginning, father is a helper and protector of mother, which is important as he contextualizes maternal care. Then it is the one that separates the mother–baby fusion.

Paternal and maternal functions

Some interesting questions have arisen from the contemporary psychological research on the specificity of functions, maternal and paternal.

A *primary maternal concern* is the term proposed by Donald Winnicott for the psychophysiological modifications that allow the mother's fine attunement to the newborn baby's needs and the exercise of her functions at this time; she intuitively identifies with the baby in order to meet her corporal and emotional needs, allowing egoic development and integration (Winnicott, 1987). This is necessary for the fostering of a "sufficiently good environment." A sufficiently good mother responds to the child, allowing for an illusion of omnipotence, the realization of hallucinations, and protection against unforeseeable anxieties which threaten the premature ego in a stage of complete dependence.

The father, in turn, has a primary function of creating conditions for the mother to exercise her function, that is, his initial function is to protect the mother, and subsequently develop the need to collaborate for the "breakup" of that mother–child fusional unit, acting in the direction of showing the existence of the external world to the baby. Strictly the father or the paternal function, makes itself responsible for the installation, in the world of the child, of the law. It is the paternal law. Along with this, in the opposite sense – not of separation, but of union – there is a symbolic structuring and linking function of the father (penis), showing not the separation but the possibility of linking between mother and father. This brings the child to a tripartite world, – child, mother, and father – linked with but different from father, that makes the world more complex. This function is called "penis as link," by Birksted-Breen (1996). There is now a space for symbolization. Good and bad, powerful and powerless, masculine and feminine can coexist, and one does not necessarily exclude the other. This is related to Melanie Klein's depressive position.

"In this condition it will be possible for the child to be able to identify himself to another as a thinking object, mother or maternal equivalent, capable of receiving in his interior and thinking situations of distress. To this capacity Bion called the container, which receives the contents of the child, split and projected anguish" (Vicente, 2006, p. 63).

The concept of parentality does not prioritize gender, but rather the functions. In principle both, father and mother, could exercise both functions.

So, psychoanalysis places us before functions. These are naturally performed by one or the other, but not always. Certain functions seem and are more natural that are exercised by the mother and others by the father. But it is not necessarily so.

Recent studies, designed for the effective research of these functions, are reported by Michael Lamb (1987). But contemporary research is unanimous in emphasizing the importance of the father in all aspects involved in caring for and raising young children. Interesting studies exist about the possibilities of involving the father in the care and education of the children, some designed to quantify the time father passes with the children and the activities they have together.

Lamb (1987) points out that paternal involvement can take place at three levels: engagement, accessibility, and responsibility, depending on the parent's involvement with the child. The first assumes that the father can feed, help feed, and later do homework, etc. The second is less intense; for example, the child plays in the room while he cooks, or he even sits in the room while she plays. The third has to do with taking responsibility for well-being and care, for example making arrangements, arranging clothes, etc.

It is relevant in the research group addressed by Lamb that although mothers are usually associated with caring for the child and men with playing, several authors point out that we cannot say that men are less capable of caring for children.

Lamb points out that research has shown that in the newborn period, the skills to care for the child are similar, there being no difference in skills between mother and father. And, contrary to the notion of "maternal instinct," research shows that skills are acquired on the job, both by mothers and fathers.

In general, the difference between mother and father lies in the fact that mothers are on the job more often as parents, so it is not surprising that they become more sensitive to the child. Lamb's thesis is that this can be reversed if the father becomes responsible for such care.

What usually occurs is that parents, with their lack of experience, become less sensitive and feel less confident about their abilities and give space to their mothers, so that they take on more and more responsibilities, including why they feel which is their function.

This would be the process by which the discrepancy of care between parents and mothers is great. But when parents are placed in the role of primary caregiver, for example, unemployed or widowed, they are perfectly capable of acquiring the necessary skills.

This set of data operates to corroborate the possibility that both genders exercise both parental functions.

The psychoanalyst Donald Winnicott, in turn, emphasizes a mother's need to be protected by the father. The initial protective environment includes both father and mother (Lamb, 2004, pp. 1–32), which is the support for the latter. Things are fine-tuned, sleep is light. There is also a transformation in the relationship of the mother with her own mother, and an opportunity to work out old conflicts which are still unresolved.

Apart from this primary maternal care, we can be talking about functions not necessarily related to biology; the concept of parentality prioritizes the roles to the detriment of the essential differences between them. Bringing a child into the world is not enough to make genitors into parents. The birth (physical fact) has to be transformed into filiation (social fact), "so that, inserted into a symbolic organization (psychological fact), the child constitutes himself/herself as a subject" (Cecarelli, 2007).

McDougall (1995) points to the importance of the parent being active, vital, dynamic, with a love of liberty, able to identify desires and needs of the child and who can usher them into the world. They might also be homo- or heterosexuals.

These diverse developments aid in the understanding of perspectives and possibilities which are referred to as "social parenthood." There is no ideal familial organization, there are only those which are more harmonious in given social times. Parenthood, from the psychological perspective, is always constructed and familial ties with children are guided by organizations of affect.

References

Amarilla, S.D.A. (2014). *O afeto como paradigma da parentalidade*. Curitiba: Juruá.

Arantes, U. (2014). A agonia de Édipo: Notas de leitura sobre pais e parentalidade. *Ide, 37*(58), 123–131, São Paulo.

Ariès, P. (1975). *História social da criança e da família*. Rio de Janeiro: Zahar.

Arnold, T.W. (1935). Apologia for jurisprudence. *Yale Law Journal, 44*(5), 729–753.

Ayto, J. (2008). *Word Origins*. London: A & C Black.

Baumgartner, E., & Menard, P. (1996). *Dictionnaire étymologique et historique de la langue française*. Paris: Librairie General Française.

Birksted-Breen, D. (1996). Phallus, penis and mental space. *The International journal of psycho-analysis, 77*(4), 649–657.

Ceccarelli, P.R. (2007). Novas configurações familiares: Mitos e verdades. *Jornal de Psicanálise, 40*(72), 89–102.

Ehrenzweig, A.A. (1971). *Psychoanalytic Jurisprudence on Ethics, Aesthetics, and Law – on Crime, Tort, and Procedure*. New York: Oceana Publications.

Faure-Pragier, S. (2011). Rester psychanalyste face au chaos des nouvelles filiations. *Revue Française de Psychanalyse, 75*(4), 1063–1080.

Frank, J. (1930). *Law and the Modern Mind*. New York: Coward-McCann.

——— (1931). Are judges human? Part two: As through a class darkly. *University of Pennsylvania Law Review and American Law Register, 80*(2), 233–267.

——— (1973). *Courts on Trial: Myth and Reality in American Justice.* Princeton, NJ: Princeton University Press.

Freud, S. (1906/1996). A psicanálise e a determinação dos fatos nos processos jurídicos. In S. Freud, *Edição Standard Brasileira das Obras Psicológicas Completas de S. Freud* (J. Salomão, Trad. Vol. 9, pp. 95–108). Rio de Janeiro: Imago. (Obra original publicada em 1906).

——— (1959). Family romances. In *The Standard Edition of the Complete Psychological Works of Sigmund Freud*, Volume IX (1906–1908): Jensen's 'Gradiva'and Other Works.

——— (1996). Totem e tabu (Totem and taboo). In S. Freud, *Edição Standard Brasileira das Obras Psicológicas Completas de S. Freud* (J. Salomão, Trad. Vol. 13). Rio de Janeiro: Imago. (Obra original publicada em 1912–1913).

Goldstein, J., Solnit, A., & Freud, A. (1973). *The Best Interest of the Child. The Least Detrimental Alternative.* New York: Free Press.

Hironaka, G. (2000). *Direito civil: estudos.* Belo Horizonte: Del Rey.

Kelsen, H. (1986). *Teoria geral das normas* (J. F. Duarte, Trad.). Porto Alegre: Sergio Antonio Fabris Editor. (Obra original publicada em 1979).

Kernberg, O., Selzer, M., Koenigsberg, H., & Appelbaum, A. (1991). *Psicoterapia psicodinâmica de pacientes borderline.* Porto Alegre: Artes Médicas.

Lamb, M.E. (1987). Introduction. The emergent American father. In M.E. Lamb, *The Father's Role; cross cultural perspectives* (pp. 4–23). New Jersey: Lawrence Erlbaum.

——— (2004). The role of the father: An Introduction. In M. Lamb (Ed.), *The Role of the Father in Child Development* (pp. 1–31). New Jersey: John Wiley and Sons.

Lebovici, S. (2004). Diálogo entre Letícia Solis Ponton e Serge Lebovici. In L. Solis-Ponton (org.), *Ser pai, ser mãe: parentalidade, desafio para o próximo milênio* (pp. 21–28). São Paulo: Casa do Psicólogo.

Legendre, P. (1974). *The Other Dimension of the Law.* In P. Goodrich & D.G. Carlson (Eds.), *Essays on Psychoanalysis and Jurisprudence.* Ann Arbor, MI: Paris: Le Seuil.

Lisboa, M., Vicente, L.B., & Barroso, Z. (2005). *Saúde e violência contra as mulheres.* Lisbon: Direcção-Geral de Saúde.

McDougall, J. (1995). *The Many Faces of Eros.* London: Free Associations Press.

Montagna, P. (1982). *Emoções expressas no ambiente familiar e evolução da esquizofrenia* (Dissertação de mestrado). Faculdade de Medicina da Universidade de São Paulo, São Paulo.

——— (2015). Parentalidade. ———In C. Lagrasta Neto & J. F. Simões, *Dicionário de Direito de família* (pp. 776–780). São Paulo: Atlas.

——— (2019). Parental alienation and Parental Alienation Syndrome. Chapter 12 of this volume.

Pereira, R.C. (2014). *Dicionário de Direito de família e sucessões*. São Paulo: Saraiva.

Pollock, G. (1961). Mourning and adaptation. *International Journal of Psychoanalysis*, *42*, 341–361.

Racamier, P., de Sens, C., & Carretier, R. (1961). La mère, lénfant das les pshychoses du postpartum. *Evolution Psychiatrique*, *XXVI*, 525–570.

Silveira Bueno, F. (1966). *Grande dicionário etimológico prosódico da língua portuguesa*: São Paulo: Saraiva.

Solis-Ponton, L. (2004). A Construção da Parentalidade. In L. Solis-Ponton (org.), *Ser pai, ser mãe – parentalidade: um desafio para o terceiro milênio* (pp. 29–40). São Paulo, Casa do Psicólogo.

Vaughn, C., & Leff, J. (1976). The influence of family and social factors on the course of psychiatric illness: A comparison of schizophrenic and neurotic patients. *British Journal of Psychiatry*, *129*, 125–127.

Vicente, L.B. (2000) A Depressão na Criança. Lisboa: Tese de Doutoramento em Psiquiatria e Saude Mental. Tese de Doutoramento em Psiquiatria e Saude Mental. Faculdade de Medicina de Lisboa.

——— (2003). Custos com a saúde psicológica. In M. Lisboa, I. Carmo, L.B. Vicente, & A. Nóvoa (Eds.), *Os custos sociais e económicos da violência contra as mulheres* (pp. 67–76). Lisbon: Comissão para a Igualdade e para os Direitos das Mulheres, Presidência do Concelho de Ministros.

——— (2005). Produção criativa ou linguagem do imaginário uma reaproximação freudiana a Leonardo da Vinci. *Revista Portuguesa de Psicanálise*, *25*, 175–192.

——— (2006). A escuta: do olhar ao tocar (pp. 61–68). In *Caderno do bebé*. Lisbon: Fim de Século.

——— (2017). *Prefácio*. In O. Van Doellinger (Ed.), *Corpo e identidade: Perspetiva psicodinâmica da unidade somatopsíquica* (pp. VII–XII). Lisbon: Lidel.

Winnicott, D. (1987). *Babies and Their Mothers*. Boston, MA: Addison-Wesley.

Chapter 11

Evaluating parental capacities

A model inspired by psychoanalysis

Louis Brunet

Introduction

In custody and child access disputes, a clinician may be asked to assess the parents' parenting abilities. A judge may want to know if the parents have the psychological capacity to take good care of their children. But what does that mean?

Nomothetic diagnostic models such as DSM are in no way helpful in assessing an individual's parenting capacities, let alone assessing their ability to meet the psychological needs of their child. Nomothetic diagnostic systems are designed to identify psychopathologies from a range of symptoms; not to evaluate psychological "capacities." Such a diagnostic system is all the more useless since we know that parents with psychopathologies can nevertheless take care of their children. In addition, most of the work on parental care shows that despite psychological difficulties or the presence of parental psychopathology, it is important to allow children to have access to both parents (Goldstein, Freud, & Solnit, 1973). It is therefore not with a simple psychological diagnosis and even less with a DSM diagnosis that the clinician can assess and describe the "positive" ability of a parent to respond adequately to the general needs and psychological needs of his children. The clinician wishes to be able to evaluate and understand much more subtle aspects of the parents' personality than a mere diagnosis of the presence or absence of symptoms or syndromes.

Although psychologists, psychiatrists, and other clinicians practicing in the field of child custody assessment have for the most part good training in adult assessment, and in child assessment, such an assessment is something else than a set of individual diagnoses. First, an assessment in child custody and access rights concerns the triangle

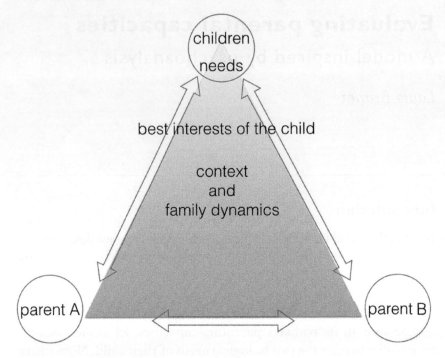

Figure 11.1 Triangle of child custody assessment.

made up of both parents and the child (or children), the evaluation of each of these three persons constituting the three points of the triangle (see Figure 11.1) (APA, 1994; Shapiro, 1984). But not only must such custody assessment procedure capture the personalities and psychological characteristics of each of the individuals involved, but it must evaluate what is happening within the triangle, that is, the family context, the family dynamic (often described as a systemic perspective regardless of the theory used) as well as the reciprocal dynamic effects that each individual has on each other. The aim here is to understand the relationship between each member of the family and to come to infer what is the best solution to meet the needs of children in this crisis that will inevitably affect them.

Psychological custody assessment is not about which parent has the "best personality" or "best parenting ability," which in any case cannot be measured with any accuracy.

The purpose of this set of psychological assessments within a child custody expertise is to assess if the parents have the capacity to respond to the psychological and developmental needs of the children. It is an attempt to determine whether the parent is capable of ensuring the child's development, psychological well-being and physical well-being and, if so, whether one of the parents cannot really respond to these imperatives. But beyond an illusory comparison of parents, it is important to understand and explain the harmony between the specific psychological needs of the child and the parent's ability to meet those needs.

The methodology in psycholegal assessment for child custody obviously requires psychological assessment of the parents and that of the child, but in addition to the personality characteristics of each of them, this assessment aims to evaluate the parent–child relationship and the parental capacities to respond to the usual or specific psychological needs that the assessment of the child has shown. However, both in clinical practice and in scientific texts on the topic, it seems impossible to find a clear definition of the concept of "parental capacity" that would be agreed upon, let alone an agreement on the best methodology to evaluate it. In addition, the clinician must not confuse the observation of the parent–child interaction with an assessment of the relationship between the child and his parent.

As summarized in Figure 11.2, this chapter attempts to propose a model for child custody assessment through

- assessment of the parent–child relationship
- observation of parent–child interactions
- assessment of parental capacities inspired by psychoanalysis, particularly by the concept of "pliable medium"

Parent assessment elements

In general, professional guidelines and child custody manuals suggest assessing a number of psychological factors of the parent (personality, psychopathology, relationship skills, etc.).

Brunet, Sabourin, and Létourneau (2014) propose to evaluate the following elements:

- the parent's personality structure (conflicts, defenses, identity, possibility of a psychopathology, relational abilities), personal, mental and relational characteristics

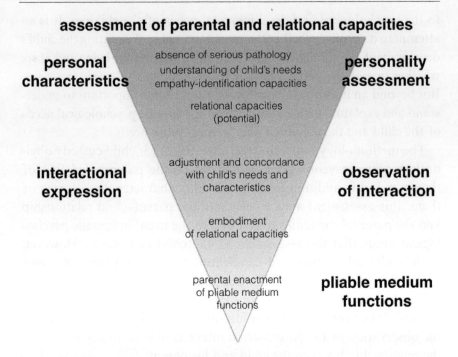

assessment of parental and relational capacities

personal characteristics

personality assessment

absence of serious pathology
understanding of child's needs
empathy-identification capacities

relational capacities
(potential)

interactional expression

observation of interaction

adjustment and concordance
with child's needs and
characteristics

embodiment
of relational capacities

parental enactment
of pliable medium
functions

pliable medium functions

Figure 11.2 Assessment of parental and relational capacities.

- the presence of a conflict or an element of personality that may constitute a risk to the child
- the parent's understanding of his child's needs and personal characteristics
- the parent's personal desires and needs that may affect his or her capacity to care for the child or affects his ability to understand the child; the harmony between the parent's wishes and needs and the specific needs of the child
- the history of the care the parent has provided in the past to his child, and the responsibilities he has actually assumed before and after the separation
- the parent's perception of the separation and its causes, his adaptation to separation
- the image of the separation transmitted to the child, the image of the other parent passed on to the child, the incitement to maintain or aggravate a conflict of allegiance in the child, the possibility

given to the child to maintain a positive image and a positive identification with the other parent
- openness and ability to communicate and collaborate with the
other parent about shared parenting and to allow the child to be in
touch with the other parent
- the capacity to be a positive model for the child
- the ability to provide the child with the stability and continuity he
/ she needs
- the abilities to secure, control and educate the child

When it comes to assessing relational and parenting skills, the expert
is faced with several related concepts that must be taken into account.
He can first understand these parental and relational abilities as a
potential. In this sense, he can evaluate the intrinsic and intrapsychic
relational characteristics of the parent. Some clinicians view relational
capacities as an intrapsychic potential that belongs to the individual
and is composed of elements such as empathy, the capacity to identify
with others, to communicate, to understand the needs of the other, the
attachment capacity, etc. A clinician working within the psychoanalytic model possesses the theoretical concepts to make a judgment on
these intrapsychic aspects.

However, as part of an evaluation of parental capacities, one must
also seek to understand if and how this potential is actualized in the
real relationship to the child. How to evaluate this? Clinicians can
approach this assessment from two perspectives: the subjective experience of the parent and the observation of the parent–child interaction.

Relationship capacities assessment

Curiously, we find in some expert reports a confusion between the
observation of the parent–child interaction and the evaluation of the
relationship. Some clinicians believe that they evaluate the parent–
child relationship by observing them in interaction and by simply
describing this interaction without drawing any inference on the
adequacy of the relationship. In reality, the observation of the interaction between the child and his parent is an observation technique,
as are play techniques or projective techniques. But this observational

technique of parent–child interaction can be invaluable in assessing whether the parent understands the child's psychological needs and is able to respond with empathy; to assess relational and emotional matching between parent and child; if the clinician is able to draw inferences from his observations.

A clinician could theoretically make an observation of the parent–child interaction without making a real assessment of the parent–child relationship or parenting abilities. The technique should not be confused with the complexity of a relationship assessment. Parent–child interaction is a manifestation of the parent–child relationship. It is therefore of a different conceptual level. The parent–child relationship is a broad concept that includes both the relational characteristics and potential of each of the individuals involved, and the actualization of that relationship into a series of behaviors and attitudes.

For the clinician, to observe is not to evaluate. He may observe the parent–child interaction, but his job at this point is not to take the observation of this interaction at the mere descriptive level, but rather to use the observation of their interaction as one of the sources of information to evaluate the characteristics of the relationship. Observing this parent–child interaction can provide invaluable information on the actualization of parental capacities and on the psychological effects that these relational characteristics of the parent provokes in the child (as well as the effects the child has on the parent).

The evaluation of the parent–child relationship is a complex process that can be achieved by using several sources since it involves assessing both intrinsic individual aspects of the parent as well as inter-relational aspects. Since the relationship is partly composed of individual and intrapsychic components, these components can be partially assessed through the parent's personality, through interviews or diagnostic tools, by the evaluation of the mental representations the parent has of his child, by the assessment of one's empathy and capacity for identification, etc. However, while assessing the intrapsychic and individual components of the relationship, the clinician also attempts to assess how these abilities actualize in the actual relationship with the child; he attempts to evaluate how the adjustment between these intrapsychic characteristics and the child is done. It is for the evaluation of this attunement to the needs of the child that the observation of the parent–child interaction becomes so useful.

But what should the clinician observe in the parent–child interaction and what inferences can he draw on the parent's ability to respond to his child's psychological needs?

In concrete terms, the observation of the parent–child interaction can be done according to a free methodology or a directed methodology. The first model leaves the parent and the child totally free to do whatever they want, without instructions and the clinician observes their interaction without intervening. By analogy, this method is similar to free association. The clinician installs the parent and the child in a room containing games, craft and drawing materials, small characters, and suggests they can play together. The clinician can then observe the contribution of each. He may observe the passivity and activity of each one, he observes how conflicts are born and how they are resolved, he can see how each one tries to "please", to "direct", to collaborate, or control. He can see how the parent can verbally contain and control the child rather than impose his control by authority or rigidly. He can observe the harmony, understanding, and empathy between the parent and the child.

Some prefer to use a more formal directed methodology where the parent is specifically asked to perform certain tasks that allow for easy observation of parenting skills (collaborative games, control or decision games, drawings, etc.). Clinicians who are trained at using projective assessment techniques can ask the parent-child pair to create a story together, using projective instruments like the "Thematic Apperception Test," the "Family Apperception Test" or any other similar instrument; or to make a collaborative drawing. Thus, the clinician can both make inferences about the projective contents brought by the parent and the child but also about the relational processes that take place between them to create and agree on the story or the drawing.

Finally, some clinicians prefer to make this kind of observation in a natural environment (the parent's home) to also observe the adequacy of the care environment while others prefer to observe the interaction in a professional environment where the material and the situation are controlled.

But to be able to truly infer with a certain validity the parental capacities through the observation of the interaction and to be able to evaluate the effect of the parental relationship mode on the child, as well as the effect of the child's relational mode on the parent, the clinician needs a conceptual model of parental capacities. We must acknowledge that currently there is no operationalized model of parental capacity assessment that would be widely shared, even less that would create consensus among clinicians. In reality, there is not even a widely shared definition of the very concept of parental capacity. This is why the next section proposes an understanding of the concept of parental capacity, inspired by psychoanalysis, which can guide the observation of the interaction and the evaluation of these capacities.

The concept of parental capacity and its evaluation

A model inspired by psychoanalysis

There is currently no satisfactory definition of parental capacity that is truly shared and agreed upon in psychology. Depending on the training and the theoretical orientations, a certain number of variables are considered by the clinicians as components of these parental capacities. Thus, the notions of empathy, ability to perceive the needs of the child, identification with the child, are important for most clinicians. Many expert witnesses also seek to understand whether the parent forces the child in a conflict of allegiance (which may go as far as parental alienation) or, conversely, whether the parent allows the child to maintain a positive image of the other parent.

Methodologically, some expert witnesses favor a purely intrapsychic approach, attempting to substantially assess the parent's intra-psychic components, while others focus their understanding primarily on the observation of parent-child interaction without even taking into account the individual intra-psychic characteristics of the parent.

When assessing the personality of a parent, the presence or absence of psychopathology, his or her relational abilities, what are the elements that really participate in what could be called his parenting abilities? One way of thinking about the concept of parental capacity would be, in our opinion, to be able to define a series of "psychological functions" that a parent must fulfill with his child in order for him to develop normally psychologically; therefore, to meet a series of primary needs of the child. Of course, here again we face the difficulty that psychology is divided in a multiplicity of theoretical models. But despite this obstacle we believe it possible to identify, in a way that transcends diagnostic models, a series of needs of the child and consequently a series of parental functions to meet these needs. Thus, we propose a model of parental capacities based on eight psychological functions that a parent usually fills with his child and which are necessary for his harmonious development.

The pliable medium object

In psychoanalysis the concept of object has many different meanings. Freud (1915) defined the object mainly as the "object of the drive," i.e. the object (person, self, part of the self) that permits drive satisfaction. Since Freud the various theories of object relations have expanded this conception and multiplied the ways of understanding the object. Klein has worked extensively on partial objects and splitted objects (good and bad). Klein (1946) and Bion (1962) also showed that the parent had to perform a "containing function" for the child, receiving his or her projections and detoxifying them. Winnicott (1951) then described a paradoxical characteristic through the transitional object: the latter being both the mother and not the mother, a sort of transitional space between the internal object and the external object. Winnicott (1969) has also shown that the (real) parent must fulfill real functions for the healthy development of subject/object differentiation: first allowing the child to experiment a primary narcissism in which he can believe he "creates" the object and then permitting a gradual disillusion and differentiation of his inner world and the outside world. Then psycho-analysis, following Winnicott, was interested in the functions that had to fulfill the real object, the parent, to allow the development of the psychic abilities of the child. It is these various functions that we consider "parenting abilities" for the purpose of this chapter.

René Roussillon (1991, 1997, 2001) is one of the psychoanalysts who sought to describe the parental functions necessary for the good development of the child's psyche, and in particular the development of the child's capacities of representation and symbolization, his capacity to differentiate the inner world and his internal objects from the external world and the external objects. He himself relied on Marion Milner's (1952) "pliable-medium" idea, and embodies these functions in the metaphor of modeling clay. This concept is, in a way, a more formalized and operationalized equivalent of elements described by Winnicott under the term "good enough mother." Roussillon describes that the object, the parent (the therapist), must accept to be used according to the needs of the child (or the patient). It describes a series of functions that the child needs and that must be fulfilled by the parent. In his first formulation, Roussillon (1988) described five characteristics (or functions of the object) of the pliable medium and he will add later on them. On our side we will use eight qualities or functions for the purpose of this text.

These eight functions respond to the primary psychological needs of a child to which all parents must respond almost completely when the child is very young, but whose importance decreases as the child matures. In short, when the child is very young, the parent must allow the child to have an almost flawless experience of these eight qualities and functions but gradually the parent must allow the child to experience the limits of these qualities (Brunet 2005; Winnicott 1971).

Inspired by the papers cited above, we use as Roussillon the metaphor of modeling clay or plasticine to illustrate these eight psychological functions related to parental capacity. Thus, when we see a child play with modeling clay, we can see that the value of the clay resides in a certain number of its characteristics: the clay can be manipulated with a great vigor, it will change shape but will not be destroyed, on the other hand a tiny pressure of the nail will leave a trace, it is therefore sensitive; it can be transformed to infinity but it also can return to its initial state, etc. From the illustrations that this metaphor allows, we present here a series of analogous functions that the parent must fulfill to meet the primary needs of a child and in order to promote a harmonious development of his psyche. Of course, if a parent has to fully adapt to the child and fully meet his needs (not his desires) when he is an infant, the more the child grows up, the less the parent needs to respond to it perfectly or quickly. Spontaneously and empathically, the parent will bring gradually the child to tolerate having to wait for the response of the object and he will respond less perfectly to the child's needs when he will empathically understand the child may tolerate it and is able to better "symbolize and represent" his experience.

We propose using the following eight characteristics as parameters of parental capacity, characteristics that can easily be observed through parent–child interaction or play situations:

1. consistency
2. indestructibility
3. transformation of quantity into quality
4. sensitivity
5. ability to transform
6. conditional and unconditional availability
7. capacity to be alive
8. capacity for fidelity

1. Consistency, being seizable

As in the metaphor of the modeling clay, the parent must have a quality of relational presence that allows the child to experience its presence, his solidity, and his reality. The child must be able to have the feeling of the actual presence of his parent and be able to feel that he can "touch" him both physically and emotionally. On the contrary, a failing consistency makes the child feel that his parent is elusive, fleeting, chaotic, difficult to understand, to move or to "touch." The parent must therefore make himself "seizable" by the child, both concretely and metaphorically. The child must be able to experience the physical and psychological presence of the parent, to be able to grasp it, that is, to feel that he may have at least relative power over him. The parent must be able and willing to let himself be seized and to let the child have relative power over him. But to be grasped is also to be understood and the parent must be able to transmit to the child what he feels and lives towards him and what he expects from him. Both his own image and his image of the child must not be confused or fused. The inability to believe that he can have some power over his parent can leave the child in a state of distress and futility that will have adverse consequences on his or her development. But obviously giving the child a feeling of relative power does not mean that the child must be allowed to grow up without constraint, without direction in an illusion of unlimited power. The observation of the parent–child interaction, either in a free-play situation or in a more directed situation (projective technique for example) shows how much the parent accepts to be "used" by the child and how much he is sensitive to the needs and affects of the child or, on the contrary, observe an interaction that would leave the child with the feeling that the parent is too distant and cannot be "affected," "touched" by him.

2. Indestructibility – survival

As great clinicians like Winnicott have observed, the child needs to experience that he may get angry with his parent, and even destroy him in fantasy, but that in reality his parent will not actually be destroyed. neither physically nor psychologically (Winnicott, 1969). It is therefore necessary, especially in early childhood, for the parent to allow the child to experience his demands, anger or fits, in a way that is not catastrophic, without giving the impression that the parent is being destroyed or depressed by these attacks, without giving the impression that he is incapable of tolerating it, incapable of containing it, that he has to flee or that he will take revenge. The parent must therefore survive the child's desires, anger, cries or anxieties, and convey to him the conviction that all these emotions are not destructive neither for him nor for others. It is because he has made this experience of survival of the object to the intensity of his drives that the child can then better differentiate what is from the inner world (desire, emotion, fantasy) and what is from the outside world (Winnicott, 1969). As a negative example, a depressed parent can create in his child the conviction that he must repress any anger or reproach because of the risk of aggravating his parent's condition. The child will then have to repress a large part of himself which will hinder his development. Observation of the parent–child interaction provides an excellent opportunity to observe how the parent "resists" and survives the demands and frustrations of the child, allows him to express his anger, his aggressiveness, his demands or his greed, without giving the impression that these requests are dangerous and destructive for the parent.

3. Transformation of quantity into quality

Young children often live emotions, anxieties, excitations that are intense and end in a form of discharge: shouting, crying, blows.

One of the fundamental functions of parents is to help the child to transform these raw emotional quantities into thoughts and words (primary and secondary symbolization) that make sense, to communicate his needs and emotions and thereby to create not only the capacity to "represent" what he experiences but also to develop a capacity of delay in satisfactions. Authors like Bion and Winnicott have shown, in accordance with the implications of the second Freudian model (with the concept of non-represented contents in the Id), that instinctual drives require a work of symbolization before being usable by the psyche (displacement, repression, sublimation). In order for the child to symbolize, to transform what is felt first of all as a thrust, push or a quantity, he needs his primary objects to help him perform this representation. The transformation of this quantity into quality (into representations usable by the psyche) makes it possible to give meaning to experiences, to "domesticate" primary needs and finally to adapt to the environment and society. The parent must therefore very early in the child's life, perform for him this task of identifying his emotions, his needs, his affects (through identification), and communicate it back to the child through words, so that not only will the child be able to "understand" better what he experiences but he will develop his own capacity for transformation, for representation. We see very early how infants can be calmed by empathic words. We see how parents, rather than oppose force to force, will calm a child with words. They then transform quantity into quality where other parents may feel the necessity to shout or repress and so respond to quantity by quantity, to raw emotion by emotion. Observation of the parent–child interaction shows how effectively a parent can use words to calm, direct, control, help the child, especially when the child is excited, nervous, irritated, dissatisfied, or demanding. Some parents are unable to help the child make sense of all this and create a dynamic of opposition, of restriction of spontaneity. Some parents' only solution is to oppose force to force and domination to spontaneity.

4. Sensitivity and empathy

It is good and important that the parent is able to be resistant and that he is able to help the child to understand that he will not be destroyed by the intensity of his drives. But this must not be experienced at the expense of sensitivity.

Just as the nail on the modeling clay leaves a visible trace, the child needs to see, to have the proof, that he can touch his parent emotionally, that he can make him feel what he feels himself, to see that he can have an emotional impact on his parent, to make him laugh as well as to make him sad or worried, to please him as to displease, thus verifying not only how important he is to his parents but witnessing the emotional sensitivity and empathy of his parent.

Some parents may be too sensitive and make the child believe they are destroyed or risk being destroyed by their emotions or their demands (the case of a parent who is depressed or who fears the aggressiveness of his child for example). On the other side, others may not be sensitive enough to the experiences and needs of their child. These two pitfalls can be problematic. Parents are usually able to interpret the meaning of the child's tears: is it hunger, pain or sadness? Parents usually succeed in being sensitive to the emotions of the child even if the child is not able to formulate them clearly.

A parent transmitting to his child that he cannot be reached, or "touched," can provoke an equivalent of the mental state described in the "still face experiment" (Tronick and Weinberg 1997): after a period when the child becomes hyperactive to stimulate and reach his parent, he then seems to resign himself in a position of silent despair which will have significant negative repercussions on his development. The child needs not only to be able to touch his parent, to transmit emotional states that he often does not understand himself (which happens even among teenagers) but he also needs an empathic return, a reflexive response from the parent showing that he has received and understood his condition.

5. Ability to transform

As play dough can be folded, rolled, transformed to represent what the subject wishes to portray, the parent, to a certain extent, must be able to accommodate the child's needs and take the appropriate form that will meet his needs. The parent must therefore be able to adapt to the child, rather than being rigid and having the same attitude at all times. At times and under certain circumstances a child may need to regress or be comforted while at other times it may be possible to ask for more self-control, for example. Is the parent able to become the kind of object that the child needs at this particular moment in his life? Can he fulfill the function that the child needs in relation to what he experiences in that particular day or does he exhibit an identical attitude regardless of what the child is living and caring about? The parent must therefore adapt who he is, what he provides to the child as well as its requirements according to the child's condition, the circumstances of life and the development of his child. Of course, if the parent has to fully adapt to the child as an infant, he must naturally reduce this perfect adaptation gradually as the child develops his capacity for delay and psychological maturation.

6. Conditional and unconditional availability

As a corollary to sensitivity and parental transformability, the parent must be available to the child. However, while the availability must be almost total and unconditional while the child is an infant, this availability must gradually become partial, notably by introducing delays, and this availability will become conditional (especially to the good behavior of the child) when he is more mature and has developed the ability of delay. On the side of the child, it is obviously a progressive learning and on the side of the parent, he must be careful not to try to push his child too early towards too much autonomy. The child learns, gradually, that he has a role to play in interpersonal relationships to be loved, to obtain an adequate response from the object. It is a function where each of the two protagonists has an influence on the attitude of the other: the child has a role to play in making the parent available and the parent must respond with sufficient availability to the requests and needs of the child. The parent must also convey to the child that it is worthwhile to ask and hope for an answer to his needs. If a parent can hardly afford to be unavailable to the needs of his child when he is an infant, he must, however, help him acquire the capacity for delay. But some parents would like the child to be self-sufficient too early, which risks provoking a pseudo-autonomy or, on the contrary, undue anxiety about absence and separation. On the other hand, some parents may want to protect their child by continuing for too long to have a total and rapid availability, thus impeding the development of autonomy and the capacity to live delay and absence.

7. *Capacity to be alive*

The parent must be able to demonstrate that he is "alive" not so much physically of course, which is obvious, but psychically, or as Winnicott said, "creatively." This necessity comes from the fact that the child, especially in the first few years of life, can easily believe that his anger, requests or emotions can psychologically damage his parent. At first, the vital capacities of the parent bring a denial to the destructiveness (Winnicott, 1969) but also make the child experience that to enter into relationship brings life to each one.

There can be a dead end, when a parent who, without being clinically depressed, still seems "psychologically dead," without enthusiasm, without energy or creativity which can provoke a tremendous insecurity in their child. The child can then develop the need to "heal care parent" to become too reasonable too early or too independent.

8. *Capacity for fidelity*

Several theories of personality refer with different words to the need for the child to live the fidelity, constancy, and permanence of his parent. Such experiences are not entirely related to the development of a purely inherent capacity of the child. This experience also comes from the real contribution of the parent. The parent must put in place the conditions for the child to experience the constancy of his parent. On the one hand, the parent must be relatively constant in his attitude, coherent, but not rigid. To use the general metaphor, despite all the manipulations that he makes to the clay, the child must faithfully find, the next morning, the man or the animal he modeled the day before. The modeling clay will not lose its shape during the night. In the same way he must also find the same parent; not only will he not have disappeared (permanence of the object), but he will be coherent with himself in spite of its flexibility (fidelity and constancy of the object).

Unfortunately, we see children who have great difficulty in internalizing their parents, internalizing their values and rules, or who are constantly worried about the disappearance of their significant persons because their parental experiences have not allowed them to live this experience of parental fidelity, the parent having been too changeable or incoherent. This is a pitfall we encounter with some borderline parents who are constantly changing in the interaction to the child according to the emotional mood they live.

The object to be symbolized and the object to symbolize

The psychoanalytic concept of object first of all refers to what will be complementary to the drive: the object will make possible the satisfaction of the drive. In early psychoanalytic theories the object was essentially an internal representation, a notion which led analysts like Klein to describe partial objects and splitted objects. But at this time the focus was on the presence of an internal object. However, Winnicott rightly described the fact that a baby alone does not exist and that first of all the baby's life consists of the union of a "baby-environment." Winnicott thus showed that the illusion of undifferentiation, the illusion that he creates the object (Freud's primary narcissism) was possible only if the real person, the parent, fulfilled his functions in such a perfect way that he allowed the child to live this illusion. He therefore described the paradox that the child needs a real presence of a sufficiently good object that meets almost perfectly the needs of the child so that it lives "subjectively" a state of primary narcissism. Then this object will gradually allow disillusionment and abandonment of this primary narcissism. Winnicott introduced the idea of the necessary functions of the real person so that the representations of objects can gradually be created and differentiated from the subject.

The child must construct internal representations of objects from his parental relations, but these constructions cannot be done without being initiated and supported by his parents. The parent has a dual role facing these developmental and identity needs of the child. The parent must both be "internalized" by the child in various ways (as an ideal, as a model, as a prohibiting principle, as a "thinking" person, etc.) and therefore "exist inside" the child. But to help the child internalize him, he must set up the conditions of such internalization and have an attitude that can support this internalization. These tasks are complex. The parent must first be sufficiently present (quality of the presence) so that the infant interiorizes him with his qualities and his functions but he must also know how to fade away, to make himself disappear (Winnicott's idea of being alone in the presence of the mother), as the child is more and more able to tolerate the distance and the absence so that internalization is transformed into autonomy.

Or course the eight parental functions described above may be present in varying degrees and not all of them have equal importance according to the parents' characteristics and the parent-child "coupling." But all these qualities, to be useful, must be lived in a meaningful relationship. So, if the child must "symbolize" and internalize the object, the parent must also be an object "to symbolize," that is to say, to fulfill the functions allowing the child to be able to internalize him and also to develop for himself these same psychic functions that his parent fulfilled.

Regarding the observation of these functions in the parent–child interaction, we must understand that the younger the child is, the more perfect the parent must perform these functions. Consequently, he must not continue to fill these functions perfectly throughout the child's life. This "perfect attunement" must gradually be replaced by an attunement in which "everyone has to put his own." From a situation where the responsibility for relational attunement belongs completely to the parent, when the infant is very young, the responsibility must gradually become shared as the child's psychic growth progresses. Two pitfalls must be avoided: that of bringing too quickly the limits of this tuning and that of keeping the child too long in a relationship where the parent would fulfill these functions perfectly. The attunement must take into account the age of the child and the circumstances of life because it goes without saying that when the child is in a difficult situation (individual or family crisis, a new school, parents' divorce, illness, etc.) he will experience a certain amount of regression which will require the parent to fulfill these functions more fully again.

References

APA (1994). Guidelines for child custody evaluations in divorce proceedings

Bion, W.R. (1962). A theory of thinking. *International Journal of Psychoanalysis* *43*, 306–310.

Brunet, L. (2005). Les manifestations de l'archaïque et les fonctions de l'analyste, *Revue canadienne de psychanalyse*, *13*(1), 57–76.

Brunet, L., Sabourin, M., & Létourneau, P.-Y. (2014). La garde d'enfants et les droits d'accès. in, L'expertise psycholégale. Balises méthodologiques et déontologiques. *Les Presses de l'Université du Québec* (Louis Brunet, éditeur), 125–153.

Freud, S. (1915). Instincts and their Vicissitudes. *The Standard Edition of the Complete Psychological Works of Sigmund Freud, Volume XIV (1914–1916): On the History of the Psycho-Analytic Movement, Papers on Metapsychology and Other Works*, 109–140.

Goldstein, J., Freud, A., & Solnit, A.J. (1973). *Beyond the Best Interests of the Child*. New York: Free Press.

Klein, M. (1946). Notes on some schizoid mechanisms. In *Developments in Psycho-Analysis*. London: Hogarth Press.

Milner, M. (1952). The role of illusion in symbol formation. In *The Suppressed Madness of Sane Men: Forty-Four Years of Exploring Psychoanalysis*. New Library of Psychoanalysis, pp. 83–114.

Roussillon, R. (1988). Le médium malléable, la représentation de la représentation et la pulsion d'emprise. *Revue belge de psychanalyse*, *13*, 71–87.

——— (1991). Un paradoxe de la représentation: le médium malléable et la pulsion d'emprise. In *Paradoxes et situations limites de la psychanalyse* (pp. 130–146). Paris, Presses Universitaires de France.

——— (1997). La fonction symbolisante de l'objet. *Revue française de psychanalyse*, *61*(2), 355–694.

——— (2001). L'objet « médium malléable » et la conscience de soi. *L'autre*, *2*, 241–254.

Shapiro, T. (1984). Psychological Evaluation and Expert Testimony: A Practical Guide to Forensic Work. New York: Van Nostrand Reinhold.

Tronick, E.Z., & Weinberg, M.K. (1997). Depressed mothers and infants: Failure to form dyadic states of consciousness. In L. Murray & P. Cooper (Ed.), *Postpartum Depression and Child Development* (pp. 54–84). New York: Guilford Press.

Winnicott, D.W. (1951). *Transitional Objects and Transitional Phenomena. Collected Papers. Through Paediatrics to Psycho-Analysis*. New York: Basic Books.

——— (1969). The use of an object. *International Journal of Psycho-Analysis*, *50*, 711–716.

——— (1971). *Jeu et Réalité: L'espace potentiel*. Paris: Payot.

Chapter 12

Parental alienation and Parental Alienation Syndrome

Plinio Montagna

Initial considerations

Parental alienation is a process that transcends cultures: nowadays, its presence has been identified in many different countries (Giancarlo & Rottmann, 2015). Although it is not restricted to situations of divorce, the phenomenon manifests itself more openly in these circumstances. In general, it is a global, multicultural issue where *"parental conflict is at the forefront of separation, rather than the wellbeing of children"* (Jaffe, Thakkar, & Piron, 2017).

The matter was first brought to the attention of the psycho-juridical world by the American child and forensic psychiatrist Richard Gardner, who described what he called Parental Alienation Syndrome (PAS) (Gardner, 1985). He acknowledged that parental alienation behaviors did occur prior to the time he described them, but noted their increase in the second half of the twentieth century at times when legal changes accompanied social changes in families (Gardner 1985).

In the 1980s, he began to observe children who started to antagonize and mistreat one of their parents who had been a good parent prior to divorce. Even if there was a previous history of a good bond between the child and the parent, they refused contact and started to denigrate or repudiate him or her. The child's distorted perceptions were similar to the other parent's ideas (whom Gardner called the "alienator"), and were also similar to behaviors of other children in the same condition. They were following the alienator parent's ideas, influenced by their state of mind and disposition against their partners. He claimed that they were being programmed or brainwashed.

Gardner named the set of symptoms presented by the child Parental Alienation Syndrome, contending that the aetiology was programming by the alienating genitor through brainwashing. He then proposed that symptoms and signs (the child's behaviors) combined with the common aetiology (programming, brainwashing by the alienating genitor) characterized a syndrome, the Parental Alienation Syndrome.

On the other hand, the child also contributes to the syndrome through actively adherent behaviors to the parent who denigrates the other one; these are the children's symptoms.

PAS manifestations in children due to the alienating genitor's programming had three stages: mild, moderate, and severe. They are: a demoralization campaign (which encompasses all the other symptoms); weak or absurd justifications for deprecation; increasing absence of ambivalence; independence phenomenon; deliberate support to the alienating parent; absence of guilt; borrowed scenarios; and generalization of the alienated Family (Gardner, 1998) – each escalating with increasing severity. There are also difficulties in visitations, behavior during these times, increased bond with the alienating parent, and problems with the bond with the alienated parent (Gardner, 1998).

Gardner's work influenced the psychojuridical milieu of many countries, including the creation of laws based on the ideas he brought about the theme. Publications proliferated in countries like England, Germany, Australia, France, Switzerland, Argentina, and Brazil.

In Brazil, for example, a law inspired by the ideas about PAS seeks to more efficiently regulate children's relationships with their parents after separation, dealing directly with the families' values and the social and cultural values involved, although these symptoms may not exactly coincide with the syndrome. This relates to divorces but also to conditions where separations or ruptures do not exist and aims to protect the children by restoring their relationship with the other genitor; punishments can even be reversal of custody and loss of parental power (Brockhausen, 2011, p. 11).

In fact, in the second half of the twentieth century when Gardner studied those families facing divorce, familial social values and family itself underwent intense changes, which placed both of these in question. These changes included a significant increase in the divorce rate in the USA and other countries during the 1970s, peaking in the 1980s, along with burgeoning legal disputes for child custody in the litigious ones.

The classical nuclear patriarchal model was beginning to undergo modifications that influenced the inner core of the family institution, including fathers with a more active role in child rearing and wives participating in the family budget as a result of their working outside the household. Legal changes included modifications in laws related to child custody, increasing the possibility that this was exercised by the father.

Before that, even if the man was still considered "the head of the family" and woman the "chief of the house" (Sarti, 2007, p. 28), the authority of women concerning general matters could not be undervalued. Men's roles of mediating between family and society did not exclude the women's guardianship and protection of the family. On the other hand, this kept women in a condition of vulnerability, as the relationship with the outside world was in some way always mediated by her husband.

Prior to that, it used to be taken for granted in cases of divorce that mothers were naturally more apt to take care of their children and suited to be their guardians by the very fact of being women. This was no longer tacitly accepted. Fathers started to be closer to their children and more active towards them. Psychoanalysis saw "parentality" as a construct between parent and child rather than biologically given, with the influence of work by Lebovici (2004) in France, where the neologism "parentalité" was created. Lamb and others conjectured that the abilities of maternal roles could be developed "on the job" and were not only given by nature.

Court decisions about child custody would then look for elements indicative of which parent would be better suited for custody, deciding in the best interests of the child.

A set of works by Joseph Goldstein, Sonja Goldstein, Albert Solnit, and Anna Freud published in 1973 and 1979, with a revision published in 1996 about this, that is "the best interests of the child," became very influential.

As to the books, Freud invites the reader to "put him/herself in a child's skin, the infant, the toddler, the pré-schooler, the schoolchild, the teenager, to consider what ought to be the guiding principles to decide. Placement decisions should safeguard the child's needs for continuity of relationships, reflect the child's sense of time, take into account the Law's incapacity to make long range predictions and manage family relationships, and provide the least detrimental available safeguarding the child's growth and development. Taking a cautious stance, the authors affirm later: "Because the best interests standard did not in and of itself define what it is that a child needs, the authors propose the placement standard should be one that provides the least detrimental available alternative to safeguarding a child's growth and development" (Goldstein, Freud, & Solnit, 1973, p. 50). It was clear that custody had to be discussed and evaluated in each case, not automatically awarded to the mother.

The new paradigm for guardianship was now based on effective search for the aptitude of each of the parents. Rather than focusing on gender, the parenting capacity of each gender should be evaluated. The best alternative could be staying with the father.

Also public policies that took into account greater equality between the sexes and shared custody became more common. This influenced, according to Gardner, some women responding with refusal and trying, in cases of divorce, to keep the child and turning him or her against the father.

These changes happened in several countries, since the role of women changed all over in connection with them getting into the labor force of the society and due to the incentive of fathers being more present and collaborative in raising their children.

As the granting of maternal custody ceased to be automatic in divorce litigation, fathers' requests for guardianship increased exponentially, as they now envisaged the possibility of gaining custody of their children. The number of litigious divorces increased, peaking in the 1980s.

Spouses had to show their perfect custodial capacity, and men would try to show evidence of maternal deficiencies in their roles as mothers.

A possible reaction from mothers was to try to get the children close to them and to move them emotionally away from their fathers.

So, the corollary reaction of many women was to seek to ensure the fidelity of the children to themselves through behaviors that have been called parental alienation, as this refers to strategies used by one parent to keep away or distance the child from the other parent. The alienating parent can constantly denigrate or express negativity towards the other and try to obstruct the relationship between the child and that parent, that is the litigant or former spouse. They can use programming or brainwashing.

Changes in parental roles also help us to explain that the parental search for equality in the exercise of the function has resulted in a rapid increase in visiting and custody litigation, triggering a war between the genders. The mothers, with the threat of matriarchal primacy, began to generate alienating behaviors in their children, engaging them in the judicial battle.

It is important to see parental alienating behaviors as one type of psychological violence or abuse. These behaviors are chiefly found in high-conflict families and chiefly coupled with a variable degree of intensity and frequency. On the other hand, extreme situations like drug addiction, acting out, severe somatic problems, can lead to an intolerable level of tension experienced by the couple, resulting in changes in how the pair exercises the containing function.

The documentary *The Death Invented* (Minas, 2003) highlights the testimony of children of separated couples who for many years were unable to contact their parents because of the effectiveness of the alienating behaviors of the mother after a long period of exercise of active separation from the father, coinciding with a brainwashing by the mother. In adult life, they were able to come back into contact with them. All of them indicate how they had been "blinded" to the possibility that the father did not have characteristics as negative as those pointed out by the mothers, and they emphasized that they truly believed in what the mother told them. These were used to inoculate the children with the certainty that their fathers did not like or care about them in the situation, but would "embark" on this narrative, even because fidelity to the mother was essential to ensure that her love would be maintained.

We see then that part of the contributions to the syndrome may be the child itself because of his or her need to preserve the bond with the alienating parent (usually the mother), who behaves like a tyrant.[1] This shows the complexity of the psychodynamics and demonstrates a possible occurrence of a "folie à deux" relation. The question of loyalty to the alienating parent usually has paramount importance in the course of children's behaviors.[2]

Case 1: A typical parental alienation syndrome of intense severity. Parental visits to the two children were only possible with the presence of bailiffs, since the mother tried to completely prevent contact between the ex-spouse and the children, who were already severely programmed. One of the sons, a pre-teen music lover and guitarist, received a sophisticated, new guitar as a birthday present from the father. Upon receiving the gift, the son breaks the guitar on the wall and physically attacks the father, cursing him. The episode sealed the estrangement of his father, who gave up visiting his children because he could no longer bear to be mistreated by them. He walked away with the hope that someday things might change and the children would have some openness to a friendly relationship with him.

Case 2: The father could only locate his daughter, kidnapped by his mother, to another country, through Interpol. When he reached the child at the court of this other country, the child behaved in such a way that it seemed that she scarcely recognized him, treating him like a stranger. Here, when the court granted the custody of the child to the father, it took quite a time of coexistence with him in order to be possible, re-establishing a father–daughter relationship without the obstacles that existed before.

The severity of alienation varies greatly. The variable that most clearly demonstrates the escalation of this is ambivalence. As the degree of alienation grows, the child adopts the point of view of the alienating parent. He or she incorporates it in an ambivalent way, but gradually this gives way to an attitude of total identification. There comes a point when her (or him) contributes to alienating attitudes in a personal way. Any ambivalence is denied.

The child invents situations and scenarios that do not exist and may even overcome the accusations of the alienating parent. He or she becomes an "independent thinker," who associates personally with the accusations against the alienated parent.

The often cruel manifestations are apparently devoid of guilt feelings. From this point the reversal of the situation becomes more difficult. The threshold delimiting a non-return point may have been exceeded. Besides the implantation of false memories, false accusations of sexual abuse are not infrequent.

Parental alienation behaviors may have a very complex composition and multiple origins, both intra- and inter-psychic. A basic ingredient of parental alienation behaviors is *resentment*; in many cases it can be its trigger or the very basis for it. Bitterness can be harbored for many years, for several reasons, such as narcissistic wounds and humiliations in the past in the form of memories of particular personal injury or injuries. Feelings of humiliation, perhaps vulnerability and terror feed the force for revenge.

A partner can feel entitled to revenge, the right to retaliation is obvious from his or her point of view. It makes sense that an effective revenge is excluding the partner from child rearing and blocking contact between the parent and the son or daughter. Through revenge, humiliation is reversed; resentment is solved.

Along with this, the inability to renounce control over objects, with the consequent inability to experience a true separation, also matters; this is a characteristic of narcissistic object relations (Steiner, 1990). Parts of the self mingle with parts of the object in an undifferentiated set that leaves no room for true separation. Projective identification may come to be at stake and the ex-spouse is fiercely accused of some characteristic or behavior that belongs to the accuser. The psychic mechanism includes projection and action against the other while identified with the self.

From the child's point of view, a divorce, or even the presence of constant litigation in a situation of family dysfunction, can provoke intense emotional turbulence. The complexity arising from feelings of different natures, which blend together, comes into play. The tension between the feelings of diverse natures is present.

It is not just about love and hate. The constructive and destructive forces of one's personality will come into play, creating tensions that will need to be internally balanced. Hard internal psychological work may be necessary, even if the child can distinguish between the abandonment of the spouse and abandonment of him or herself.

This work of mourning becomes impossible on the part of the child. For such mourning to happen, it is necessary to recognize the positive qualities of the object. Here, there is no integration between good and bad, the manichaeist posture of the alienating parent will force the permanence of a constant schizoparanoid position. The distortion of judgment ends up weakening not only the object relation but also the integration of the ego, made vulnerable by the distorted contact with both internal and external reality.

A possible prior idealization falls to the ground and is reversed to its opposite, the total disqualification of the object, justifying the destructive attacks. The libido is invested in hatred and, fed by the alienating parent, becomes an overvalued object, resulting in the restructuring of the objectal bond.

The relation to the alienating parent, frequently the mother, in its turn resembles Stockholm Syndrome, in which hostages displayed no hostile feelings to the hostage takers, and further, feared the police more than the captors. It is a totally distorted transference relationship, that consists of negative feelings from the hostages towards the authorities, positive feelings towards the hostage takers and positive feelings reciprocated by the hostage taker towards the hostage.

It is necessary to say that it is usually assumed that this identification with the aggressor may enhance the chance of survival in hostage situations. It has been equated to identification with the parent of the same sex in the Oedipal situation (Kuleshnik, 1984).

The child can be terrified about the possibility of defying the alienating parent's command, which is later internalized as self-censorship. Obedience is necessary as the threat of being left is real; helplessness is knocking at the child's door. This may unconsciously evoke Winnicott's "fear of breakdown" (Winnicott, 1974), a breakdown of defenses originally set up to ward off unthinkable anxieties. Ego organization is threatened.

Ogden argues that the central point in the fear of breakdown "is that feeling states that are tolerable in the context of the mother-infant bond are primitive agonies when the infant must experience them on his own (2014). The child avoids disconnection with the mother. An unbearable "falling forever," expressed by Winnicott, can be compared to the agony experienced by the astronaut in Stanley Kubrick's film, *2001: A Space Odyssey*, in which he floats alone into endless, silent, empty space after the umbilical cord to the spacecraft is severed.

In the presence of conflicts of loyalty with their inevitable ambivalence, the solution to the fear of disintegration of mind that may arise and the protection from psychic pain lies in clinging to an object. The alienating one is chosen. The child recovers the possibility of distinguishing the good from the bad; there is a good parent and an evil one. Hostility will be directed to one of them and affection to the other, exempting the child from ambivalence or ambiguousness. Schizoid conflict escapes are, after all, always at hand and used more easily.

Furthermore, the child's reaction, denying that he or she is being programmed, may also carry a protective role, contributing to attenuating his potential guilty feelings and creating a new circle of self-protection in the process – alienating parent and child (Gardner, 1998, p. 96).

In clinical practice, it is important to consider the ego strength of the child involved in alienating actions by one parent and the defensive purpose of the relation with her or him. Abrupt alienation of defenses may lead to profound melancholic states and even to suicidal ideas.

According to Gardner, it is more probable that mothers alienate their children than fathers, which does not mean that they do not try to do so, but that mothers tend to be more effective (1998, p. 127). In clinical and forensic practice, it is much more frequent to come across alienator mothers than fathers.

It is more frequent, in many countries, that children live with mothers instead of fathers, after a divorce. This is also true in severe PAS, when the child has split off from parents' figures and lacks ambivalence.

Fear of being left alone, loyalty, envy, jealousy, cults, low self-esteem, and depression may also be at stake in a child's response to a mother's alienating behavior. Divorce, as a moment which changes the family group, leads to the rupture of the container function of the family. The container passes through transformation and becomes distorted, changeable, disorganized, disrupted, broken, failing. Bergozhi compares this to the anamorphic pictures we find in art, where the picture is "projected onto a curve mirror and likened to the *trompe d'oeil* style" (Bergozhi, 2014, p. 202).

The sloughing of parental containers (in Bion's sense) may bring to the fore intense, aggressive, and eventually disruptive behaviors on the part of one of the spouses. Usually these behaviors characterize a reaction of the spouse who feels victimized by the situation. An aphorism of the author is: "Shame is to the container what guilt is to the content." The shame-carrying spouse is the symptom carrier.

It is worth mentioning that most cases of parental alienation occur from the pre-adolescent age to actual adolescence (up to 15 years of age). Sometimes the process of parental alienation, inevitably also composed by projective identification as the narcissistic accusation that the other does not care for the child, can be reversed against the accuser.

Although the ill effects of the false accusations may be recognized by laws in several countries, parental alienation poses the question that removing the child from living with the alienator may be worse for the child, which often makes it difficult to properly treat the problem.

It is worth considering other elements involved in alienating behaviors:

a) The overprotection of the child, which relates to factors like insecurity, low self-esteem, or even the impossibility of mourning. All of which should always be kept in mind.

b) Sadistic and psychotic elements of the alienator's mind. Harold Searles's work, "The Effort to Drive the Other Person Crazy: An Element in the Etiology of Schizophrenia" (1959), examines the extension and results of what seems to be pathological interaction. It shows the ways through which one person can influence the other to cause mental problems. The torturing aspect of parental alienation behavior fits in this box.

c) Cross-projective identifications usually seal the closeness of couples, eventually making them seem alike, sometimes even physically, as is often observed. This "twinning" operation also presents itself as underlying destructive assaults. When the couple breaks up, this narcissistic skin is broken, and the underground aggression may ignite (Anzieu, 1996, p. 84).

d) Jealousy, which may be associated with oral possessiveness and the desire to own the partner, ex-partner, mother, or father. Similarly, the wish for domination and complete control over the love object may play a role.

   Jealousy may be increased tremendously when the ex-partner starts with a new partner. This decidedly shows that the relationship has come to an end.

e) Envy, which may be fueled by or arise in the context of constriction and deprivation, as Harris points out (2018), suggesting subtle transmissions of social and psychic dynamics from parents to children.

f) Dependence, even a financial one. The rupture of the family, with threats to security and fear of falling below the prior standard of living, is pinpointed by Riviere in widowhood in her work from 1937 (Riviere, 1945/1937, 1945). This may still be true, today, in many cases, and is relevant also in cases of divorce. She says: "To some extent, this reaction is a primary, instinctive one, like that of an animal fighting to preserve its own, and furious at being robbed. But to a great extent hate and resentment increase because they can be used to soothe the wounded pride of the sufferer and allay her anxieties" (Riviere, 1945/1937, p. 216).

g) A devaluation of women by men, catastrophic in some cases, may account for distance and abandonment. Kernberg claims it may be related to envy of the mother and necessity to take revenge on her (1995).

These elements contribute to a wish for a symbolic murder of the (alienated) parent, most of the time the man.

It must be stressed that one condition for the diagnosis of Parental Alienation Syndrome is that the alienated parent is a good parent, dedicated to the child. And it must also be stressed that Parental Alienation Syndrome is a relational pathology (Brockhausen, 2011, p. 51); it is related to divorce and loss of custody.

Children become mere tools of aggressiveness directed towards the ex-partner. They end up accepting as true everything they are informed of. They identify with the guardian parent, who comes to take complete control. They become inseparable, in a sick symbiosis. The other is now considered an intruder, an intruder to be driven away at any cost. This set of maneuvers gives pleasure to the keeper of the guard, in his trajectory of promoting the ruin of the old spouse or companion (2011, p. 51).

For example, we have, in Brazil, a law ruling the rights of children and adolescents considers that a parent alienation violates the fundamental right of the child or adolescent to healthy family life, damages the re-establishment of affection in relations with the parent and the family group, and constitutes moral abuse against the child or adolescent.

This definition is wider than Gardner's definition, as it addresses behaviors and not syndromes, so that it is not necessary that the child start to reject the genitor to the point that the law needs to intervene, there is no mention of the word syndrome. The function of the judiciary's intervention shall be to avoid the development of the process (2011, p. 61).

On the other hand, it is not rare for a litigant to accuse the other one of parental alienation as a tactic just meant to press the opponent.

Parental Alienation does not have an entrance in the DSM or the International Classification of Diseases. But, the DSM-V lists "Problems Related to Family Upbringing," which includes Parent-Child Relational Problem, the Sibling Relational Problem, Upbringing Away from Parent, Child Affected by and Other Problems Related to Primary Support Group.

Among these, Disruption of Family by Separation or Divorce, Uncomplicated Bereavement and mainly High Expressed Emotion Level within the family, all bring space to think about high-conflict parents and parental alienation.

It must be said that Parental Alienation Syndrome is not necessarily irreversible; provided that it is treated correctly and with specialized professionals, many children can recover from their previous alienated state. The documentary *Invented Death* clearly shows this.

Notes

1 Some dictators require orphaned children to put together their personal protective guard because, in this way, they would ensure exclusive fidelity to themselves, as protector, without dividing it with any effective parent.
2 Loyalty often determines the central reference for changes of impossibility of changes of people in emigration.

References

Anzieu, D. (1996). La scène de ménage. In *L'Amour de la Haine, Nouvelle Revue de Psychanalyse, 33*, 201–209.

Benghozi, P. (2014). Anamorphosis, sloughing of containers and family psychical transformations. In A.M. Nicolo, P. Benghozi, & D. Lucarelli, *Families in Transformation: A Psychoanalytical Approach* (pp. 199–218). London: Karnac.

Brockhausen, T. (2011). SAP e Psicanálise no Campo Psicojurídico de um amor exaltado ao dom do amor. Mastership thesis presented to the Institute of Psychology of São Paulo University.

Gardner, R.A. (1985). Recent Trends in Divorce and Custody Litigation.

——— (1998). The Parental Alienation Syndrome.

Giancarlo, C., & Rottmann, K. (2015). Kids come last: The effect of family law involvement in parental alienation. *International Journal of Interdisciplinary Social Sciences: Annual Review* (May), *9*, 27–42.

Goldstein J., Freud, A., & Solnit, A.J. (1973). *Beyond the Best Interests of the Child.* New York: Free Press.

——— (1979). *Before the Best Interests of the Child.* New York: Free Press.

——— (1996). *The Best Interests of the Child.* New York: Free Press.

Jaffe, A.M., Thakkar, M.J., & Piron, P. (2017). Denial of ambivalence as a hallmark of parental alienaion. *Cogent Psychology*, *4*, 1–15, 1327144. htps:dói.org/10.1080/2331908.20017.1327144

Kernberg, O. (1995). Psicopatologia daas Relações Amorosas. Porto Alegre: Artes Médicas.

Kuleshnik, I. (1984). The Stockholm Syndrome: Toward an understanding. *Social Action & The Law*, *10*(2), 37–42.

Lebovici, S. (2004). Dialogo Letícia Solis Ponton e Serge Lebovici. In *Parentalidade, Um Desafio para o Terceiro Milênio* (pp. 21–46). São Paulo, Casa do Psicólogo.

Minas, A. (2003). A Morte Inventada. Filme Documentário, Rio de Janeiro.

Ogden, T. (2014). O Medo do Colapso e a Vida Não Vivda. *International Journal of Psychoanalysis*, *95*, 205–223. Livro Anual de Psicanálise, XXX, 77–93.

Riviere, J. (1945/1937). Hate, greed and aggression. In A. Hughes (Ed.), *The Inner Wold and Joan Riviere* (pp. 168–206). London: Karnac.

——— (1945). The bereaved wife. In A. Hughes (Ed.), *The Inner Wold and Joan Riviere* (pp. 204–226). London: Karnac.

Sarti, C. (2007). Famílias Enredadas. In A.R. Acosta & M.A. Vitale (Eds.), *Famílias: redes, laços e políticas públicas.* São Paulo: Cortez.

Searles, H. (1959). The effort to drive the other person crazy: An element in the etiology of schizophrenia. *British Journal of Medical Psychology*, *32*, 1–18. JURIS, Rio Grande, v. 27, n. 2, p. 119–138, 2017.

Steiner, J. (1990). *Organizaciones Patologicas como obstáculos para el duelo: el rol de la culpa insuportable.* Libro Anual de Psicanálisis, 59–66.

Winnicott, D.W. (1974). Fear of breakdown. *International Review of Psycho-Analysis*, *1*, 103–107.

Chapter 13

Law and psychoanalysis in processes of adoption

Cynthia Ladvocat and Eliana Mello

Adoption in mythology and history

The literature of Greek mythology tells us about children who escaped from death, were adopted and had a place in history. On the myth of Oedipus, his father Laius, the king of Thebes, was warned by the Oracle of Delphi about the curse that would take the son to kill his father and to marry with his mother, Jocasta. Laius abandoned his son, who was received by a pastor and baptized as Oedipus and adopted by the king of Corinth. Oedipus, aware of the curse, escapes and kills Laius, unaware that he was his father and marries Jocasta, not knowing that she was his mother. Jocasta commits suicide and Oedipus stabbed out his eyes. According to Sorosky, Baran, & Reuben (1989), Oedipus's mourning over his need to understand the mystery of his birth and myths are full of references to mysteries about origins. Adoption is probably the most universal method used by society at all times to ensure the continuity of the family. Regarding illegitimacy, we observe the myth of Hercules, who was the most celebrated hero of Greco-Roman culture. Hercules was the bastard son of Zeus, Jupiter to the Romans, with the mortal Alcmene. Hera, the wife of Zeus, hated the fruit of his husband's infidelity. To appease the wrath of his wife, Zeus baptized the boy as Hercules, with the meaning of "Glory of Hera." Hercules was a demigod, with human, divine, and strong attributes. Yet his existence continued to inflame his "foster mother," which led to the madness and murder of his wife and children, believing they were his enemies.

Regarding the myth of Romulus and Remus, we know that Amulius, to secure the throne, assassinates the descendants of Numitor and forces his niece Rhea to become a virgin priestess. She becomes pregnant with sons of god Mars, giving birth to brothers Romulus and Remus. As punishment, Amulius arrests Rhea and throws her children in the Tiber River, and they are suckled by a she-wolf. Faustolo finds the boys and years later reveals to Romulus his history, who departs in search of his origins. The twins set out to establish a city of their own. Romulus wanted to call it Rome and build it on the Palatine while Remus wanted to call the city Remora and base it on the Aventine.

In the sacred book we find the record on Moses with the first documented reference of an international adoption. A Hebrew woman gave birth to a son during the period that King Pharaoh had ordered all the baby boys to be killed to control the population. She placed the baby on the banks of the Nile. Termulus, daughter of the Egyptian pharaoh, took the child out of the reeds and adopted Moses, who was raised by the royal family and became a faithful and blessed servant of God. In the New Testament, the only son of God, Jesus Christ, was conceived through the Holy Spirit instead of the seed of man. He was adopted by the husband of His mother, Joseph. Therefore, for Christians, adoption is a powerful basis for paternity and masculine identity, Jesus Christ being an adopted son.

Pharaoh's choice in ancient Egypt was made through adoption. Among the students of the School of Life attached to the great temples, the most promising ones were chosen for adoption by the Royal House and trained until one arrived at the rank of co-reigning and being sacred like Pharaoh, which was one of the causes of the longevity of the Egyptian civilization.

According to Figueiredo (2006), the history of humanity reveals records from ancient peoples, when the adoption was aimed at perpetuating the gods and family worship. Since antiquity the abandonment of children occurs as the paterfamilias had the right to accept or refuse a child to live in their house, and even had the right to decide on the life and death of a baby. In Rome, with its laws as the basis of culture, the family was a social and political construction and adoption was a means of fortifying alliances, creating hereditary lines and perpetuating domestic worship to the gods of the family. By the "Laws of Manu," who nature did not bear children, mother are eligible to adopt a son to perpetuate the funeral rites. In Greek society, after adoption, there was the complete disruption of the adopted with his origin, not even being able to give funerals to the biological father.

In the primitive civilizations of the peoples of Greece and Rome, adoption met religious longings, since the dead depended on the funeral rites practiced by their descendants for peace of mind in the afterlife. In the case of sterile women, the marriage could be annulled, with adoption being a means for the family to escape the dreaded misfortune. Adoption took place through initiation into the worship of the domestic religion in a sacred ceremony. The adopted child could no longer enter the home of the biological family, unless he had a child and left the child in his or her place with the adoptive family, having to break ties with that child. The Code of Hammurabi, during the Babylonian dynasty (1750–1685 BC) marked the first legal codification on adoption, which could be revoked if there was ingratitude of the adopted son. If he told his adoptive parents that they were not his parents, his tongue would be cut off and if he wanted to return to his origins, his eyes would be withdrawn.

In Athens the purpose of adoption was to ensure the continuity of domestic worship and prevent the extinction of the family. During the second century BC through the second century AD, adoption was a solemn act when the biological parents delivered the child. In Rome, adoption reached a political purpose, besides the religious cult. The adoption also had the purpose of perpetuating the head of the family, so that the warlike deeds had continuity. The adoptee, lacking ties to kinship, should show his fighter qualities in return for his name.

According to Weber (1998), in the Middle Ages by influence of Canon Law, adoption remained unknown, as the Catholic Church manifested a series of cautions. Christianity has removed the fear of death without male descent in funeral rituals. Priests saw adoption as a transgression of marriage and a legitimate affiliation, as well as being able to recognize adulterous or incestuous children, which was forbidden. The transfer of titles by way of adoption contradicted the economic interests of the feudal lords and resulted in a long period of obscurity. There was a significant reduction in the practice of adoption, which no longer accommodated new customs nor was further contemplated in ecclesiastical legislation. From the practice of adoption in Rome, there only survived the right of *imitatio naturae*, by the Christian sentiment of paternity and the protection of those who could not have children. However, there was an environment of disregard for childhood and there was no need to protect the child.

We have found references to adoption in the Code of Christian V in the year 1683, in the Prussian Code of 1751, and in the Codex Maximilianeus in 1756. These laws required a written contract and influenced the Napoleonic Code. In Roman law, there was the acquisition of the "father power," but in Hispano-Portuguese law, through profiling, the heir could have his succession rights, had they been confirmed by the prince. In the origins of the Napoleonic Code, we know that in the year 1796, Josefina, a widow with two children, married General Napoleon Bonaparte. He was very fond of his children and adopted them officially, not allowing them to be called adopted children. During the French Revolution, adoption became part of the Civil Code and evolved from the adopter's interest to the interest of orphaned children.

According to Atalaio (2017), in pre-Islamic Arabia adoption was common practice. The prophet Muhammad himself was adopted by his uncle after his orphanage and later, in turn, adopted the slave Zaid. Since then The Quran adoption was progressively banned in the countries of Muslim confession. Countries governed by the "common law" imposed prohibitive rules on adoption, owing to the inalienability of parental responsibility. In countries of Muslim confession, adoption is prohibited by imposition of The Quran and the resulting Sharia. In these countries, adoption has been replaced by another figure, Kafalah, with natural filiation being the only form of family ties. The institution of Kafalah does not establish relations of kinship and successions. Adoption of State's pupils and abandoned children authorizes material and educational care.

After the First World War , with so many orphaned and abandoned children, adoption became understood as a solution to the well-being of children without parents. However, after the Second World War, culture reinforced the adoption of young children, due to the irreversibility of the effects caused by precarious initial development.

In legal treaties since the Napoleonic period, adoption appears as an imitation of nature, a fictional relationship of fatherhood and sonship children, a fictional bond of fatherhood, which still permeate beliefs about adoptions to this day. What happens in relation to maternity?

Introduction

The current question of the Western world concerns the social phe-nomenon that still leads to the abandonment of children. There is a need for a process that provides as quickly as possible for the care and protection of these children who are at risk or in institutions. Legal adoptions intermediated by courts have reduced the problems associated with adoption, including psychological assistance to the biological mother in her desire to surrender her child, although many abandon them to their own fate.

Adoption is internationally recognized as paramount to the interest and protection of children and adolescents. It must be irreversible and granted to individuals or couples, regardless of their sexual orienta-tion. Since 1993, an agreement legitimized by the Hague Convention, supports the process of international adoption between countries and ensures the registration of the nationality of the adopted child. Adoption in several countries can defend the records of the child to be adopted in a closed or open system. In confidential or closed adoption, the child's story is available to adopters only prior to the adoption sentence. Once the process is finished, the records are legally sealed. Through this system foster parents prevent interference from the biological family, protect the child from stigma illegitimacy, and strengthen adoptive bonds. In open adoption, the contact between the biological family and adoptive parent brings positive results if agreed between the parties. By avoiding secrets, adoptive parents also avoid negative fantasy and guilt over the birth mother, increase the sense of belonging to the adoptive family, and facilitate information about health and genetic inheritance.

There is a controversy between open and closed adoptions, but apart from a country's law, we must address the secrets about a child's biography before adoption. The fact that the records are closed should not be associated with the denial of a life story. In practice, we know that access to the real story aims at completing an empty and fan-ciful space that interferes with the construction of the child's identity. It is important to outline that considering biological origin does not mean placing the child face-to-face with his/her biological mother as advocated by the supporters of the open adoption. When informa-tion about the child's past is clear, affective bonds are strengthened and biological bonds become part of the symbolically elaborated past story. In clinical therapeutic practice we know that in adult life it is possible to encounter the birth family, which is not necessarily harmful to the adopted individual.

The motivations for adoption

Considering the concept of affective bonding and the diversity of family configurations, there should be no distinction between forms of biological or adoptive filiation. Both are found in various cultures, valued, denied or privileged in different ways. However, blood ties and heredities are still part of the great myths that permeate adoptive families. The work on adoption raises some points on issues related to adoption in the psychic and social spheres. First, the decision to adopt a child can come after years of failed attempts to have a child. After one or both of the partners is found to be infertile, it is finally decided to adopt a child. This is a complex decision that involves accepting that you cannot give birth to one's own baby. A narcissistic wound sets in and only when it starts healing the couple is able to face the adoption process. And this process will be very painful until the moment of the arrival of the baby. Why painful? Because in addition to the couple closing the scar of their narcissism wound, the couple will come across a whole bureaucracy until the outcome of having their dream baby. We are talking about a dream that confronts the real baby. What does it mean? Gestation takes nine months to produce a baby. In the adoption process time is indeterminate. It means having to sustain a desire during all this waiting time. In Brazil, for example, the bureaucratic process is still quite Kafkaesque. This is the point to ask why a child already placed to be adopted also has to wait so long to find his/her future parents? We know that the earlier a child is adopted, the easier it is for the whole family. We also know that the birth of a child changes the dynamics of the couple and when this child is a child generated by desire and not generated by the natural process, which will produce effects in all family members. And the narcissistic wound can reopen to the extent that this child does not look like either partner. And even if a child's desire is greater than their parents' narcissism, this child still has to confront the story of his/her own birth.

There are many ways of forming family bonds. Fertility is the bridge between generations and reflects the parents' desire to find in their son or daughter their genetic traits. People and couples suffer when they encounter infertility that causes deep marks in the psyche. They need to elaborate gestation mourning in order to seek assisted reproduction through embryos of biological parents or anonymous donors. We can make the analogy between this procedure and adoption, because a member of the couple should "adopt" a child with whom he or she does not have any genetic link. Of course, in the face of the new ways of having a child the issue of adoption will be given a new lease of life: when a woman freezes her egg and it is fertilized by sperm of a stranger, she is also dealing with the issue of adoption. The biological father is in sperm DNA.

We may think that in a very short period of time adoption will be the rule not the exception. We do not know yet what are the future effects on these children resulting from "test tubes": genetics has progressed in such a way that the limit of the ethics of procreation has been lost. The "Brave New World" has arrived, that is, we will be dealing with a problem: what place will children have if not being generated through a sexual relationship? This is a problem already experienced by adopted children and their adoptive parents.

Faced with the failure of the assisted reproduction, the individual may choose to substitute the biological bonds for adoptive bonds and the transformation of the *need* to a child for the *desire* of a child, which demands a symbolic fecundity of adoption, which concerns the imaginary life. According to Galli and Viero (2002), when the mind cannot cope with suffering for the lost child, the marks of the failure of assisted reproduction and the negative repercussions can interfere in the relation with the son/daughter who will be adopted.

The adoptive family configuration

Family configurations are varied across cultures. In anthropology there is no difference between adoption and gestation, since they are possible forms of affiliation. However, nowadays we find myths and prejudices about adoptive status, perhaps because the child represents a constant reminder of the reason why parents are adoptive.

Adoption promotes this encounter in the symbolic and in culture, but even today it is possible to identify secrets that affect the development of the child. According to Hamad (2002), it is important to elaborate the adoption of a real child by the unconscious aspects that contribute to the imaginary of an idealized child, especially if the child is in the place of a lost biological child, not conceived. In the case of a biological child, this identification is natural, but in the case of adoption it is important that the mother identifies herself with the child.

Winnicott (1997) points out that the absence of the mother is a very painful experience for the child, who needs loving care of a sufficiently good mother or a substitute mother. And he stresses that we cannot arrange an adoption for the cure of neurotic adults. Some parents are distressed and hide the child's origins by a number of factors. The child who cannot bear the knowledge of adoption reveals questions about illegitimacy and difficulties from interferences in his/her initial care. In fact, biological parents are unknown and unattainable. There is for the child a mystery between fantasy and reality, as well as emotions that cannot be lived or left behind. In any case, this child will always be adopted but with a safe environmental provision can overcome his/her difficulties.

For adoptive parents the child's biography should be considered from adoption. If the child realizes the difficulty in approaching his/her origins, he/she will construct his/her fantasies, his/her myths and prejudices. Children need to know their story based on real facts, even if they fantasize about it. And in case there are no objective data, this gap will exist, not by omission or secrecy, but by the limits imposed by the reality of the biography. Adoptive parents have fears that the child's possible difficulties are associated with heredity, so they prefer not to talk about the child's past. According to Dolto (1998), when parents hide the child's story, they fantasize that in this way the child who knows nothing can become a *biological* child.

The child, on the other hand, from a victim of his parents' lies and omissions can become an accomplice to this story and develop a prejudice about his/her status as an adoptee. He may feel indebted and keep secrets about his/her fantasies in what his/her life would be like if he/she were not adopted. The unconscious records are lost and the child is silent so that his/her complicity guarantees his/her belonging to the family.

According to Galli (2002), the phantoms that inhabit the fantasy of the child find in the form of the invisible its persecutory and inexplicable character. Working with the child is not intended to erase pre-adoptive history or painful episodes of the past, but to elaborate his/her impasses, defenses, and resistances on his/her history according to acceptable conditions, aiming for stability until adulthood.

The analytical process

The initial attendance with the parents of the child aims at knowing their difficulties and the child's life, which can generate resistance to situations that are not consciously related to adoption, but should be contextualized preventively. The adoptive mother can engage in an imaginary competition with the birth mother. She, the infertile mother, without the ability to generate a child, may feel bad about the fertility of women in general. And she may feel punished by true mothers, by the biological mother of the child, and by her own mother for her competitive desires, including the analyst, being a woman, and with children.

It is important to analyze how parents pose fears about the child's origins. And it must certainly be considered a history of early failures with the rupture of the maternal bond, by decision of the mother herself, by decision of justice or by some fatality. The analyst makes a survey about the migratory path from gestation to adoption, which includes the institutional reception if it happened, the adaptation to the new family, the conditions on the disclosure of adoption and the problems presented, even in a preliminary diagnosis unrelated to adoption.

Freud (1909) did not address the subject of adoption in his work, but rather about the Family Romance with the fantasy of lesser-value affiliation, of being an adoptive child, which would justify the dislike of the parents. Freud conceptualizes, at this time, the adoption as a fantasy of illegitimacy. In his text, he describes it as being a common fantasy, the fantasy of being adopted. Such fantasy becomes stronger in the passage from childhood to puberty. And why would it be an almost universal fantasy? It would be a way to lessen the feeling of guilt because of Oedipal incestuous fantasies. In this way, the feeling of guilt is attenuated as well as the de-idealization that occurs in this period in relation to the parents. In general, the child starts to idealize the other family and wonders why he/she is not the son/daughter of that other father/mother, who is/are so much cooler.

Winnicott (1997) and Kernberg (1985), Hamad (2002), and Galli (2002) contributed to Freud's theory, not as the child's fantasy to be adopted, but about the child's family novel that is actually adopted and so projects on the two pairs of parents, the adoptive and the biological. It is important to note that the familiar novel is activated in the transfer, which is intense and projected in the setting. The child rejects, attacks, and projects good and bad feelings in the person of the analyst. Or can develop an ideal-analyst-mother dependency relationship and wish to be adopted by the analyst. According to Levinzon (2000), the secret in liking the analyst and not letting the parents perceive it is lived as a forbidden love, a fact that is not understood by the parents, generating resistance to the treatment.

The development of the adopted child presents a differential factor, because there are mysteries about the linking plot, with the double belonging of the parenting that includes the two parental images. Based on Kernberg's theory of the adoption triad (1985), the Oedipal triad involves the biological family and the adoptive family. The fantasies about his/her family novel reflect the real vicissitudes of his/her life story, and there might be a tendency to overvalue or devalue this pair of parents. The symbolic representation of the biological parents contains projections and it is possible to triangulate only in the fantasy, because they are absent in reality. The concept of limbo emphasizes the time between the rupture with the mother of origin and the encounter with the substitute mother. His/her biography refers to this period of limbo before the child is adopted. Just like the adoptive parents before the adoption living in a parental limbo.

The treatment represents a whole, stable, and flexible therapeutic space for the children to express affections for the elaboration of traumas in their life story, in addition to the narcissistic wounds inherent to their adoptive condition. The analytical work unlocks fixations, so that the child's identity can mature, even without known biological parents, which represents a trauma that must be elaborated. The child can swing in the direction of affection in good and bad elements to the two pairs of parents, sometimes rejecting the biological parents and sometimes rejecting the adoptive parents. The child's conflicts can arise in the form of drawings and jokes. The theme of abandonment and rejection is a way for him/her to elaborate and find within himself/herself a place for the absence of her biological parents.

During the crisis of adolescence, the curiosity of the young adult turns to his/her origins. The search for biological parents is one of the biggest fears of adoptive parents. The analytical treatment of such difficult subjects helps him/her not to actually find his/her biological mother, for this quest can be elaborated symbolically.

The failures in adoptive bonding

The great dreaded scene of professionals working with adoption is the child's return. However, the field of adoption must predict failures in adoptive bonding and, consequently, in the analyst's sense of failure over the return of the child by the custodian. Factors that have not been treated early should be identified and are affecting adoptive parents who think about giving up their child's adoption. In these extreme cases, the child is returned because the parents consider that his/her problems are related to heredity. They feel powerless, suffer with their ambivalences, and project idealized and persecutory objects upon the child. They may reject the child or feel rejected, revealing unconscious narcissistic dissatisfaction about a real child and desired child. The abandonment of adoption is understood by them as the only possible solution to the impasse.

Adoption is irrevocable, but guardianship is revocable. If adoption allows the fixing of the most deficient internal aspects, adoption failures can lead to a fragility of personality structure. The return is an exception, in the most serious cases the attendance is an emergency with the objective of understanding this desire of return. The breaking of the adopted bond reveals the sad reality of the abandonment of the child, who suffers again with rejection. The child's feeling is equivalent to that of the abused child. It will have to readapt again to the institutional life and can begin to direct destructive desires against the biological parents, and ambivalent feelings against the adoptive parents (Galli & Viero, 2002). In practice with international adoption, although adopters are available the child can express his/her desire not to be adopted by foreign parents, sometimes because he/she has lived in the institution for many years and feels attached to employees and other children. In that case, the judge accepts his/her wish and does not authorize him/her to leave the country.

According to Winnicott (1997), a child can recover from the loss and guilt that he/she would have, even when in fact he/she did not contribute to the event. Clinical attendance greatly contributes to the reversal of the parents' decision to return the child to justice. It addresses, when possible, the tragic repercussions of this abandonment revived in the child's story, which despite the stigma of having been returned, he/she can be adopted by another family.

The adoption clinic

Working with adopted patients brings us to relevant issues about the need for a child and the desire for a child. The following examples demonstrate some of the intrinsic vicissitudes related to adoptive issues, which need to be carefully addressed in the psychoanalytic process.

Case 1: A couple seeks attendance to meet their 3-year-old daughter. The child had a symptom of stripping off her clothes in public. And this was causing the couple anguish over not knowing how to deal with this situation. This child was the daughter of the adoptive father's daughter, that is, the adoptive father was the child's grandfather. His wife from a second marriage was the adoptive mother. The child lived in the same house as her biological mother, who was her sister. Faced with this familiar situation, the child, with this symptom, was aimed at the stripping off this story. In the sessions she said that she thought her sister was her mother. The child repeated this version through playing. It is noteworthy that from the first interview the adoptive mother was chased by the phantom of her daughter to know the true origin. She emphasized that it was impossible for her that her daughter knew the truth. According to her words: "I have no longer the age to have a child of mine." More and more threatened her daughter came, namely that she was not her biological mother, decided to run away with the child.

On the eve of the child's session, the mother makes a phone call to the analyst saying she was no longer in Rio de Janeiro. And that she was moving with her daughter out of the country.

This illustration is to show that the issue of adoption is not a rose garden, as the media often make people believe. In addition to the bureaucracy widely advocated by lawmakers in the adoption process, it is often quite insane as well. Lawmakers argue that couples do not want to adopt older children and that this increases waiting time and besides the fact they make a pejorative personal judgment of future parents. Almost imputing the responsibility of non-adoption to this couple demand.

We know that the waiting process also presents other problems: it often causes people to stop adopting legally. And then the process of the child's illegal adoption begins. The couple enters into agreement with a pregnant woman, through contacts parallel to the law and an arrangement is made. The couple will be informed when the pregnant woman is about to give birth. In this way, the couple will have the new-born baby as expected by them. They accompany the pregnant woman during pregnancy, financially assume all the medical expenses and any other expenses that involve the birth of the baby.

The sooner a child is adopted, the easier he/she will feel belonging the family. It is not only because they want small children, but mainly because one knows that the older the child, the more he/she will have the marks of abandonment.

To have a child is a decision that mobilizes any couple. The arrival of a child changes all the dynamics of a couple in any case: adopted or not. In other words, this process involves several affections: the child will be around with the phantom of its origin. And parents with their phantoms about biological parents. In clinical practice with the mothers who adopted their children, the adoption scar is never closed.

Case 2: Attendance of a woman who had adopted a child shortly after losing a child in a risky pregnancy. The patient had eclampsia and almost died. And because of that she was prevented from having children. She decided to adopt a child. She looked for analysis treatment because of the ambivalence towards her daughter: on the one hand she loved her deeply and on the other she rejected her in the same measure. She claimed that as well as the daughter not looking like her physically, she also did not have a similar personality. Her daughter was six at the time. And according to her, her daughter was agitated and messy. And she went on to say that "it must be because of the biological mother." One day, she brought her daughter to the session. And astonishingly she was physically identical to her mother!

In practice, the adopted children end up resembling their adoptive parents. And when children are adopted in a process within legal boundaries the issues of adoptive parents become more softened. When adoption takes place illegally, persecutory fantasies increase because they feel they "have stolen the child from the true mother." And as the adoptive mother carries this phantom she unconsciously transmits it to her child, thus generating a reciprocal feeling of distrust.

Case 3: Case of three adopted children and there was also the phantom of "robbery," another phantom in relation to the father figure. The mother, who adopted the children, was single and adopted them at an advanced age, around 52. This generated in the children a feeling of inferiority: being adopted and without father. In addition, there was a feeling of shame for she was much older than the mothers of their friends. Whenever the mother went to school she was confused as if she were their grandmother. Both had symptoms of rejection to the mother, undermining her authority. Both had very serious learning problems: one could not learn how to read and the other one could not retain anything he learned. "If my origin is surrounded by mists, automatically, I will cloud any knowledge!"

Case 4: Patient at the early stage of adolescence changed his surname after being molested by his father at the end of his childhood and beginning of his puberty. This way he tried to get rid of his incestuous guilt and mostly tried to save the father from being an abuser.

According to Lacan (1972), when a patient complained that he did not want to be born, and wanted to have other parents, Lacan answered: "You chose to be born and have these parents." We fully agree with the Lacanian theory that every human being is responsible for his/her own history. We are marked by helplessness and constitutional failure. That is, no one complements no one, there is always a gap between me and the other.

We know that the mother–baby relationship is a relation that has three elements: the mother, the baby, and the phallus. That is, there is not the famous pair: mother and baby. The baby is to the mother a symbolic and mainly imaginary relation of "to be the mother's phallus." That is, the girl when she renounces the Oedipus with her mother, the Oedipus is always with the mother for the girl and for the boy, and turns to the father to receive "a baby" from him.

We are, therefore, considering the Freudian equation: baby-penis-money-faeces. And it is this desire that will later materialize with motherhood. And in that sense, every adopted child or biological daughter will suffer the effects of how her mother and her father subjectivated their story of origin.

Case 5: A couple adopts a small boy and years later, upon learning that there was a 7-year-old sister in the institution, they chose to adopt her. Faced with the numerous problems of this girl, they decided to return her to the institution about a year later. Therapeutic intervention helped these parents to review their own difficulties, realizing the girl acted just to test the love of the new family and that they did not have to give up their daughter to keep their marriage. Years later, they learned that there was yet another institutionalized 13-year-old sister. And they preferred not to continue with the analytical treatment, but despite the many problems they faced, they finally returned this third child to the institution.

Case 6: Couple keeps the secret of adoption until the son is 30 years old. The son has realized since childhood that there were secrets about his life. He did not feel loved, he fought a lot with his parents. He was very insecure and jealous of his wife and imagined she cheated on him. His professional life and financial situation were chaotic. He worked for his parents' company and had a habit of excessive spending. The parents felt guilty and paid all his bills. The late revelation of adoption occurred by the time he had received an inheritance left by his birth mother. Afraid of being abandoned by their son when he discovered his origins, they sought family treatment. The man met his entire biological family and after years of analysis he deemed his adoptive parents as his true parents.

Case 7: A couple looked after a 12-year-old adoptive daughter surrounded by protection and care. A very aggressive and controlling father, who did not admit talking about the adoption. The mother was insecure and a submissive wife, not free to go out with her daughter without the husband. The daughter sometimes asked to sleep in her parents' bed, and the mother went to sleep in another room. The girl was cheated by a pedophile on the Internet and ran away from home. She was abused and prostituted. Weeks later she was captured by a federal police officer. The girl thought that whoever was saving her was her biological father. She returned to the clinical attendance in love with the pedophile and very afraid of her father, who said that "she was now ready for sexual life" and as punishment could not have access to the Internet anymore. This father was identified, at the time of the process, as an abuser of the daughter. The parents were frightened by the repercussions of the case, and moved to another city to "let time erase the whole story."

These illustrative examples of clinical practice show that adoption problems affect adoptive parents much more, and consequently children react and rebel in symptomatic behaviors. The analytical work proves its efficiency in relation to the individual adopted concerning the symbolic place of his origins, and also concerning the adoptive parents relatively to the awareness of their fears.

Conclusion

We can confirm in clinical experience the suffering of parents and adoptive children. In fact, every child has to be adopted by the parents. That is, all parents have fantasies about their children and when they are born they will have to give up the idealized child of their dreams to adopt the one that is there!

What is traumatic for a child is not the fact of being adopted; it is rather how this is transmitted and lived by the family. And often, adoption takes the responsibility for all problems with children. If this were the case, the child not adopted would be a symptomless and harmonic child in his/her family.

In clinical practice attendance we find that children, adolescents, and even adults reveal real traumatic events that have invaded their lives and need to be expressed and elaborated upon. Listening, the insightfully looks, and psychoanalytic thinking consider that parenting and adoption membership need to be addressed. It is important that the myths, secrets, and the biography of the child can find a place in both the symbolic and reality. The treatment is not intended to remove the marks and specificities of adoption, but rather to address the repercussions of those marks.

As psychoanalysts, we know that the figure of the father is a symbolic figure and that the paternal function can be exercised only by the mother or only by the father. It is what allows a couple of men or women to adopt and exercise motherhood and fatherhood. In other words, the issue of adoption is often more difficult for adoptive parents than for adopted children. Because for the adopted child, when newborn, the only family it knows is the adoptive family. The weight of the phantom lies in the subjectivity of the adoptive.

References

Atalaio, R. (2017). Adoção Internacional e o Superior Interesse da Criança. Universidade de Lisboa. Faculdade de Direito, Mestrado Profissionalizante Ciências Jurídico. Forenses.

Dolto, F. (1998). *O destino das crianças*. São Paulo: Martins Fontes.

Figueiredo, L. (2006). *Adoção internacional: Doutrina e Prática*. Curitiba: Juruá.

Freud, S. (1909). Romances Familiares (Family Romances). In *Edição Standart Brasileira das Obras Completas*. Rio de Janeiro: Imago Editora.

Galli, J., & Viero, F. (2002). *Fallimenti adottivi, prevenzione e riparazione*. Rome: Armando Editore.

Hamad, N. (2002). *A criança adotiva e suas famílias*. Rio de Janeiro: Companhia de Freud.

Kernberg, P. (1985). Child analysis with a severely disturbed adopted child. *International Journal of Psychotherapy, II*, 277–299.

Lacan, J. (1972). Escritos. Campinas, Editora Siglo.

Levinzon, G. (2000). *A Criança Adotiva na Psicoterapia Psicanalítica*. São Paulo: Editora Escuta.

Sorosky, A., Baran, A., & Reuben, P. (1989). *The Adoption Triangle*. San Antonio, TX: Corona Publishing.

Weber, L. (1998). *Laços de Ternura: Pesquisas e histórias de adoção*. Curitiba: Ed Santa Monica.

Winnicott, D. (1997). Duas crianças adotadas & Armadilhas da Adoção & A adolescência das crianças adotadas. In R. Shepherd, J. Johns, & H.T. Robinson, *D. W. Winnicott – Pensando sobre crianças*. Porto Alegre: Artemed.

Chapter 14

The psychopathology of litigious divorce

Adrian Cesar Besuschio

Introduction

Divorce or litigious separation represents a very specific personal situation within the bond between two members of the human couple. The existence of diverse conflicts of greater or lesser seriousness within such a bond might obstruct or render the continuation of cohabitation inadvisable. As of that point, very often to their own surprise, both members discover that they will encounter important difficulties in order to be able to separate.

I suggest designating litigious divorce or separation as one specific form of object relationship, a bond in which each of the members of the couple represents to the other an object of anaclitic character – of backing and support that stem from difficulties already present within their historical records of attachment bonds.

The manner in which they express themselves may reach varying degrees of conflict. The couple's family members or friends in certain instances may intervene, and may summon police or civil or criminal forces, which is sometimes necessitated and sometimes not. Many of these cases are included in what is termed "domestic violence" or "violence of genre" and they become notorious over a diverse media of communication.

The number of years in which the couple has been together or the presence of children is not important – what matters is the entirety of the circumstances, and the intensity and "passion" that both members of the couple have experienced since the beginning of their attachment.

This is how couples who have been together for decades and those whose courtships have passed in a flash, might break out into a crisis involving violence and aggression – a common indicator of psycho-pathology of a distinctive and personal character.

Presentation

These cases may present in the form of marriages within which there exists the following difficulties in the habitual sharing of life: jealousies towards their own children or of relationships with each other's family members; and difficulty in accepting job assignments, new job assignments, or assignments that impel travelling abroad or long absences from home.

Harassing, limitations to each other's freedoms for the good of the relationship, control, and up to a certain extent, mutual submission, might be some of the means sustained by these united couples, but at the same time heavily encumbered by a degree of indisposition. This can be perceived in tense feelings about the components of sharing a life, ill treatment, reprisals against "disobedience" which takes the form of disregarding one another's presence, threats, and artful control over the children.

The life story of these couples usually has to do with intense feelings about the attachment, a sudden and intense experience of falling in love where each believes they have found the precise person they ever wanted in life, sealing a love pact for eternity. These are cases in which life sharing usually starts early in the relationship.

Before long, the respective families begin to notice attitudes of one party towards the other that are akin to obsession. Frequent jealousies distort family and social relationships with the couple very often becoming remote from groups they belong to socially, in order to avoid interference.

Throughout the couple's everyday life, neighbors and close relations become witnesses to frequent fights, disrespectful verbalizations and scandal where nobody dares intervene. Sometimes the spectators remain paralyzed before a couple that seems untouchable to any person outside the dyad.

This panorama of disintegration usually generates symptoms in the children, through their witnessing, traumatically, the violent outbursts of aggression which become everyday behavior in these couples. It can be observed that both members of the couple turn out to be complementary in the manner and mechanisms they use to process their affection.

The threat of abandonment, actual or imaginary, leads to a burgeoning anguish. Anxieties are used as barricades to avoid the loss of the object, who becomes characterized as a brace and protector against moral devaluation and pain.

It is for this reason that when finally they do decide to separate, each one interposes multiple obstacles to dissolving the bond legally. Within young couples, there is harassment, persecution, hounding, and threatening in order to prevent that another individual should become possessor of the object, by showing much more interest in the object in respect to the moments they had both shared.

In Argentina, in the cases of formally constituted marriages, where only one of the parties applies for divorce, the Judge of the Civil Court dictates dissolution of the bond without needing existence of cause, such as adultery, absence of spouse obligation, lack of marital cohabitation proved by witnesses, etc., as per the new Civil Code issued by law in 2015.

The problem in arrangements of this nature comes up at the time of laying out the rule for visiting timetables if there were children from the marriage, the children's maintenance, and the distribution of inheritance goods. It is there where legal causes arise that would keep the couple together by means of specifying the heading of a legal file, multiple hearings and mediations, where it is usually very difficult to come to agreements over long periods, even years.

Course of events

The couple which is going through the procedures of litigious divorce becomes a personal and specific form of object relationship, a bond in which each one of the members of the couple represents to the other an appraised, necessitated, and transitional object, with whom at the same time each one shall protect himself against his own separation/abandonment and engulfment anxieties.

Following the conceptualization of this object relationship proposed by Fairbairn (1970) and within our midst, by Basili (1990a, 1990b), the appraised, necessitated and transitional object would be one of both types of bad objects (for these authors there exist two kinds of bad objects: accepted bad objects and rejected bad objects), in the subject's inside world through which the psychopathology becomes constituted. To the minds of these authors, differing from Klein (1977) and Bion (1962), psychopathology comes about from an excess of bad objects, and not due to the lack of good objects or absence of objects.

The excess of bad objects in the subject's inner world is represented in the couples' various types of experimenting, conflicting, violent, and litigious separations. In these cases both members would present personality features that supplement that of the other. The histories of these couples show that as far back as the beginning, each one chose the other for supplementary and specular features, sometimes through massive identification in reference to previous life experience such as aggressive features of childhood experiences, mistreatment or domestic violence in childhood, or previous and systematic bond failures in romantic life. Disturbance in identity, in self-esteem and in ego integration are observable in these cases as well as the utilization of primitive defense mechanisms, primitive dissociation and scission instead of repression.

Pre-Oedipal mechanisms dominate: omnipotent control of the object and emotional instability are present right from the start. At the beginning of the relationship the members of the couple experience infatuation to a degree of excess, jealousies, possessiveness, and scandal when faced with the slightest menace of fancied or actual loss of the bond. Graphic, television or radio broadcasting media often take up these cases and make them public.

Each member approaches the life of the other with the purpose of filling a gap. The arrival of that object on the scene is experienced as a saving grace – the prize that the previous adverse psychological experiences seemed to have derailed. Previously hopeless, both members of the couple thought that the love object, the "Saviour," would never come. It is often possible to observe that previous problems in the regulation of self-esteem in both members are present within this pathology.

A dyad is created, in which, by means of projective identification and the double dissociation within both the Ego and within the object, each one of the members of the couple supports the other. Each one recovers in the other a lost object, which acquires the character of a transitional, supportive, and anxiety-controlling object, comparable to those basic suppositions proposed by Bion for groups (mating, attacking, escaping, and dependence). The prevailing psychic mechanisms of this couple manifest as the diffusion of identity syndrome (Eriksson, 1969) – specifically, the narcissistic object relationship peculiar to this pathology is relevant here.

The physical proximity inherent to the human couple, some time into the relationship, begins to generate in each mental phenomena which can be linked to the conflict of closeness and distance. In order to control this, unconscious mechanisms are implemented, which have to do with the compulsion to repeat, transformation within the contrary and return against one's self. In this way there is a return to bad objects, or to the repressed, proceeding from fixations and childhood remembrances.

The process often begins with alternating double statements of values, followed closely by the onset of ambivalence – thanks to which, each one of the members of the couple projects feelings of love and/or of hate, the outcome being that the other will never be able to tell why the strife began nor even when he himself started it up with his couple.

The presence of children within the family does not attenuate the picture. On the contrary, they become necessary participants and spectators of their parents' narcissistic competition in which both subjects seek omnipotent control over the object.

The syndrome of Parental Alienation, unforeseen by the members of the couple, is used as a battering ram in competitive attacks in what becomes, finally, the battle between sexes. The children end up by occupying the place of excluded aspects of the members of the couple – becoming a kind of scenery of projections, introjections, and dissociations. These become, finally, distortions in the parents' bond with the minors, and paradoxical behavioral reactions ensue.

In a libidinally motivated attack, in the aid of aggression, the man usually appeals to his strength while the woman makes an appeal to her cunning, resulting in explosive interactions that surprise and worry the majority of spectators (neighbors, close relatives, friends, etc.).

The couple would remain "paralyzed" by means of the mechanism of the projection of inductive counter identification – thanks to which they remain "not knowing what to do." The essence of this couple's bond means that remain usually in a state of long paralysis, and, despite the scandalous behavior, cannot decide whether they should separate or continue to live together.

In the midst of the need and desire to sustain the bond, aggression generates guilt, which in turn leads to the point of preferring at many times destruction of the object over its loss or abandonment.

The vicious circle of sadism-masochism is thus closed – the ill-treated/stricken woman and the ill-treated/striking project their aggression onto one another and thus remain tied together by their striving to control anxieties, and engulfment/separation/abandonment on both sides.

Because of this circle of identification and projecting counter-identification, the degree of guilt and aggression imputed to the other is vastly greater than imagined as possible within oneself.

In the last attempts to avoid a rupture in the bond, the woman, in a fairly conscious manner, acts out the fantasy role described by Fairbairn as the "Pact with the Devil" – "Better bad than worse," or "Better the Devil you know," and also, better to have a Devil than none at all, "Better this than nothing." The man, on the other hand, acts out another unconscious fantasy, dealing within his own pact with God – "I prefer to be a Daemon surrounded by saints than a Saint surrounded by daemons" (1970).

Behavior against the mate and family of both may become frequent. In this stage, police or civil or criminal justice intervention might take the form of an authorized, legally regulated form of attack and simultaneously provide protection over those persons and goods concerned.

Metapsychology

As mentioned in previous paragraphs, litigious divorce usually occurs in bonds where the personalities are supplementary to one another, and where both characters display identities, self-esteem and ego integration disturbances.

There exist common features in these circumstances, such as the use of primitive defense mechanisms, dissociation and primitive fission, as opposed to repression. Couples who perform rowdy separations frequently make use and abuse of their identification projective hold on the other party.

The status of the human couple bond means that there is often a reappearance of aspects of each member's own parents, and each member contributes to a microsymbiosis of these aspects. The threat to the dissolution of this symbiosis generates anxieties about abandonment, and paranoid fears of engulfment, and often, of confusion. In the case of these couples, members of which persist upon a condition of childhood dependence, divorce represents a traumatic situation that would favor the return of internalized bad object.

The dreaded separation would become linked with a repetition of an original separation of good and bad family objects, and is all the more painful and warded off.

Following from this, the anguish of separation is the most distinctive feature of the frequent crises experienced by the couple – specifically the doomed attempts to prevent the rupture of the symbiosis.

Alterations in the sense of fact, psychosomatic illnesses, perversions, episodes of creativity, etc., or a return to a more archaic symbiosis than the one more recently experienced, at the end, are some of the ways the couple unconsciously undertakes in the process of litigious divorce.

Loss of an object in the objective outside world may motivate the subject to blame himself for her burdens on the object, once again, as a means of sustaining the relationship to the object and to keep under control the anguish of separation.

The emotional experiences of the litigiously divorcing subject can help elucidate the schizoid phenomenon which, in Argentina, Basili proposed be named "conflicto esquizoide" (schizoid conflict) – "Fear of approach for fear of later abandonment."

Schizoid conflict and litigious divorce

Schizoid conflict, as described by Basili, and based on Fairbairn's schizoid phenomenon, is the double dissociation within the Ego and the Object specific to the pre-Oedipal, dyadic, and universal stage – which is resignified in the Oedipus Conflict. This conflict is systematically distorted within the pathology of litigious divorce and is especially useful to the study of all pre-oedipal pathology.

Psychoanalytically, the pathology is defined by abandonment and engulfment anxieties (in Fairbairn's terms: separation and locking up); the defense mechanism is primitive dissociation in a double effect, as this dissociation takes place in both the Ego and in the Object.

The unconscious fantasy of both couple members is the achievement of being loved, accepted – not to be abandoned by the object regardless of whether that object is bad, because its value is measured by another criterion. Omnipotent control of the object is the main defense used in litigious divorce.

The subject in the process of litigious divorce looks upon their experience of estrangement from the object as "bad"; she takes note that she must stay vigilant about the threat of losing what they have achieved (walk, find one's own feet). Separating would mean a return to mother, to be trapped and engulfed by her (engulfment anxiety).

Using a clinical criterion it is possible to observe separation-abandonment anxieties with paranoid contents within the couple (in order to keep an optimal distance from the object, the object is projected onto the outside world); or hypochondriasis (in order to maintain an optimal distance from the object, it is projected onto the image of the body); or confusion of the contents of engulfment anxieties (loss of sense of boundaries between Ego-Object, Ego not Ego, etc.). In all of these cases, omnipotent control is exercised, from and towards the object.

The members of the litigiously divorcing couple present with pathologies that really border on borderline pathology, because of their chronic alteration in self-esteem regulation, abandonment anxieties in them are not felt as such, but as self-devaluation. In order to control these anxieties the patient resorts to primitive splitting of the bad object into two objects, the one accepted and the one rejected. The lost objects in the real, outside world are usually sexuality and work.

Fairbairn tells us in his book *Psychoanalytical Studies of the Personality* (1970, p. 51) that schizoid phenomena arise when there are problems with the child achieving security in:

a) being loved by his parents
b) their acceptance of his love

The child's capacity to give up his childhood dependence without harming his ability to trust is based on the possibility of obtaining sufficient assurance of safety during the original period of dependence. If the child experiences too much anguish in his resignation of childhood dependence, he will lose all hope of obtaining satisfaction of his needs.

Anguish associated with separation manifests as fear of isolation (abandonment); whereas, with identification, it becomes a fear of becoming locked up (engulfment).

In the litigiously divorcing couple the schizoid conflict was often badly worked out as of the pre-Oedipal period, and, consequently, the resignification in the Oedipus phase becomes distorted.

The collapse of the couple lived as a traumatic case is constituted by childhood dependence of each of the spouses with the object, and typically the problem with childhood dependence for the members of this couple is with the anguish of separation: the dependent subject cannot find a substitute for its object.

Narcissistic fits of temper, threats, scandalous legal and police accusations represent a desperate intent to maintain the bond, even if it has to be by means of aggression – loss of the object would incur too much loss of self-esteem and identity.

In the case of those individuals that insist upon that condition of childhood dependence, the marriage or human bond represents a quasi-traumatic situation, with the return of bad internalized objects, and the failure of repression.

This return takes the form of jealous passion, persecution and scenes in which aggression dominates the picture with one of the spouses deeming it necessary to request security measures such as peripheric forces restrictions, telephone or digital communication restrictions, police custody, etc.

It is often the case that these individuals have no prior criminal records or past legal history. One legal file should maintain within its heading the name of both, united and together, even if it were to make it appear to be normal before the judge who acts in the case ("Better the Devil you know" and "Better a Devil than none at all").

The anguish of separation always bears the mark of birth trauma, and any post-natal experience that should provoke separation anxiety will assume, in some regard, the significance of the trauma of birth.

That primary separation can become active under certain conditions, for example, in the case of divorce.

Medical-legal considerations

When there exists a proposal of separation, if there are children involved frequently it is the woman that initiates the move; the man's experience is usually that of loss, abandonment, devaluation, aggression, an injury to his narcissism and personal pride.

Clinically, to avoid an underlying depression might mean making room for different kinds of action within the unceasing emotional crescendo.

When faced with imminent rupture, the most frequent actions taken by both parties might be verbally aggressive scenes, violence, aggression towards physical objects, aggression towards pets, pyromania, threats, jealousies, paranoia which many times require the professional intervention of a psychiatrist or of the police, and implementation of isolation in respect to conflict focus points by means of confinement to a mental institution, exclusion from home, and perimetrical exclusion ordered by a judge.

As therapists, when and if references should come to our knowledge, for example by means of family interviews throughout the hospitalization period that each one is both victim and victimizer of the other, confirming the presence within the litigious or rowdy divorces of Celani Syndrome or the ill-treater/ill-treated.

In such cases it shall be indispensable to seek the presence of justice, a petition of higher degree capable of organizing the case in order to avoid greater hindrance. The Supreme Court of Justice created the Department of Domestic Violence in 2014 for the specific purpose of handling these cases. The department is staffed by a psychologist, a lawyer, and a specialist in social assistance. They have a system by which they put together all the instances in which a person may have performed acts of violence. This is done by means of a report that documents all offenses, making it possible to find out whether an incident is isolated or part of a pattern.

In regard to the statistics of this department, 42 percent of people cease to act by means of perimetrical restriction. The remaining

58 percent do not heed this Order of Justice and the case may end in serious action: criminal offenses against the physical integrity of the person and of the person's company, custodians, etc. One of the intentions of the interdisciplinary team is that this 58 percent of cases becomes smaller in the future. According to other statistics from this department, divorce cases are generally initiated in equal proportion by both parties (man and woman).

Exclusion from home, peripherical exclusion and banning of telephone or electronic communication are immediately instrumented and a case is initiated at the appropriate law court office.

Often one of the aggressors responds to this with persecutory guilt, with the intention of avoiding greater punishment than that of loss of the bond and of the protecting object. The presence of depressive guilt, which deals with object restoration, is more rare in couples that reach such a point of violence.

The swiftness and flow of the legal procedures of divorce implemented in Argentina as of 2015 by means of what is called "Express Divorce" allows for the judge to dictate a divorce sentence with the request of only one of the spouses, without the need of hearings. In these cases, more legal, medical, and psychological events often follow after the sentence is dictated.

In these instances, it is not necessary to prove causes such as adultery, suspension in the sharing of a life, marriage debit, etc. This was abolished in the new Civil Code. The visiting timetables and distribution of family assets have to be negotiated after the divorce sentence is dictated, and the intervention of a lawyer is necessary for each one of the parties under litigation.

Clinical case

Julio, a 50-year-old lawyer, is hospitalized in a clinic in Buenos Aires after a police intervention resulting from a series of crimes he has committed, including forcing open the door to his luxury apartment and setting fire to the living-room curtains with whisky, thereby destroying everything in the apartment. He is married to Sylvia, 46 and a retired ballet dancer. They are a successful couple with four children, the youngest in his teens and the others adults at university.

After multiple marital disputes involving threats and jealousy, Sylvia suggests separation to Julio who does not accept.

In the hospital waiting room, Sylvia is obviously upset and worried. She tries to show me Julio's threats recorded on her cellphone's voice-mail, which would explain why she left the apartment before Julio got there. She informs me that he said he would "set fire to all and to every-body, to me and himself."

In the days following Julio's discharge from the hospital, direct family members of both spouses arrive for a succession of visits. Each visitor systematically attempts to defend his own relative against the other spouse. As soon as Julio is discharged, he goes to find his wife's psychiatrist, a mutual friend of theirs whom he also threatens to kill. Several years later, he makes intimidating calls to a sportsman who has begun a love affair with Sylvia, who has not communicated with Julio for a number of years.

In his analysis, Julio mentions different childhood episodes involving his mother and father. His parents had fled during the Second World War when they were young, migrating from Yugoslavia to Argentina. Among various hardships he experienced as a child, Julio mentions instances of hunger as well as the sacrifices his family made so that he could complete his public education and attend university, becoming his parents' great pride ("They made a fortune of ten pesos bills").

Julio's memories include scenes of having been sexually abused by one of his cousins and of having been ill-treated by his parents throughout a period of great emotional turmoil and conflict in the family. He says that the situation of Sylvia's family, also from Argentina, was even worse. He and his father-in-law fought continu-ously until the latter's death. The two families were enemies for years until the divorce took place.

Conclusions

As of August 2015, when the new Civil and Commercial Code came into effect in Argentina, couples in circumstances such as these could divorce by means of judicial sentence in less than a month, implying the capacity of a third party, in this case the intervening judge, to terminate the bond and thus generate an end to the relationship. In practice, this third-party involvement would indicate assistance in undoing these traumatic and pathological bonds.

Psychodynamically, the awareness of a judicial sentence, which is public and can radically alter a person's civil status, would serve as an ego organizer. This awareness would impact thought and behavior, making room for the emotional housing of a traumatic situation, leading to a more favorable resolution of these types of conflict.

References

Basili, R.M. (1990a). Utilidad del diagnóstico psicoanalítico en el tratamiento de las personalidades narcisistas graves. *Nuestra experiencia clínica. Revista de Psicoanálisis, 47*(1), 153–176.

Basili, R.M. (1990b). Desarrollos en las Escuelas Psicoanalíticas Británicas sobre las Personalidades Narcisistas Graves. *Nuestra Experiencia. Revista de Psicoanálisis, 47*(1),1087–1112.

Bion, W. R. (1962). Aprendiendo de la experiencia. Buenos Aires: Paidós.

Erikson, E.H. (1969). El problema de la identidad del Yo. *Revista Uruguaya de Psicoanálisis 5*(2–3), 267–338.

Fairbairn, W.R.D. (1970). *Estudio Psicoanalítico de la Personalidad (Psychological Studies of the Personality)*. Third edition. Buenos Aires: Horne.

Part IV

Psychoanalysis and legal action and interaction

Introduction

Plinio Montagna and Adrienne Harris

This part might be seen as addressing the most complex, often sometimes creative and sometimes problematic encounters of psychoanalysis and legal theory and practice. In this series of chapters, emanating from different social and cultural settings, we can see the powerful new ideas and projects and practice that can emerge from this powerful encounter of disciplines.

Let us start by noticing the complexity of the interweave of disciplines. The law and psychoanalysis can seem opposite in different ways. Legal experiences can be adversarial, the contemplative reflective space of psychoanalysis can seem quite foreign to the embattled engagements that occur in various legal spaces: courtroom, legislature, lawyer's office, etc.

Looked at another way, psychoanalysis contains and privileges the powerful undercurrents of subjectivity, the most lawless and tumultuous aspects of unconscious experience while the legal realm operates under the lodestar of reason and logical argument.

The chapters in this part live in this creative and potent set of contradictions, contradictions which turn out to be necessary tools for a number of important problems and experiences in legal practice. The first three parts of this book examine the power of these disciplines – law and psychoanalysis – to illuminate political issues on a global scale, the powerful productive encounter of law and psychoanalysis on personal and family life. This part examines the force of this interdisciplinarity on the practice of the law itself.

Rakesh Shukla's chapter will take a European, North and South American reader into the often less familiar world of the caste system in India. The lessons that emerge from this chapter will be all too familiar: the degree to which the legal system can anchor racist and dehumanizing practices and the role of various disciplines, moral argument and psychological deconstruction in the undoing of the law-lessness of the law in regard to humanity and subjectivity.

The chapter by Estela Welldon and Ronald Doctor brings together case reports and theoretical arguments involving legal and psychiatric categories and judgment in areas of extraordinary difficulty and challenge. Their argument is that we need a psychoanalytic lens to work on the difficult, terrifying problems of motivation and intentionality in cases where murder and self murder are not always easy to disentangle. Here we can see the law and psychoanalysis as necessary partners, perhaps because they are always in some powerful tension with each other. The complexity of unconscious motivation, on one hand, and on conscious or mindful responsibility will perhaps always be at odds. Each discipline, in a sense, reminds the other of what is hardest to think about. All these intellectual and moral problems live and pulse in situations of the utmost gravity and importance, involving questions of safety (often of people we are enjoined to protect, that is, underage children), rights, and responsibilities.

Chapter 17, jointly authored by Corzo and Axelrod, takes on the important task of thinking psychoanalytically about concepts not usually discussed in this way in a legal context. Corruption, betrayal, and perversion are familiar terms within a clinical context but here are offered for us to think about in regard to legal process. The authors ask us to think about where and how unconscious motivations and experiences, often outside awareness, need to be considered in the context of legal proceedings.

The last two chapters (18 and 19) address the particular demands and challenges on the practicing psychoanalysts who finds himself or herself in the demanding situation of expert witness or forensic practice. Here we see the encounter of the law and psychoanalysis at its most creative and at its most ethically challenging. It is precisely at the built-in points of tension between these two disciplines that powerful projects and work will emerge. We can see that, in practice, in either discipline, contradiction and the often unexpected tensions and conflicts are the site of potential new emergence and development in both arenas.

Chapter 15

Quest for justice

Psychoanalytical explorations with judges

Rakesh Shukla

> It has always been an ideal desire of analysts to win over two
> people for our discipline: teachers and judges.
>
> Sigmund Freud (1934)

The promise of law is the deliverance of impartial justice. Law as a discipline stresses rationality, logic, and intellect and as a consequence, a considerable body of jurisprudence has developed to check arbitrariness, which is regarded as the anti-thesis of equality in human actions. All of us in an osmosis-like process tend to imbibe to a greater or lesser degree, the biases, prejudices, and stereotypes of the race, community, caste, religion, gender, and class in which we have been raised. Legal systems assume that an individual appointed as judge functions impartially, but there is unfortunately no way of being miraculously free from prejudices, biases, and stereotypes. Likewise, the apprehensions, anxieties, and fears of the individual judge are as likely to impact the working and interpretation of laws. The disjunction between the judiciary and the predominant majority of the persons caught in the legal machinery, especially those from the lower socio-economic classes, the subordinate castes and the subaltern tribes and communities in India further impacts the inequitable working out of law.

A case in point is the recent nationwide uprising in India by the marginalized and exploited communities, the Scheduled Castes (SC) and Scheduled Tribes (ST), who have historically been discriminated against in India. The SC and ST are listed in a specific schedule of the Constitution of India in order to correct centuries of inequality. Vigorous protests by these communities took place in April 2018 against a Supreme Court judgment perceived to be diluting the special law, the Scheduled Castes and Tribes (Prevention of Atrocities) Act, 1987 (SC/ST Act) according to which perpetrators of atrocities against these subaltern sections could not get anticipatory bail from courts. The headlines in national dailies read "9 Die as massive Dalit protests across country turn violent"[1] or "SC's dilution of SC/ST Act caused great damage"[2] and are indicative of the gap between the marginalized populations and the Indian judiciary. *Dalit*– which literally means "oppressed" in several Indian languages – is an empowering term used by the political movements of the castes at the bottom of the caste hierarchy, including former "untouchables."[3] A pointer to the relationship of the judiciary to caste is the recent Bombay High Court directive to the Information and Broadcasting Ministry and the Press Council of India to issue an advisory to the media to avoid the word "*dalit*" in their reports.[4] There is very little representation in the judiciary of the communities affected by these rulings. The National Commission of Schedule Castes (2011) notes: "Even today in 2011 there are only 24 judges belonging to SC/STs against a total of 850 judges in all the 21 high courts, but 14 out of the 21 high courts do not have a single SC/ST judge. Similarly, there is not a single judge belonging to SC/STs in the Supreme Court where the strength of judges is 31" (p. 7).

There are sections in any society who proclaim their hatred against particular categories of persons as their agenda. In a polarizing trend there is increasing loud articulation of hate and lynching of Muslims in some parts of India by Hindu extremist organizations formed with the conscious agenda of hierarchies based on religion, with Hindu supremacy a guiding force. In a similar vein there are upper caste organizations with a proclaimed agenda of caste superiority. However, an exception or two apart, few judges would consciously think, "I am against workers" or "I think Muslims are bad" or "Homosexuals are disgusting," yet these ingrained notions impact judicial behavior and functioning. The seeds of biases, prejudices, and origins lie in and operate at an unconscious level. However, there is no formal acknowledgement by the legal systems the world over, of the role of the unconscious in law. Yet, in practice, any encounter with the legal system inevitably brings home the bearing of the unconscious and the irrational in law. Seasoned lawyers from experience know the impact of the visual image on the judge. In matrimonial disputes, lawyers routinely advise the woman not to wear her "Sunday best" for court appearances as the sight of a well-dressed woman may influence the quantum of money fixed by the judge as maintenance from the husband. In turn, the husband may well be advised to present a pitiful appearance before the court to evoke sympathy so as not have to pay a high monthly maintenance to his wife.

Apart from decisions in specific disputes or the determination of guilt or innocence of an individual accused of an offence, the impact of the unconscious can be seen in almost all spheres of law. Human rights jurisprudence, constitutional validity of legislations to the very drafting and working of the laws seem majorly impacted by the unacknowledged irrational and unconscious. Taking Freud's (1905) conception in the context of "dream work," the psychoanalytic frame offers us pointers to move from the "manifest" to the "latent" in law.

The question of shared assumptions

In the arena of psychoanalysis, phrases like "conscious" and "unconscious," "affect" and "associations" are commonly used, based on shared assumptions and premises. However, the minute we take the frame to another field, the assumptions can no longer be taken to be universal. In a sense the basic principles or premises of psychoanalysis have to be first established through everyday experiences of persons.

Many of us as lawyers, litigants or observers in court may have witnessed or been a party to an irritable exchange between the judge and a lawyer. All of us are human and irritation, anger, frustration, and perceived provocation, influence rational thought. At times the judge may be heard to observe that he/she never lets such exchanges with counsel impact the adjudication on the merits of the case to the detriment of the interests of the parties involved in the litigation. This could be due to the image of a judge as a person unaffected by emotions in the discharge of judicial functions. This self-image may make a thought like "As a judge I get affected by angry exchanges" intolerable, and the thought gets suppressed and denied at a conscious level. The suppressed emotions impact mental functioning and the discharge of judicial duties. Almost everyone else present in court, barring the judge, senses *"Judge sahib naraz ho gaye hain"* (the judge has become angry) and a price may have to be paid.

A more meaningful paradigm could be to acknowledge the feelings engendered by the angry exchange and take them on board at the conscious level. Feelings which are suppressed are not amenable to processing and yet continue to impact human actions. Once feelings are in the conscious domain they can be processed in the psyche. A judge after acknowledging feelings of irritability may take a sip of water and think, "Maybe it is better not to pass a final order today" or "Maybe I should adjourn this case today" or "Maybe I should *recuse* myself from this case." It makes possible conscious choice to reduce the impact of the angry and irritable feeling engendered by the exchange which could adversely affect adjudication on the merits of the case.

Opening windows

It is these everyday examples which help in opening the window towards the movement from the manifest conscious to the hidden unconscious. A special responsibility rests on individuals placed in judicial positions to try and reduce the impact of personal biases, prejudices, and stereotypes in order to promote impartiality. Gender, caste, class, race, religion, nationalism, and sexual orientations are some of the likely areas of play of these notions.

Judicial training is oriented towards following and being guided by the observations and judgments of superior courts. Fortunately, in a first, the Supreme Court of India in a judgment has acknowledged the possibility of unconscious prejudice on the part of the judges.[5] The Punjab and Haryana High Court had ordered the termination of the pregnancy of an adult woman who had not given her consent for the procedure. The woman had been categorized as "mentally retarded," and consent was deemed to be irrelevant. Reversing the High Court order, the Honourable Chief Justice of India (CJI) observed: "this case also presents an opportunity to confront some social stereotypes and prejudices that operate to the detriment of mentally retarded persons. Without reference to the present proceedings, *we must admit that even medical experts and judges are unconsciously susceptible to these prejudices*" [author's emphasis]. The CJI went on to perceptively observe: "It would also be proper to emphasize that persons who are found to be in a condition of borderline, mild or moderate mental retardation are capable of being good parents."

Psychoanalysis and the Mexican judicial experiment

In talking of psychoanalysis and law, it is fitting to discuss the experiment of Judge Carrancá in Mexico, about whom Gallo (2012) observes, "One of the most original and eccentric readers Freud had anywhere in the world was Raúl Carrancá y Trujillo, a Mexican judge who studied in Spain, returned to Mexico City in the 1930s, and worked tirelessly to reform the judicial system by, in part, incorporating psychoanalytical ideas into the legal profession." (p. 253).

Carrancá (1934), a Mexican judge and great admirer of Freud referring to him as "that intrepid explorer of the human soul and its dark, subterranean recesses" (p.125), in an unprecedented move placed defendants who were referred to him in a chair, sat behind them and invited them to explore their fears, fantasies, anxieties, dreams and anxieties in order to arrive at the truth. In the Mexican legal system –unlike the Indian and the British– the judge has investigative functions. The judge published his experiment in the journal *Criminilia*. Gallo (2012) informs us, "Soon after 'A legal experiment with psychoanalytic techniques' appeared in *Criminalia*, Carrancá mailed a copy to Freud. Freud responded with a gracious – albeit brief – letter, telling the Mexican judge that he had read his article with great interest and approved of the efforts to find new applications for psychoanalysis, and that 'it has always been an ideal desire for the psychoanalyst to win two people for our discipline: teachers of youth and judges'" (p. 257).

The role of analyst to the defendant played by Judge Carrancá would be impermissible in India, where the role of the judge is that of an impartial referee between adversaries. The inquisitorial system followed in Mexico gave space to Judge Carrancá to play the analyst-therapist to the accused-defendant.

The case of the accused in the famous Leon Trotsky[6] murder case was allotted to Carrancá. The assassin confessed to the crime claiming disillusionment with Trotsky as the motive and the matter could have ended there. However, Judge Carrancá was keen to explore the motive and the identity of the perpetrator who appeared to be using an alias. This time around, the judge, rather than conducting the analysis himself, directed a criminologist and a forensic psychiatrist to explore the unconscious motives of the assassin.

Freud died in 1939 and would have turned in his grave at the verdict in the Trotsky case in 1943 holding "Oedipus Complex" as the motive for the murder. When called upon to give an expert opinion in the Halsmann case, Freud (1931) writes, "Precisely because it is always present, the Oedipus Complex is not suited to provide a decision on the question of guilt" (p. 252). The inquisitorial system providing leeway for Carrancá to play analyst apart, the use of psychoanalytical tools like free association, the explorations of dreams and fantasies of the defendant and the violation of the basic tenet of confidentiality inherent in the mixing up the judicial and analytical role, is unlikely to serve the interests of justice.

Law in praxis

> *Tu kehta pothi kee lekhi, main kehta ankhan kee dekhi.*
> (You speak that which is written in books, I speak that which is seen by the eye.)
>
> Kabir[7]

Incarceration in jail involves the curtailment of the vital rights to life and liberty of the individual. The essential principles of Anglo-Saxon jurisprudence like "presumption of innocence," "burden of proof on prosecution," "objective evaluation of evidence," and "proving beyond reasonable doubt" were evolved and crystallized over time and are irreproachable. In practice, these high principles of law are played out in hundreds of courtrooms in India, mediated through the agency of a judge, an individual prey to human foibles, idiosyncrasies, pride, prejudices, and egotism.

A person arraigned for theft may in appearance fit the very stereotype of a drug addict in the mind of the judge and evoke a gut feeling, *"smackiya hai, isi ne chori kee hogi"* ("the guy is a smack addict, must have committed the theft"). The "gut feeling" impacts and influences in a vital manner the application of the legal principles like the presumption of evidence, the evaluation of evidence and the determination of innocence or guilt in the theft case. However, judicial training does not have any component of taking this gut feeling "on board," in the sense of acknowledgment, awareness, and processing of the feelings evoked with a view to a fair application of the legal maxims to the case of the apparent "drug addict" already condemned as guilty, even before the start of the trial and presentation of evidence to establish the offence.

Apart from individual cases, the unconscious at play can be seen in the adjudication of the constitutional validity of laws touching upon nationalism, gender and sexuality including sexual orientation. National security laws in India such as the "Terrorist and Disruptive Activities (Prevention) Act," 1985,[8] the "Prevention of Terrorism Act," 2002[9] and the "Armed Forces (Special Powers) Act," 1956,[10] which impact civil liberties and democratic rights, have been challenged in the courts but have been consistently upheld as constitutionally valid by the Supreme Court of India. The judgments delivered by the courts upholding the laws are on the manifest level about aspects of the fundamental rights to life, liberty, freedom of speech, and expression and reasonable restrictions to be imposed on these rights on the ground of public morality, public order, and national security. Love for mother and motherland; anxieties of disintegration of the country, particularly poignant in the context of the partition of India in 1947; and the internal image of the brave son of Mother India in the psyche of the judges, are some of the unacknowledged factors which impact the adjudication of constitutionality of such laws.

Yet, judges by definition are deemed to be free from personal biases, prejudices, and stereotypes as soon as they occupy the judicial chair. Healy (1950) reviewing *Courts on Trial: Myths and Reality in American Justice* by Jerome Frank (1949)observes: "The virile chapter on The Cult of the Robe shows what Judge Frank is after, namely, to have an intelligent public understand 'that the springs of decision in judges' do not 'differ from the springs of decision in other men'. The wearing of the robe and legal jargon tend to becloud that fact" (p. 238). What then are the possibilities of intervention?

Affect and free association workshops

Applying the psychoanalytic frame giving primacy to "affect" followed by "free association," I conducted a series of workshops on "Minimizing the impact of biases, prejudices and stereotypes in the judicial-decision making process" at the National Judicial Academy,

Bhopal; the Delhi Judicial Academy, New Delhi and the Karnataka Judicial Academy, Bengaluru in India. The workshops were targeted at newly-recruited judges as well as senior judges attending refresher courses. The senior judges had been in service for up to 15–20 years.

We begin with open-ended queries about individuals who feel they are totally free from biases and prejudices to those feeling a little biased and prejudiced. It is rare for a participant to take up the gauntlet of being an extremely prejudiced individual. Participants volunteer to share, and mention the biases they are aware of and we proceed to establish the distinction between conscious and unconscious biases.

Predominantly, images and words were projected on the screen and in the first round the participant-judges were to get in touch with their feelings. The judicial role being cerebral, getting in touch with one's feelings and articulating them requires effort on the part of the individual and is one of the objectives of the workshop. In the second round of reactions, the participants were to express the associations to the images. The images selected were keeping in mind the intersect of class, caste, gender, sexuality, and sexual orientation. Some of the images projected on the screen were: Mother; Black; White; Peaceful Protest Picture; Criminal; Bearded Keffiyeh Man; Man inhaling from foil; Schedule Caste; Sexy Woman; Homosexual; Dowry; Celebrity, Naxalite;[11] and Fair Handsome Man. To illustrate some points we take up responses to three of the images projected on the screen.

Mother and Bearded Keffiyeh[12] Man

The image depicting or symbolizing "Mother" evoked feelings of "Care, Affection, Comfort, Respect, Obedience, Security, Devotion, Patience, Pride, Sacrifice, Strength, Pamper, Kindness, Compassion, Happy, Nurturance, and Solicitude. The image of a bearded man with a keffiyeh evoked feelings of Suspicion, Fear, Anger, Terror, Curiosity, Hate, Caution, Contempt, Shock, Surprise, Aggression, Worry, Horror, and Anxiety."

The free associations of the participants to "Mother" were in the nature of: Great sense of security; My mother; Life's First teacher; Can endure anything; Most respected; Goddess; Guiding light; Missing her; Food; Guidance; She is one who created; Energy of life; "*Dantna*" (trans. scolding); Selfless; Our Mother; Responsible; Dedicated; Teaching me religious things; Most lovable; Should be respected; Sacrifice; Ask for anything; Life-giving soul; Life-giving teacher.

The free associations of the participants to the Bearded Keffiyeh Man were: Muslim; Fundamentalism; Arab; Basketball player; Looks like a terrorist; Needs help; Needs to be put behind bars; Osama; "*Kattar*" (trans. hardcore); Who is he looking at; Thank God not staring at me; Terrorist; *Akshardham*;[13] Criminal; Threatening; Needs to be educated; Orthodox; Human beings; Fanatic; Belief in own religion; "band" (trans. closed); Desperate; Son of Osama bin Laden; Directionless; Needs help; Insecurity; Religious man; What is he up to; *Intifada*; *Al-Qaeda*; Cruel; Religious identity; Dissatisfied; Terror will he create; Harm; Explosives; Creation of God; Allah; Pious; Cleric; Distance; Curious who is he; Ghetto. In a somewhat similar vein the word "Naxalite," referring to the armed left-wing revolutionary movements in India, evoked feelings of: Terror, Fear, Dilemma, Anger, Sympathy, Hatred, Repulsion, Curiosity, Injustice, Pity, Insecurity, Hate, Violence, Anguish.

At the level of "affect" the feelings evoked by Mother and Bearded Keffiyeh Man seem to fall into neat categories: all the positive feelings with the Mother image and the negative with the Bearded Keffiyeh Man. The value-loaded sharpness of the contrast was similar to feelings evoked by the two colors Black and White. At the level of free associations the Scolding Mother is the closest to a negative. In the case of the Bearded Keffiyeh Man the most benign associations were basketball player, Pious, Creation of God, and at the other end of the spectrum were Hate, Osama, Cruel, and Create Terror.

The participant-judges were invited to share their experiences of trying the accused under anti-terror laws and for offences like sedition. Sharing of feelings by the participants of anxiety and/or fear evoked at setting eyes on an accused individual who fits the very stereotype of a "terrorist" helped in weaving in the inter-connections between the emotions and the free associations evoked in the workshop and the possible impact of their feelings on the trial process. Participants sharing the mobilization of positive feelings of love, affection, security for life-giving mother, and motherland along with the negative feelings of horror, fear, and terror evoked by the Bearded Keffiyeh Man assist in illustrating the playing out of these emotions in courtrooms.

Unconscious fears of rape and pillage by gun-toting "Terrorists" and "Naxalites" and fantasies of the brave "Lion" son protecting mother and motherland appear to play their role in the apparent objective processes of legal trials. Baccheta (2004) writes: "As Andrew Parker et al. [1992] have amply demonstrated, in so many nationalisms across the globe the territorial component is associated with, or symbolized as, a chaste female body, often a mother or motherly figure. The notion of her potential violation by foreign invaders is also widespread" (p. 27). I elsewhere observe: "The vague inimical forces get reified in the stereotype of the bloodthirsty bearded AK-47 toting "terrorist" out to destroy. Childhood fantasies of protecting mother against the bad father may mesh in with those of the macho boy soldier and brave patriot son defending the Mother Nation. The plethora of feelings which may get provoked impact fair, balanced and rational application of mind with regard to the validity of such laws" (Shukla, 2011, p. 349).

"Unnatural sex" and homosexuality

An image depicting two men holding hands in an apparent homosexual relation evoked the following feelings: Sick; Deprived; Not again; Abnormal; Aversion; Repulsive; Helplessness; No feeling; Neutral; Secrecy; Lust; Bad; Empathy; Ignore; Compassion; Passion; Disgust; Deviance; Discomfort; Sympathy; Hatred; Uncomfortable; Inhuman; Revulsion; Confusion; Pity; Blank; Curiosity.

Coming to thoughts, the free associations of the participant-judges were: Proper treatment; Love and care; getting between; Delhi High Court; Discouragement; Defiance; Deviation; Perversion; Each his own; HIV; Latest issue; Let them live; Social stigma; Legalize their relation; Offence against nature; Gender; Transgender; Hostel; Unnatural; Psycho; Abnormal; Diseased; Ailment; Difference; Their own wish; Interference; Accepting variety; Shameful; How could they enjoy it?; Distorted; Aberrations; Deviants; Abnormal; Discrimination; Naz Foundation; Type of sex; Unusual; Justice Murali; Immoral; Unnatural; Illegal; Feeling of person; Justice Shah; Adverse to nature; Mental sickness; Different people.

The Indian Penal Code, 1860, drafted by the British, criminalized homosexuality under Section 377 as "unnatural sex." The Delhi High Court in a landmark judgment in the *Naz Foundation v Govt. of NCT of Delhi* case (2009) excluded homosexual sex among consenting adults from the ambit of the offence. However, the Supreme Court on appeal overturned the verdict in the *Suresh Kumar Koushal v Naz Foundation* case in 2013 and held Section 377 of the IPC to be constitutionally valid and applicable even to consensual adult homosexual acts, again rendering a significant section of society as "criminals." After a wait of five long years, on September 6, 2018, the Supreme Court in the recent landmark judgment in the dancer-choreographer *Navtej Singh Johar* case decriminalized same-sex adult relationships. The Supreme Court reversed its own earlier judgment of 2013, terming it as "arbitrary, fallacious and retrograde." The Supreme Court termed the British-era Section 377 of the Indian Penal Code as "irrational, indefensible and arbitrary." The court held criminalizing consensual sexual acts between adults as unconstitutional and said that "The majoritarian views and popular morality cannot dictate constitutional rights." The changing positions give us an indication of the powerful role which subjective factors in the psyche of a judge may play in adjudicating on merits in the apparent legal paradigm of fundamental rights to life, liberty, equality, speech and expression and constitutionally permissible reasonable restrictions.

The conscious and unconscious notions of the individuals performing the judicial function about "natural–unnatural sex"; heterosexuality-homosexuality-bi-sexuality; "normal sex"–"abnormal sex" impact adjudication in this arena. Feelings of disgust at homosexuality and penalizing homosexual acts among consenting adults may well stem from unacknowledged homosexual attractions of an individual. Lack of acknowledgment of one's own homosexual inclinations could impact decisions in the arena of sexuality. Reaching a certain minimal comfort level with regard to sexuality, processing anxieties about differences and diversities in the area of gender identity and sexual orientation, are a *sine qua non* for a balanced judicial temperament. These factors also come into play in cases involving the validity of exclusion of marital rape from the offence of rape or the issue of adultery as an offence or the validity of the non-prosecution of the woman under the adultery law, issues presently under challenge in the Supreme Court of India.

Caste and psyche

According to traditional Hindu thought there are four castes with the *Brahmin* originating from the head; the *Kshatriya* from the arms; the *Vaishya* from the thighs; and the *Shudras* from the feet. The hierarchy corresponds to the correlates of Knowledge, Defence, Sustenance, and Service respectively.

Caste, which is a unique and predominant feature of Indian society, transcends the Hindu religion and has permeated Christianity, Islam, and Sikhism. It is both blatant and lurking under the surface and is generally accessible to most Indians at all times. It is a volatile and sensitive issue today and in the workshops with judges, caste remained the most difficult area in which to access emotions evoked in the participants. Leaving aside an exception or two, participants chose to give politically correct answers. Judges trying cases under anti-discriminatory laws like the Protection of Civil Rights Act, 1956 and the SC/ST (Prevention of Atrocities) Act, 1989, are trying with the full force of conscious logic and rationality at their command to be impartial. Yet the judgments and interpretations of the provisions of the two legislations in the cases reflect the unconscious caste biases.[14]

The complaint of Justice Karnan of the then Madras High Court to the National Commission of Schedule Castes in 2011 came in useful as an illustration in my attempts to access and process unconscious caste biases in workshops with judges. Justice Karnan, who is a Dalit, complained that: "The judge, sitting cross-legged next to me, touched me with his shoes deliberately and then said sorry. Two other judges were watching it smiling," he said. Justice Karnan claimed that he was discriminated against on basis of caste at several get-togethers such as full court meeting, high tea, and dinner.[15]

The brother judge may have touched his shoe intentionally to humiliate or it may have been accidental. Likewise the two judges may have been watching and enjoying Justice Karnan's humiliation or it may be possible that they might have been smiling at a joke entirely unrelated to Justice Karnan. As a measure to diffuse tensions, Justice Karnan was transferred to Calcutta High Court. However, matters escalated, Justice Karnan accused the seven judges of the Supreme Court bench who issued contempt notices against him and also "convicted" them of offences under the SC/ST Act. In a step unprecedented in judicial history, the Supreme Court of India found Justice Karnan guilty of contempt of court and sentenced him to six months' imprisonment. The direction by the Supreme Court for a psychiatric examination of Justice Karnan did not help and seems to have been perceived by the judge as a persecutory attack. In contrast to aspects of psychiatry with mental illness as pathology, perhaps, therapy-counselling sessions from a psychoanalytical approach which looks upon the "pathological" as part of the spectrum of the "normal," may have been a more con-structive avenue to explore in Justice Karnan's case.

Individual sessions with judicial officer

From a psychoanalytic approach with an implicit assumption about the availability of an endless number of sessions, I was in a dilemma about taking up an assignment with the limit of a maximum of five sessions of therapy with a judicial officer. Taking inspiration from the colorful Ukrainian proverb "He who doesn't risk, doesn't drink champagne" – the equivalent of the sedate English proverb "nothing ventured, nothing gained" – I accepted the engagement. The setting was the Judicial Academy and the High Court headed by the Chief Justice, the superintending authority for subordinate judicial officers, had directed retraining of the magistrate. The therapy sessions were being paid for by the Academy, not the judicial officer. Much like concerned parents who want to know about the session of the child, the persons-in-charge met me before and after the session. Assuring confidentiality to the client-magistrate would inspire little confidence under the circumstances. Sensitively, the authorities understood and waived the requirement of meeting them pre- and post-session.

I will attempt to flag some of the issues which arose in the sessions. Legal details like provisions of law and reported judgments of courts including citations in combination with a flowery and convoluted manner of talking took up lot of space in the session. A fascination, almost like a craving or greed for the language and wordplay of law, reflected in a phrase like "I didn't get satiated," referring to the law course. The preoccupation with detail and wordplay as a defense to stave off lurking distressful feelings could be an avenue to explore.

Much like the elephant in the room which no one is talking about, there was no mention by the Magistrate of the reason he was here in the session. The leave of the officer had been cancelled as a punitive measure and he was instead sent for training by the Chief Justice. In the sessions, the Chief Justice came across as an inspirational mentoring figure whose approval meant much to the youthful magistrate. Along with feeling that his action was justified, was the emotion that "they know better" with regard to the punitive measure taken by the authorities. Possibly, the anger or rage fleetingly surfaced as resentment against his father-in-law and against old lawyers appearing before the young magistrate.

As part of judicial training, the motto not to be a 9am to 5pm judge, but to be a 24-hour judge was inculcated. This in turn seems to have fed a grandiose self which looked upon colleagues as well as at personnel from investigation agencies with contempt, leading to friction at work. There were also problems in the marriage, though the wife's complaints had been put on hold by the protective Chief Justice. The crisis in the marriage was related in a calm manner without pain and anguish. Possibly, day in and day out using the formal legal language of courts can have a distancing from emotions effect on the personality. Phrases like "matrimonial relations" instead of "my marriage" or "spouse" compared to the intimacy of "partner" or "wife" creep and spread into the personal arena. The emotional distancing could play a role and contribute to relationship problems. Given the setting of five sessions as part of a punitive order along with anxiety about the therapist "spilling the beans," creating a safe, secure holding space for painful and distressing emotions to play out and work through integral to therapy was difficult to achieve in the circumstances.

Balint groups and individual sessions

Intra-psychic processes like our inner feelings of hostility getting split and converted into perceptions of the "other" as hostile to us; or denial of our feelings of humiliation leading to perceiving the actions of the other as slights; or suppressed feelings of guilt leading to feelings of being accused are at play in all of us. Judges are the same as the rest of us and there is no reason to suppose that processes of denial, splitting, and projection are not at play in them. Freud (1906) cautions that judges may "'be led astray by a neurotic who, although he is innocent, reacts as if he were guilty, because a lurking sense of guilt that already exists in him seizes upon the accusation made in the particular instance' (p. 113). Providing a facilitating space for observing these processes through *Balint groups* equips the individual to better perform the judicial function.

Balint groups initiated by Hungarian-British psychoanalyst Michael Balint were spaces where about eight to ten doctors met at regular intervals along with a facilitator and one or two cases were presented focusing on the non-medical aspects. *Balint* groups for judges would provide a space not to discuss legal aspects but to explore feelings in a non-judgmental space. It would offer an opportunity to reflect on work as well as a space to articulate anxieties and frustrations. It could lead to increased self-awareness, more capacity to reflect on themselves and the usefulness of examining one's own reactions. To illustrate, a mother who is a judge in child custody matters may find her maternal feelings evoked and invariably feel inclined to give custody to the mother, regardless of the merits. The legal system offers no space for the articulation of the "non-legal" responses evoked in judges who are as human as anyone else. A space for naming the feeling, elaborating and processing the emotion could lead to improved judicial functioning as well as judges being better equipped to address the psychological aspects of issues like trauma testimony.[16] Experiencing the creativity of a group and greater professional satisfaction could be other possible positive outcomes.

When parents are stressed in their quasi-judicial functions of arbitrating quarrels amongst children, the quantum multiplier in the stress and strain in deciding life and death matters, day in and day out, cannot be imagined. Healy (1950) observes that Frank (1949) advocates that judges "should undergo at least a short period of psychoanalysis that they may acquire knowledge of themselves and thereby learn to control to some extent their own otherwise unavoidable preconceptions and biases" (p. 238). Individual therapy sessions for judges would offer spaces to observe biases and prejudices, get in touch with feelings in the nature of slights, humiliation, and helplessness as well as take on board feelings of grandiosity and omnipotence. These emotions could thus possibly be processed better and lessen the impact on judicial behavior and action.

Notes

1 Times of India, April 3, 2018.
2 Times of India, April 13, 2018.
3 Untouchability was prohibited post-Independence by Article 17 of the Constitution of India, as well as a specific legislation titled "The Untouchability Offences Act" passed in 1955 (renamed in 1976 as "Protection of Civil Rights Act"). However, untouchability continues to be practiced in several pockets across the country.
4 "HC to Govt: Ask media to avoid 'Dalit' word." *Times of India*, June 7, 2018.
5 *Suchita Srivastava v Chandigarh Administration*, 2009 (11) SCALE 813.
6 Trotsky, exiled in Mexico, was widely suspected to have been assassinated on the directives of Stalin.
7 Fifteenth-century mystic poet with biting criticism of Hindu and Islamic practices in couplets referred to as "*dohas.*"
8 *Kartar Singh v State of Punjab* (1994) 3 SCC 569.
9 *Peoples' Union for Civil Liberties v Union of India* (2004) (9) SCC 580.
10 *Naga Peoples' Movement for Human Rights v Union of India* (1998) 2 SCC 109.
11 The term "Naxalite" is derived from Naxalbari village in West Bengal, India, the site of an armed peasant revolt in 1967.
12 Traditional headdress in West Asia, originating from Kufa, Iraq, typically worn to protect against sunburn, dust, and sand.
13 Akshardham temple in Gandhinagar, Gujarat, India was attacked by two armed men on September, 24, 2002, killing 30 people.
14 For examples of caste bias reflected in judgments under the two anti-discriminatory laws, see "Judicial Pronouncements and Caste" by Shukla, R. (2006).
15 Dalit judges targeted, says Justice Karnan. *Times of India*, November 4, 2007.
16 For trauma testimony and law, see "Trauma survivors meet the Law: Explorations in India," Shukla (2016).

References

Baccheta, P. (2004). *Gender in the Hindu Nation, RSS women as ideologues.* New Delhi: Women Unlimited (an associate of Kalifor Women).

Carrancá y Trujillo, R. (1934). Un ensayo judicial de la psicotécnica. *Criminalia 6* (Feb): 125.

Frank, J. (1949). *Courts on Trial. Myths and Realities in American Justice.* Princeton, NJ: Princeton University Press.

Freud, S. (1905). *Jokes and Their Relation to the Unconscious.* Standard Edition VIII.

———— (1906). *Psychoanalysis and Legal Evidence.* Standard Edition, IX.

———— (1931). *The Expert Opinion in the Halsmann Case.* Standard Edition XXI.

———— (1934). Letter to Carrancá y Trujillo, February 13, 1934. *Criminalia,* *8* (April), 160. (Reproduced in with English translation by Gallo, R. (ibid.).

Gallo, R. (2012). A wild Freudian in Mexico: Raúl Carrancá Y Trujillo. *Psychoanalysis and History, 14*(2), 253–267.

Healy, W. (1950). Courts on trial. Myths and realities in American Justice by Jerome Frank. Review. *Psychoanalytic Quarterly, 19,* 437–438.

Kartar Singh v State of Punjab (1994). 3 Supreme Court Cases 569. Lucknow, India: Eastern Book Company.

Naga People's Movement for Human Rights v Union of India (1998). 2 Supreme Court Cases 109. Lucknow, India: Eastern Book Company.

National Commission of Schedule Castes (2011). A Report on Reservation in Judiciary. http://ncsc.nic.in/files/Reservation%20in%20Judiciary.pdf, retrieved September 6, 2018.

Naz Foundation v Govt. of NCT of Delhi (2009). 160 Delhi Law times 277. D.L.T. Publications Private Limited, Delhi, India.

Navtej Singh Johar v Union of India Writ Petition (2018). (Criminal) No. 76 of 2016. www.livelaw.in/breaking-sc-strikes-down-157-year-old-law-criminalizing-consensual-homo-sexual-acts-between-adults-holds-section-377-ipc-unconstitutional/, retrieved July 9, 2018.

Parker, A., Russo, M., Sommer, D., & Yaeger, P. (1992). *Nationalisms and Sexualities.* New York: Routledge.

Peoples' Union for Civil Liberties v Union of India (2004). (9) Supreme Court Cases 580. Lucknow, India: Eastern Book Company.

Shukla, R. (2006). Judicial pronouncements and caste. *Economic and Political Weekly,* October 21.

———— (2011). Judging sedition: The case of the good doctor. *Int. J. Appl. Psychoanal. Studies 8*(4), 346–352.

———— (2016). Trauma survivors meet the law: Explorations in India. *Int. J. Appl. Psychoanal. Studies 13*(3), 271–275.

Suresh Kumar Koushal v Naz Foundation (2014). 1 Supreme Court Cases 1. The judgment was delivered on December 11, 2013 and reported in the law reporter in 2014. Eastern Book Company, Lucknow, India.

Chapter 16

Fear of death or of murder?

Challenges confronted in the modified psychoanalytic setting established by forensic psychotherapy

Estela V. Welldon and Ronald Doctor

Introduction

The fear, not only of death, but also of murder could be closely related in the forensic patient when gross, unconscious, archaic memories of loss and despair may be evoked by transferential interpretations within therapeutic relationships. This could produce compelling and potent feelings of revenge and acting out, which would need to be contained. When the fear of death occurs in the therapist's countertransference feelings, beyond the secure settings of forensic psychotherapy, massive acting out may occur in the therapist to counteract his or her own threat of death. Karl A. Menninger (1938) wondered: "Is it hard for the reader to believe that suicides are sometimes committed to forestall the committing of murder? There is no doubt about it. Nor is there any doubt that murder is sometimes committed to avert suicide."

It is the enactment on the part of the patient, which defines forensic psychotherapy, and it is significant that even the most apparently insane violence has a meaning in the mind of the person who commits it. There is a need to be aware of this meaning and to learn from it in an attempt to prevent further violence (Doctor, 2003). Moreover, the "psychotherapy involved in forensic psychotherapy is different from other forms precisely because society is, willy-nilly, involved" (Welldon, 2011). Forensic psychotherapy goes beyond the special relationship between patient and psychotherapist. It is a triangular situation: patient, psychotherapist, and society. In parallel, there is the "existence of the triangular process of power dynamics in social roles such as the bully, the victim and the bystander, (sometimes intervening as rescuer), where the bystander becomes the audience of the bully-victim drama" (Welldon, 2015). The bystander role is important but remains often unrecognized. Psychotherapists can become part of this dynamic.

In this chapter, we shall draw on clinical material to demonstrate the enormous challenges facing the patient and the therapist in dealing with the fear of annihilation. This is especially so when therapists are confronted with patients who inform them that they have a gun. We will discuss two patients, a man and a woman, with disordered personalities bordering on psychosis and perversion, and we will illustrate the triangular situations inherent in forensic psychotherapy. We will place particular emphasis on their sadism and destructiveness and on how they evoke countertransference feelings and responses that may be difficult to tolerate.

Symington (1980) states that it is possible to classify the responses aroused by the patient with personality disorder under three headings: collusion, disbelief, and condemnation; those are defences used by the professionals to protect themselves from very disagreeable feelings. He notes that the personality disordered and, in particular, the psychopathic patient in treatment will use every means to get us to do something other than give interpretations. Such a patient makes a desperate appeal to us to either collude with him or, through projective identification, he stirs our own sadism. Our attempt to deal with our sadism then leads to the other two responses: either disbelief or condemnation.

The psychopath despises the person who holds onto an illusion that he is good; unconsciously he knows that this is a rejection of an important part of him and will always give a strong clue about the hidden side of his character. To adhere to the evidence, rather than disbelieve, requires us to accept our own sadism. It may be more comfortable to believe that he and we are good. The other reaction is to deny our sadism by projecting it back into the psychopath who is a particularly suitable scapegoat. To relate with neither disbelief nor condemnation is extremely difficult, as seen in the response aroused by the psychopath who goes into a psychiatric hospital where he is met with disbelief and in the prison where he meets condemnation.

In the clinical vignettes that follow, it would be important to note the gender-related differences in the patients. In men, the focus of violence and perversion is on the phallic body whereas in women it is on the containing body and their use of children narcissistically, as extensions of the body.

In the first instance, Ronald Doctor is going to describe a male patient. In his encounter with him he was presented with a combined container-phallus: a bag potentially carrying a gun was placed on the table in his consulting room, which provoked a massive anxiety reaction in him.

Clinical vignette I

A 44-year-old single man, Mr C, a lab technician, was referred for a psychotherapy assessment outpatient appointment. However, an hour before his appointment I received a telephone call from his GP to say that he, the GP, had been unable to sleep the night before as Mr C had come to his consulting room that day to tell him he had a gun and was suicidal. The GP was unsure what to do (perhaps due to the bystander effect and thus unwittingly abandoning the patient) but urged the patient to keep his appointment with me the following day. Following the conversation with the GP, my heart was pounding but I decided that I would keep the appointment. An hour after the phone call from the GP, Mr C calmly walked into my office. He put a small bag on the table in my consulting room and started the interview. "My problems are complicated. I had a road traffic accident with whiplash injuries and consequent depression, followed by a nervous breakdown due to the incompetence of my solicitors." He was unable to work for a period of nine months. During those months he had attended counselling for six sessions and then the Psychiatric Outpatients Service for management of his depression with medication. Finally, he was referred to the Psychotherapy Service. He said that before the aforementioned accident he had been planning to emigrate to the USA and used very forceful language to describe his attitude to England. He had clearly been very dissatisfied with his life here for a long time. Another consequence of the accident was that he had been unable to take some examinations that would have enabled him to practice as a lab technician in the USA. However, in the long term he still planned to emigrate. He went on to tell me that his fiancé and her parents were involved in another road traffic accident a few weeks prior to our appointment and all had died from 40 percent burns. He also informed me that in fact he had another friend who had died from an arson attack a couple of years before. As a result of these four deaths he now felt very depressed every morning and had been so for the past three weeks since his fiancée's death. He said he had picked up an automatic pistol and pointed it at his head, imagining that he had a bullet in the chamber, and then pulled the trigger. He informed me that he did have bullets in the house but had not yet put them in the chamber of the gun. I blurted out, in shock, at hearing all these deaths as well as his impending suicide that he was playing Russian roulette with himself. He grinned and said that obviously I knew nothing about guns as you cannot play Russian roulette with an automatic pistol. He went on in a somewhat triumphant way: "You, being a psychiatrist, probably think I am suicidal – I am not suicidal, it is a ritual I am playing. I point the gun at my head and pull the trigger and I have played out this ritual every morning for the past three weeks to try to overcome the fear of death." Mr C said to me that he was also moonlighting for a security agency, who had issued him with the firearm, but he could not tell me anymore about it, it was a secret.

At this point in the interview, I felt very alarmed at what I was hearing and fantasized as to what was in the bag on my table. Was it his gun? Was he going to use it? To defuse my terrified mind, I asked Mr C if he could tell me about himself. He told me that his relationship with a woman came to an end in the middle of the previous year after a four-year very off-and-on relationship. He said that the woman concerned had often gone abroad without explaining where she was going and returned to the UK without telling him she was back. They then had a period together again and she would again go off. Finally, the relationship ended with a telephone conversation in which he discovered she was living in a different part of the country and was in another relationship. It was not clear whether this was the same woman as his fiancée, who had died in the car accident. He told me he was upset about this, but more in terms of injured pride, because he felt he should have ended the relationship rather than being in emotional distress at the loss of the relationship. He said that his parents, both lawyers, divorced when he was an infant. His dad remarried soon after and he never saw his father again but he knew his father had died about six years ago. He was brought up by his mother and he had one sister, married with children.

Listening to Mr C, I could feel myself in a very high state of anxiety, with thoughts of mass murder enacted by him going through my mind. I said to him that he had come today to tell me that he had a gun: he was letting me know how very serious the situation was and

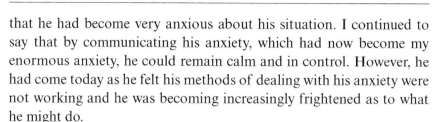
that he had become very anxious about his situation. I continued to say that by communicating his anxiety, which had now become my enormous anxiety, he could remain calm and in control. However, he had come today as he felt his methods of dealing with his anxiety were not working and he was becoming increasingly frightened as to what he might do.

A lengthy discussion followed during which I felt increasingly anxious and I continued to say that he was telling me about his gun and that this was a communication which we had to take very seriously. I think the conversation became quite fixed in my mind with the idea that he had brought his gun into the room inside the bag on my table. After considering a number of options, including handing the gun over to the security agency that he had mentioned earlier in the session, we decided that I would let the police know so that they could contact him to take the gun away. By this point I was able to think of Welldon's (2015) triangular situation and to call on the judiciary to help me with my anxiety. He said this would complicate matters but agreed with the idea that I should contact the police and I gave him another appointment in two weeks' time.

I subsequently informed the police about this patient being in possession of a gun. They thought that it was a false alarm, another example of disbelief, and doubted that he had a gun. However, the police arrived at his home in a large convoy and he let them in. After a lengthy search of his house, and to their great surprise, they found the gun, but not just one gun: there were over 100 guns in his possession!

Mr C was then seen by two psychiatrists, who differed in their opinion of whether he was psychotic, but he stood trial for possession of weapons, was convicted and was given a custodial sentence. He found his home in prison, a place secure enough to contain his murderous anxiety. Perhaps he will be able to look back over his experiences and consider that the professional response he received was appropriate at the time (Binder & McCoy, 1983).

Discussion

Mr C did not commit murder but he projected his murderous thoughts into my mind. I think he had probably reached the point of realizing he needed help in order to contain his enormous anxiety due to his murderous impulses, as he felt unable to do this on his own. He had sought help by initially going to the GP and then coming to the Psychotherapy Service. I never discovered whether he had in reality brought the gun into my consulting room, but in my mind he had brought an image of something very violent, causing me great anxiety. Perhaps that was what he wanted, someone to contain his huge anxiety, and at that moment all I could think of was that I needed help as he was more than I could contain.

I think that, in Mr C's case, a weak dependent part of the self attempted to make contact with me, but was prevented from doing so by an alliance of destructive objects. Rosenfeld (1971) refers to this as the Narcissistic Organisation, often represented as the unconscious fantasy of a gang which can either be idealized or feel very persecutory and thus represents itself as a helper or a tyrannical persecutor. In fact, it takes over the personality and prevents development and growth. Maybe his collection of guns was initially the idealized gang that protected him from his enormous persecutory anxieties, which were projected into the solicitors and ultimately into the whole of the UK, from which he felt he had to escape. However, with the mounting number of deaths in his life, the gang became the tyrannical persecutor driving him to come for help.

Perhaps Mr C had developed a fetish of guns and placed his gun (phallus) in the bag, which he brought into the consulting room for me to see, and attempted to reassure himself that his body and, in particular, his mind were still functioning properly. However, he might have unconsciously wanted to communicate that he was in a desperate situation and needed help. He had remained calm and superficial as I was experiencing the enormous projected anxiety that he could not bear.

Estela Welldon will now discuss a female patient. In her seminal work (1998, 2011) on female perversion, she demonstrated that she was able to listen to her patients and their stories without condemnation or disbelief. She challenged the assumption that a phallus was an essential prerequisite of perversions and introduced the notion of female perversion to describe the narcissistic use of children to extend a woman's own maltreatment of her body and to repeat an intergenerational pattern of abuse and cruelty.

Clinical vignette 2

Mrs S was treated, as an inpatient, at a medium security psychiatric unit for a period of around ten years: she received medication and electroconvulsive therapy. She attempted to kill herself and her three children on at least three occasions. She was convinced that they were harmed from birth because she had passed on genes from their Nazi grandfather and they were psychologically damaged as a result of her being a bad mother when she felt depressed and unable to care for them. She did not experience regret about these actions. On the contrary, she experienced a great deal of shame at not having succeeded: she would prefer them dead rather than have them endure the suffering she had gone through. She never envisaged including her husband in these killings.

Mrs S was the product of a violent rape in a country occupied by the Nazis. It transpired that her father was a Nazi informer. In her own words: "My birth was my family's shame. When I was born, I should have been thrown out of the window into the canal at the back of our house. Sadly, no one bothered."

Mrs S was brought up in her grandmother's home, an all-female household. Her mother and aunts constantly subjected her to humiliation and denigration, for example they addressed her as "You Nazi shit." Her "one and only good enough relationship" was that with her grandmother, who died when she was eight.

Soon after her mother's marriage, her stepfather began to physically and sexually abuse her. His male friends also joined in her sexual abuse. At the age of 14 she became pregnant, although she was not completely aware of this. She vividly remembered that she was in the bathroom with her stepfather, which we can assume was the baby's father, when the "baby came out." He took the newborn, a boy, away from her and a horrific scene then developed: first he cut off one of the baby's hands and then wrapped him up in newspaper, poured petrol all over and burnt him. He forced her to witness this. Soon after, she left home and started working in a special school helping children. Then she decided to train as a nurse.

Later, Mrs S met and married an Englishman and moved to England where they had three children. To start she managed the household and the care of her children in an adequate manner. However, following her mother's death, unresolved grief eventually caught up with her and she attempted to kill her children and herself for the first time. This attempt could be interpreted as her being "forced" to give up her mother as the "bad object" from infancy and to take it onto herself to become the "bad mother."

A second attempt followed her hysterectomy. She became chronically depressed and was treated with antidepressants. She refused to talk and didn't get out of bed for a period of almost four years, requiring electroconvulsive therapy. A few years later after gynecological repairs she became uncommunicative and refused to eat or drink. Once more she attempted to poison her children, offering them tea laced with her husband's prescribed tablets and after she took an overdose. She was detained under Section 3 of the Mental Health Act 1983, and was transferred to the Regional Secure Unit for observation and treatment. She again had electroconvulsive treatment and her depression seemed to lift. She often became violent, breaking windows and objects in the ward, and throwing objects at members of staff. On one occasion, she destroyed all her previous medical reports. She also remained intermittently suicidal.

After her first attempt to kill her children, memories and flashbacks began to torture her mercilessly. The killing of her firstborn baby boy, whom she secretly called Robert, remained consciously the main focus of all her concerns and preoccupations. This trauma was responsible for her survivor's guilt. She was not allowed to survive him and her three live children were to face the same fate. After all, in her mental representations they were not only born of her body but they were parts, extensions of her own body and mind. As she got better this nightmarish imagery revisited her more ferociously than ever with increasing suicidal ideation and homicidal feelings. She executed all her attempts to kill her children in the same way: in her feeding role as a mother, through poisoned food.

Mrs S initially received a diagnosis of a severe personality disorder, later one of severe chronic depression and eventually that of severe post-traumatic stress disorder. As such, analytical psychotherapy was considered a possibility and she was referred from a medium secure unit to the Portman Clinic for an assessment. Following a series of diagnostic consultations Mrs S started weekly psychotherapy with the understanding that it would be for a period of no longer than five years. For the first three years, she remained an inpatient and was brought to sessions escorted by two nurses in an ambulance, a two-hour drive each way. As positive changes were observed, she was permitted to spend weekends at home with her family and these visits increased in length and frequency. Once she was discharged from the medium secure unit, she began to live at home with her husband and to attend sessions on her own and of her own volition using public transport.

Mrs S often brought written material to her sessions including her own poems and dreams. These showed her to be sensitive and creative, despite being psychologically damaged. During her therapy, she also became a grandmother as her daughter had a baby girl. She kept in consistent contact with her children and regularly saw her granddaughter with whom she had a close relationship.

Mrs S's psychodynamic understanding

In the light of psychodynamic theories, Mrs S's homicidal and suicidal attempts are comprehensible. Menninger (1963, p. 240) said that all cases of violence have meaning and represent an effort to avoid something worse: "The murder is often committed in order to preserve the individual's sanity."

There are, paradoxically, other challenges to understanding her: for example, how was this woman able to mother three children in their early infancy without any gross misbehavior? One could speculate that her "one good relationship" to her grandmother facilitated some healthy identification with her during that period, which allowed her to mother babies without any serious complications.

This "good enough experience," which she also effectively used later on in becoming a grandmother of a little girl, may be responsible for her accepting the offer of therapy, experiencing me in transference as her grandmother. This capacity for identification was clearly shown during one session a year after therapy had started when she brought a written statement saying:

I own my life. And only mine.
And so I shall appreciate

my person.
And so I shall make
proper use of myself.

This was an unusual piece of writing because all her weekly written messages were usually filled with torture, terror, and emotional pain. Was she experiencing an increased sense of self-esteem? No, this had nothing to do with her – it was a picture of me! On reflection, some degree of identification with her experience of me as an accepting and self-assertive "grandmother" was in operation.

Psychotherapy took us through several phases: in Phase 1 she was bewildered at having been accepted for therapy and I was constantly challenged as she was frightened that very soon I would be fed up and give her up. At the end of the sessions, she used to refuse to leave and would get very angry at my silences.

> Why are you not prepared to answer my questions? I answer your questions. I don't know how to deal with your persistent, perturbing silence. Punishment? There is no communication possible if there is no foundation to establish mutual trust. Can we come to an understanding between us, will you let me know when you are livid with me and why? Will you explain what to expect?

She would bring all sorts of drinks, especially sugary ones that would jeopardize her diabetes, and she would check whether I was alert to this fact. She was showing her lack of trust about my capacity to "feed" her properly. This also represented her feeling uncontained and uncared for. Perhaps, more importantly, in offering those drinks to me, her desire to poison me was also present as well as her need for my interpretation about her homicidal feelings. This escalated with the alarming and disturbing presentation of a gun which she brought into the consulting room with the aim of blackmailing me into silence, since by then she felt my interpretations were too intrusive and invasive. Her intention was either to kill me or to commit suicide. In both cases, I was the offending "victim" since I had become the "perpetrator."

In Phase 2, Mrs S's enormous anger was actively directed at me, perhaps as a result of her having an incipient sense of trust in me and of her fear of becoming dependent. At first she used to get irritated;

she later on became quite explosive, throwing things like pens and paper clips. At times, her hostility was hidden under a veneer of concern.

This was followed by Phase 3 which was marked by the emergence of the pain of growing up. In one session she talked with a sense of reality about her granddaughter's physical and emotional growth: she was already aware that "very soon the baby will walk away from me in search of other, more attractive things in life." This seemed to be an appropriate time to make an interpretation indicating that a similar time would come for us. I felt we had to start a preparation for a termination of the therapy due to my impending retirement in two years' time since she believed I would be a lifeline for her, to be there with her until she died. On getting to know of the inevitability of the ending of therapy, she became listless, agitated, and angry. She told me that she dreaded her future life and that, in a concrete way, my retirement might mean her own retirement from life. She wanted to know if I was going "to put her right" before I went, or otherwise what or who was I going to offer her. She felt that any improvement on her part would fade away in no time. This, at times, I experienced in a rather pressurized, urgent way.

It was at this stage that the important role the body plays in people who have suffered severe traumas became much clearer. She talked extensively about her body, her husband's body, my body, but much more so about her first little boy's hacked hand. I believe that the little hand had become a bodily feature in between dream and hallucination, which had intermittently but consistently appeared during the sessions.

Finally, in Phase 4, Mr S began making contact with reality. She experienced a constant preoccupation about her marriage and developed an awareness of her husband's complete detachment from her and everybody else. Although he was seen as the "good man" in the family, he very much resented her improvement and her having asserted her own voice, feelings, and ideas as a result. This was the first time the conditions had been created for her to use and develop her own mind – or even have a mind at all. She desperately wanted for her family to enter family therapy but this was not supported by Social Services. It seemed that her position in life would remain that of a foreign body and her fate would be that of the dysfunctional member of an otherwise "ordinary" family.

In a way, it also became a sign of mental sanity that she was able to be in touch with the mental torture rather than regress to the "automaton" state, which had occurred after the second homicide/suicide attempt when she remained in hospital completely uncommunicative and isolated, needing electroconvulsive therapy. Interestingly, I was reminded of Ferenczi (1933, p. 163): "the abused child changes into a mechanical obedient automaton" and of Shengold's (1989, p. 25) addition: "But the automaton has murder inside."

Van der Kolk (1989) poignantly describes the phenomena that appear in these patients in relation to their deep shifts of mood when he says "trapped between feeling too much and too little." He means that these patients appeal to two different modes of behavior when facing distress and frustration: they either react with excessive anger and impulsivity or become depersonalized, "spaced out" or numb. The latter refers to the state I've described earlier as "obedient automaton."

Discussion

Mrs S made me consider that not all traumatic events can be integrated into experience. There was a limit as to how much more she could take in and it became evident that some experiences would remain untransformed in her mind. This prompted me to discuss modifications in psychotherapeutic techniques with colleagues when working with patients who have suffered from severe or early traumas leaving them with limited capacity for symbolic thought. To what extent can we make interpretations, which, although accurate, may lose all therapeutic value because such patients may experience them as penetrating and violating, and as such may be unable to digest and process them? Indeed, how much is one cajoled or forced in the transference process to become some sort of perpetrator? I believe that while one should not hide away from interpreting the negative transference, especially in the initial phase when recognition and acknowledgement of negative experiences are badly needed, the therapist should be aware as to how much patients can take in order to remain the therapist and not to become the rapist.

The process of identification with the aggressor that dominates the lives of people who have been abused becomes rather entangled in this case. The two men who appeared more ostensibly and significantly in her early life were extremely violent and sadistic and both were sexually attached to her own mother. Her biological father was responsible for her generally hated and repudiated birth. Her stepfather was responsible for her further denigration, her sexual abuse, and later became the killer of her first child. Were both amalgamated into one? Violence, sexuality, and sadism were interlinked in her psychological makeup. Her choice of partner appeared superficially to be an unusual one in that he could offer stability and support, but simultaneously he couldn't stand her being able to communicate her own feelings and so he became sadistic. It is interesting that she was never criminally charged for her attempts at killing and that although her husband elected to remain an apparently supportive and loyal family man, he consistently refused to take anything seriously. Her homicidal and suicidal attempts almost went unnoticed. Her husband was the martyr, the one who "stood" for and always took care of her. This became so unbearable that there was always a possibility she would regress to a state of profound depression and non-communication, becoming an "automaton."

Conclusion

The psychotic or perverse structure of patients such as the ones described in this chapter, is like a delusional world into which parts of the self tend to withdraw. It appears to be dominated by an omnipotent or omniscient, extremely ruthless part of the self, which creates the notion that within the delusional world there is complete painlessness but also freedom to indulge in any sadistic activity. The destructive impulses within this delusional world sometimes appear as overpoweringly cruel, threatening the rest of the self with death to assert their power but more frequently those objects appear disguised as omnipotently benevolent or life-saving, promising to provide the patient with quick ideal solutions to all their problems (Rosenfeld 1971).

Such patients often complain of a profound sense of inner emptiness and ignorance of their true identity, as if their concealment of their most inner self has been so extensive that they themselves lose contact with it. One of the most important tasks of their therapy is the establishment of a secure and substantial sense of self. In these patients, there is an attack on their origins and their history, creating a lack of narrative, a void, which they fill with their psychotic debris and with sadomasochistic abuse. This is in order to encapsulate their anxiety of death and murderous rage. With the emergent fear of death, murderous violence is triggered (Doctor, 2008).

Freud (1917) believed that the primary task of psychoanalysis was to fill in the gaps, undo the distortions and finally arrive at the true narrative of the patient's history. It is important for the patient to be able to arrive at a more complete and better knowledge and understanding of his/her history. Such knowledge can diminish the unconscious pressure to submit to the repetition compulsion and for history to be repeated in the present. In fact, Freud (1917) went further and stated that the aim of psychoanalysis is a history of the unconscious, or rather of its origins, a history of discontinuities in which the moments of burial, concealment, and then resurgence are the most important of all.

Note

The authors would like to acknowledge the editorial help of Dr Katherine Papaspirou for this chapter.

References

Binder, R.L., & McCoy, S.M. (1983). A study of patients' attitudes towards placement in seclusion. *Hospital and Community Psychiatry, 34,* 105–1054.

Britton, R. (1998). *Belief and Imagination: Explorations in Psychoanalysis.* New York: Routledge.

Darnley, B., Doctor, R., Gordon, J., & Kirtchuk, G. (2011). Psychotic processes in forensic institutions. *Psychoanalytic Psychotherapy, 25*(1), 55–68.

Doctor, R. (Ed.) (2003). *Dangerous Patients: A Psychodynamic Approach to Risk Assessment and Management.* London: Karnac.

——— (Ed.) (2008). *Murder: A Psychotherapeutic Investigation.* London: Karnac.

Ferenczi, S. (1933). The confusion of tongues between adults and the child. *In Final Contributions to the Problems and Methods of Psychoanalysis.* London: Maresfield Reprints.

Freud, S. (1917). *Mourning and Melancholia.* SE 14, 237–258.

———— (1927). *Fetishism.* SE 21, 149–157.

Menninger, K.A. (1938). *Man Against Himself.* New York: Harcourt Brace.

———— (1963). *The Vital Balance: The Life Process in Mental Health and Illness.* New York: Viking.

Rosenfeld, H. (1971). A clinical approach to the psychoanalytical theory of the life and death instincts: An investigation into the aggressive aspects of narcissism. *International Journal of Psycho-Analysis, 52,* 169–178.

Shengold, L. (1989). *Soul Murder: The effects of Child Abuse and Deprivations.* New Haven, CT: Yale University Press.

Symington, N. (1980). The response aroused by the psychopath. *International Review of Psychoanalysis, 7*(7), 291–298.

Van der Kolk, B.A. (1989). The compulsion to repeat the trauma: Re-enactment, revictimization, and masochism. *Psychiatric Clinics of North America, 12,* 389–411.

Welldon, E. (1988). *Mother Madonna Whore.* London: Guilford Press.

———— (2011). *Playing with Dynamite.* London: Karnac.

———— (2015). Forensic psychotherapy. *Psychoanalytic Psychotherapy, 29*(3), 211–227.

Chapter 17

Corruption

Instances and mechanisms involved

Rosa Corzo and Ruth Axelrod Praes

Corruption is defined by the Oxford English Dictionary (2018) as: "Dishonest or fraudulent conduct by those in power, typically involving bribery. The action or effect of making someone or something morally depraved." The worldwide organization Transparency International defines it as "the abuse of entrusted power for private gain" (2018). This definition is focused on public corruption exercised by politicians. But we all know that corruption is present among private individuals and in the corporate and business world. Corruptie (a European organization against corruption and an active participant in the International Anti-Corruption Conference Council – www. corruptie.org) completes the definition as follows: "Corruption is the misuse of entrusted power (by heritage, education, marriage, election, appointment or whatever else) for private gain" (2014).It is much easier to point out corruption whenever the events involve large sums of money and/or public figures and politicians. But major corruption thrives on a broad base of small corruption payments or bribes (even if money is not directly implicated). We believe that the underlying psychological mechanisms are the same with any corrupt act.

We know the Id is like a living mass of intense drives; it responds primarily to the domain of the instinctive and unconscious. In addition, it knows no rules, no time or space, or prohibitions, and it is governed only by the urgency for satisfaction. The psychic energy is often linked to sexuality or aggression, and its ultimate aim is to achieve immediate pleasure (Principle of Pleasure). With that in mind, we can start to imagine how strong are the ties that keep us humans from taking inappropriate advantages.

In any corrupt act, we identify seven elements:

1. Abuse or misuse of entrusted power
2. For a personal/private gain
3. Events executed in secret
4. Usually includes lying
5. Personal certainty of innocence and the conviction of deserving special treatment
6. Unawareness of any wrongdoing
7. Coexistence of two ego structures mutually exclusive

An event that is considered by some just as a "friendly turn," for others will be a "wrongdoing"; a "gift in gratitude" for some, is a "punishable pay-off" for some others. It is very difficult to talk about corruption, because it is always a hidden event. All parties involved agree to keep the affair a secret. Why? One answer could be that all parties are ashamed, thus guilt is present. This will direct us to explore the guilt and the superego. However, another answer could be that one or several parties involved are aware of how dangerous the act that is about to be committed really is, since it is forbidden by internal and/or external laws, thus it is a way to get the unconsciously needed punishment. We will elaborate on this in the paragraphs ahead.

We must consider another possibility: that one or both participants are compelled to do *things* knowing that they are *inappropriate*, and not understanding what dictates over his/her actions to do *these things* that only produce a brief comfort that lasts just long enough to alleviate a growing anxiety (Weldon, 1988). In this case, we are dealing with perversion, which we will also cover.

A third scenario could be that corruption comes from the compulsion to betray related to the frustration of failed expectations: the betrayed becomes a betrayer executing his/her right to get even.

We will examine corruption (public and private, big and small, personal and corporate) from a psychoanalytical point of view, in order to identify the instances and mechanisms involved: superego and guilt; the perversion involved in the unavoidable cleavage in the ego structures; the primitive betrayal of the mother and corruption both as a revenge and as the well-deserved payment for the deceit suffered; the personal conviction of innocence and the certainty of deserving a special treatment or attention, etc. Psychoanalysis gives us access to the unconscious where we can find the deep motivations of our fantasies and actions. We believe that a deeper understanding of corruption will help us deal with it in a wide variety of situations.

Attacks on linking

According to Sher (2010), individual and social behavior are described under the concept of *internal object*: the internalized mental images of significant people, experiences, and ideas (with intense emotions and feelings attached) influence identity formation (including belief and value systems) which in turn leads to the formation of attitudes and behaviors. On the other hand, corruption is an inversion of reality due to the inability to accept an imperfect and sometimes frustrating reality. Explained in Bion's words, the turning away from internal objects is caused by hate (H) and intolerance of knowledge (K). Corruption occurs when the individual cannot adopt a depressive position state (accepting imperfection, conflict and dissatisfaction) but stays in a paranoid-schizoid position, in which unpleasant emotions are repressed. "Corruption is about removing thinking, removing acknowledgement and indebtedness, and fostering primitive mental mechanisms" (Sher, 2010, p. 51).

Another conception also related to parent–child interactions is offered by Lamothe (2003) who states that a deprived complex plays an important role. He points out that in early development, when the child's deeply felt erotic assertions are misrecognized by significant adult caretakers. This misrecognition leads to a sense of invalidation and, as the child depends on the parents for survival, he/she adapts to the parents' recognitions, even if these are not his/her true affirmations. The parental recognitions are defined by their self-representations and longings. The child learns that possession of objects will provide comfort, security and – most of all – represent life itself. As possessions supply only a pseudo-fulfillment, the subjective feeling of satisfaction is never complete. But at the same time, the attachment to powerful parents can provide an omnipotent sense of being worthy of getting anything he/she desires, together with an unconscious sense of emptiness.

Impossibility of innocence

One of the first and most important things that we humans learn is that it is very important to get our mother's attention. That is the only way to insure our survival. According with the Theory of the Mind, learning to lie is a normal stage of development. Very early in our life, we learn to identify how others feel, think, and want. And we learn to adapt our actions in order to get what we want from others. As soon as we lose the unity illusion and our mother is recognized as a different and separated object, we "know" what she expects and how we can get her to fulfill our needs. This is how we learn how to be a human being.

In order to get her (and others') attention, we make efforts to please them and learn to lie, as our parents have lied to us "for our own good," to keep us calm and/or avoid anxiety. Hence the potential for corrupt behavior is an "integral component of our psychosocial makeup" (Sapochnik, 2003). Although primitive feelings never completely disappear, social expectations help us integrate them in our personality. But sometimes we learn to turn a blind eye to the values that frustrate our pleasures.

Superego and guilt

Through his work (1913, 1927), Freud points out the opposition between the individual drives and the requirements for a society constitution and coexistence. Particularly in "Totem and Taboo," he proposes that the Law comes out from the primitive horde: first as an attack from the group of brothers against the father, and later when they feel the filial guilt after the killing of the primal father and were besieged by remorse and fear of retaliation and punishment. One of the three psychic instances,[1] the superego, is in charge of moralization and punishment. It makes sure that the Ego complies with the rules and prohibitions imposed, keeping the Id's demands under control through discipline and fear of penalization. This critical agent is formed (Freud (1923) states in "The Ego and the ID") as an outcome of the Oedipal phase and represents the internalization of parental, social, and cultural censures and requirements. For some authors (Rincón, 2002; Potestad, 2016) corruption is the result of the lack of moral and ethical laws within the twenty-first-century capitalistic society, considered by them as the "twilight of the Superego." But we know that corruption is as old as humankind, as well as the sense of guilt expressed through the shame and secrecy surrounding a corrupt act. On the other hand, the international statistics on corruption reveal that Lutheran countries suffer a lower incidence of corruption than the Catholic or Muslim ones. We could think about the impact of some alternative means to get absolution from guilt, such as the possibility of confession, as well as influence trafficking and payments for absolution. Since these options are not available under Lutheran traditions, it becomes more difficult for the subject to rub out the guilt and start all over from scratch.

As Gellis and Lima (2011) summarize, in Freud's work "the guilt appears often related to morality and ethics, as well as the emergence of the superego and to the development and survival of civilization. … [it] sustains life gregarious, but it is also related to the subject, to the causation of neuroses."

In 1929 Freud states that "the sense of guilt is the most important problem in the development of civilization and … the price we pay for our advance in civilization is a loss of happiness through the heightening of the sense of guilt." Then he declares that our discontent in civilization arises not directly through the heightening of the sense of guilt, but rather through the heightening of the unconscious need for punishment that defends against the sense of guilt.

Too often we see patients suffering the effects of a very severe unconscious superego that is always ready to give a guilty verdict and exert severe punishments. Here, the need for punishment is present, increasing the urgency for committing punishable acts: the unconscious superego and its punitive operations oppose to the development of mature guilt and reparation, thus encouraging the execution of dangerous activities.

Some psychotherapists work under the belief that soothing the patient's superego is part of their job, in an attempt to diminish their need for punishment. Since the very need for punishment arises from an attempt to defend against the sense of guilt, these psychotherapists become accomplices by keeping unconscious the true sources of guilt. The true work should be directed to help the subject to discover the unconscious desires and phantasies that give rise to the guilt. If we can confront and bear guilt, understood as depressive anxiety or concern, the need for putting ourselves into dangerous and punishable situations, including acts of corruption, will diminish.

Perversion

Not so long ago, a renowned Mexican politician declared: "I do not believe that any President has ever wakened up thinking about how to screw up Mexico ... [but instead] always thinking about how to do things the right way" (Reséndiz, 2016). It is very common to witness statements like this one from people that have been suspected of a corrupt act. The splitting structures allow them to present an innocent façade or even an outraged one, when caught up or accused.

In his work "Three Essays on the Theory of Sexuality," Freud (1905) talks about perversion as the result of a unresolved Oedipal Complex: the 3–5 years old child is full of desire for his mother and, at the same time, wishes for the death of his father, giving him full access to his mother. However, he is afraid of being severely punished by being castrated by his father. The only way to solve these anxieties is to assume his fear of castration and to give up his incestuous desires. When the boy is unable to give up, he has to deny castration: he recognizes the danger of castration, but still he denies it: "I know it is there, but at the same time I choose to believe that it is not there." As a consequence, one part of himself never really gives up his mother (the pre-Oedipal mother stays in the unconscious), but at the same time he has to protect himself against anything that could bring back the fear of castration, such as recognizing himself as having a penis that can be cut off. In order to achieve the required denial of the truth, the subject recognizes an aspect of reality, but through a splitting in his structure, he has to deny that unbearable reality (Darwin & Moreira, 2018). Even if the term *perversion* has some moral implications and is used in a derogative sense, for the psychoanalysis this means just a disfunction in the sexual aspect of the personality: "In a more comprehensive sense, 'perversion' connotes the whole of psycho-sexual behavior that accompanies such atypical means of obtaining sexual pleasure" (Laplanche & Pontalis, 1996).

This theory built around the masculine gender child has been applied to explain both normal and perverse sexuality in boys and girls. In order to do this last, a parallel situation was assumed in the development of female sexuality, proposing the symbolic equivalence of the penis and having a baby. Freud himself declared later that female sexuality was an enigma, hoping for other psychoanalysts to solve it.

Many authors after Freud agreed on the importance of the early mother–child relationship on the core of the perversion (Weldon, 1988, 2011; Jacobs, 2008; Mahler, 1975). For them, the symbiotic phase with the pre-Oedipal mother is crucial in the development of the perverse psychopathology and deeply related to the fears of being abandoned or seduced by the mother.

It may start with a girl that has lived the abandonment and insensitive care from her mother, or recalling being treated as substitute of an absent father. These girls haven't been able to enjoy an individual development as a differentiated being, but they have always felt as an object part of their mothers. When they grow, these women become mothers and treat their children just as they were treated: as partial objects whose sole purpose is to satisfy their mother's needs and expectations. The basic trust derived from being loved and accepted as a whole person was never built, so they just have no idea about how to give that sense of being significant as a whole independent person to their children. The danger of losing the mother prevented them from reaching sexual and emotional maturity, thus complicating heterosexual relationships. This experience is relived by their children and can run for generations to come. For Weldon (1988, 2011), there is only one important difference among the masculine and feminine perverse act: while men usually act perversely towards an external partial object, women do it against themselves, their bodies or the objects considered by them as their property: their children. Their feelings of despair, defeat and incompetence as mothers can easily turn into hate and disdain for themselves and their children.

The distinctive trait in perversion is an unconscious mechanism: the subject tries to overcome the intense fear of losing the mother through the perverse act that, at the same time, reassures his/her individuality and serves as a payback to the dangerous pre-Oedipal mother for her infantile abandonment.

Recognizing themselves as victims, they easily turn into prosecutors. They feel entitled to do whatever they want, deserving a special treatment and being unable to acknowledge any wrongdoing on their part. Too often the subject is caught up in paranoid-schizoid splitting unable to acknowledge the badness and the goodness at the same time (Carveth, 2001).

Betrayal: identification and corruption

We will define betrayal as a rupture of a commitment between individual beliefs, something that was said or not, that in principle allows human beings to be in the same team, with the same ideals and on the same referral setting but that is being broken. It happens because one of the participants breaks the covenant without negotiation and thus surprising the other one.

Betrayal is the fault that breaks loyalty or fidelity, something that someone committed himself to do and was unable to comply. This fault can be the product of an oral or written commitment either implicit or not, being conscious or unconscious. It consists of a denial to a covenant either by word or action, an act of disloyalty. Going back to the subject of the country index of corruption, it is the conquered and colonized countries where the corruption is higher. As if the colonized people felt that they have the right to betray the powerful ones, because they had betrayed them in the past.

A secular definition of betrayal is a violation or breaking of a trust, contract, or confidence between an individual, group or organization that someone or others place in a person, group or organization. It is like a husband or wife committing adultery or a nation that is aligned with another nation against a common foe who then turns against the one they were aligned with and then joining the common enemy for which they had made a compact or agreement to fight against. It is the height of treachery against someone or a group that seems in direct conflict with what was first agreed upon. Benedict Arnold is a great example of someone who betrayed his country and who once was a general for the American Continental Army but defected to the British Army and became one of the greatest traitors in American history.

Akhtar (2013) asserts that betrayal is an integral component of the psychic trauma. It transcends the realm of trust-distrust leaving ingenuity and innocence aside. Akhtar does not understand why betrayal, being a topic so essential, has not been thoroughly studied by psychoanalysts. He found that the word *betrayal* appears only 18 times in Freud's writings and, of those, five times colloquially; nine in betraying oneself through slips in an unsuccessful effort to hide a secret; and the remaining four due to compulsive rituals to control the fear related to a massive paranoia.

Balint developed the concept of "basic trust" which is an affective perception that generates a natural learning experience that is difficult to sustain. In his book *The Basic Fault* (Balint, 1979) he considers that primary and adult love is based on original cathexis to objects felt as threatening or dangerous. He considers sadism and hate as secondary phenomena resulting from unavoidable frustrations. For him, harmony between subject and object requires absolute loyalty where it is not possible to allow interferences. Who is able to do it? If in the relationship between the one that exercises the maternity function predominates love over hate, and what is gratifying over what is not, the subject develops the basic feeling of trust and mistrust. He puts trust into the other's goodness and mistrust in his aggression, thus building the unconscious fantasy of the goodness of the object and of the ego. But at the same time hate is always there.

The drive to betray others is part of a psychic conflict, where the Id imposes aims to the ego. The compulsion to betray is connected with the frustration of failed expectations. Revenge, envy, jealousy, abuse, and rage are related. When there's an automatic reaction or response, no mentalization becomes useful.

No guilt is present; betrayal seems natural and can occur through denial, splitting or addiction. It can be deliberate or unintentional; installed like perversion with a specific new private law. This involves the fact that betrayal hurts. The phenomenon comes in both an active and a passive form, and the affects connected with these forms are conscious or unconscious mental pain, respectively. Betrayal is a specific form of trauma and at the same time a constituent of all psychic trauma.

Freud (1920), in "Beyond the pleasure principle," considers the existence of a protective shield against excessive excitation and when that shield suffers an externally caused fracture, trauma is produced.

We are convinced that betrayal has penetrated in this kind of fracture through related fear and anxiety, as well as need for retaliation.

In a previous work entitled "Psychodynamics of betrayal," Axelrod (2017) divided the psychodynamics of betrayal into five stages:

1. Original betrayal
2. Narcissistic betrayal
3. Dyadic betrayal
4. Oedipal betrayal
5. Social betrayal

What does betrayal mean? Most of us have been betrayed, but what does it mean to be betrayed, or to betray? They're two sides of the same coin: the betrayer that decided to break the loyalty provoking the law; and the betrayed that passively maintains silence, as an accomplice of the event.

Betraying can be a form of identification, looking for acceptance or a provocation by making fun of the other who is waiting to be unveiled. How far is betrayal and transgression from corruption?

Open issues

Whatever the psychoanalytic explanation each of us finds more suitable to explain and understand the question of corruption in general or a specific corrupt act (guilt, superego, perversion, betrayal, splitting, revenge, etc.), it is our aim to find out the roots and unconscious motivations, rather than prosecuting or judging. Both ourselves, our patients, and the society as a whole can benefit from a deeper understanding of the instances and mechanisms involved in any corrupt act. No one is innocent. We all are involved as active or passive participants, as witnesses, accomplices or victims. Knowledge gives us the responsibility of helping others to better understand and try to prevent such severe dysfunctions or, at least, try to stop these endless repetitions.

Note

1 Freud stated that the human psyche is be divided into the conscious and unconscious mind. Later he introduced another way to study the

psyche: the Id, which represents the unconscious mind, rises up from biologically determined needs, and comprises all drives and unconscious motivations. The superego represents the regulations and prohibitions inherited from the parents and imposed by society's traditional morals and taboos. Finally, the Ego that is in contact with the external reality receives both external and internal perceptions and is in charge of keeping a balance among the demands of the Id, the regulations and prohibitions from the superego, and the limits imposed by the external reality, all in order to achieve a better living for the subject.

References

Akhtar, S. (2013). *Betrayal: Developmental, Literary and Clinical Realms*. London: Karnac.

Axelrod, R. (2017). *Psicodinamia de la traición* at "El cuerpo del psicoanálisis y el psicoanálisis del cuerpo." Axelrod & Montilla, Mèxico (Eds.), De Textos Mexicanos.

Ballint, M. (1969). *The Basic Fault*. New York: Brunner/Mazel.

Carveth, D. (2001). The unconscious need for punishment: Expression or evasion of the sense of guilt. *Psychoanalytic Studies*, *3*(1), 9–21, https://doi.org/10.1080/14608950020026827

Corruptie (2014). www.corruptie.org/en/corruption/what-is-corruption/

Darwin, C., & Moreira, J. (2018). *The Verleugnung in Freud: Textual Analysis And Hermeneutical Considerations, Psicologia USP*, *29*(1), Sao Paulo.

Freud, S. (1905). *Tres ensayos de teoria sexual*. Obras completas de Sigmund Freud, Vol. VII. Buenos Aires: Amorrortu Ed.

——— *Totem y Tabú* (1913). Obras completas de Sigmund Freud, Vol. XIII, Buenos Aires: Amorrortu Ed.

——— (1920). *Más allá del principio del placer (Beyond the pleasure principle)*, Obras completas de Sigmund Freud, Vol. XVIII. Buenos Aires: Amorrortu Ed.

——— (1923). *El yo y el ello. Obras completes de Sigmund Freud, Vol. XIX*. Buenos Aires: Amorrortu Ed.

——— (1927). *El porvenir de una ilusión*. Obras completas de Sigmund Freud, Vol. XXI. Buenos Aires: Amorrortu Ed.

——— (1929). *El malestar en la cultura*. Obras completas de Sigmund Freud, Vol. XXI. Buenos Aires: Amorrortu Ed.

Gellis A., & Lima, M.I. (2011). Sense of guilt in Freudian work: universal and unconscious. Psicol. USP, *22*(3), São Paulo, July/Sept.

Jacobs, A. (2008). *On Matricide*. New York: Columbia University Press.

Lamothe, R. (2003). Poor Ebenezer: Avarice as corruption of the erotic and search for a transformative object. *Psychoanal. Rev.*, *90*(1), 23–43.

Laplanche, J., & Pontalis, J.B. (1996). *Diccionario de Psicoanálisis*. Barcelona: Ediciones Paidós Ibérica.

Mahler, M. (1975). *El Nacimiento psicológico del infante humano*. Buenos Aires: Marymar Ediciones.

Oxford English Dictionary (2018). https://en.oxforddictionaries.com/definition/corruption

Potestad, F. (2016). *Crepúsculo del Superyó y corrupción*, www.deia.eus /2016/ 05/04/ opinion/tribuna-abierta/crepusculo-del-superyo-y-corrupcion

Reséndiz, F. (2016). *No President wakes up thinking about how to screw up Mexico*, El Universal dairy, section Nation, Politics, October 25, 2016.

Rincón, L. (2002). *Reflexiones sobre la corrupción*, Fepal – XXIV Congreso Latinoamericano de Psicoanálisis "Permanencias y cambios en la experiencia psicoanalítica" – Montevideo, Uruguay, Septiembre 2002.

Sapochnik, C. (2003). Corruption: Oedipal configuration as social mechanism. *Organ. Soc. Dyn.*, *3*(2),177–190.

Sher, M. (2010). Corruption, aberration or an inevitable part of the Human Condition? Insights from a "Tavistock" Approach. *Organ. Soc. Dyn.*, *10*(1), 40–55.

Transparency International (2018). Found at www.transparency.org/what-is-corruption/

Weldon, E. (1988). *Madre, virgen, puta: Un estudio de la perversión femenina*. Madrid: Prismática.

——— (2011). *Jugar con dinamita. Una comprensión psicoanalítica de las perversiones, la violencia y la criminalidad*. Madrid: Prismática.

Chapter 18

The psychoanalyst as expert witness

Robert L. Pyles

Could we possibly imagine a more alien environment for psycho-analysis than the courtroom? Perhaps only the actual battlefield! Psychoanalysis, as we were trained, depends on the neutrality of the consulting room, the quiet contemplation and careful attentiveness of the therapist to the patient. So why on earth would a psychoanalyst involve him or herself in such matters, and what would we possibly have to contribute?

Well, as it turns out, quite a lot. As with individual patients, legal cases involve individuals caught up in the intense emotional drama of human interactions, that lend themselves quite nicely to the exact same analytic approach in which we are more experienced than any other group. The cases themselves are quite often perfectly riveting in terms of trying to understand why these people behaved, and continue to behave, in the way that they do, and the outcome of the case quite often depends on being able to convey that understanding to the judge and jury.

The other issue, which is no small matter, is that of financial com-pensation. This is one of the few areas where psychoanalysts can get fees comparable to legal fees. In the USA, "expert witness" fees are generally four to five times what a therapy hour would bring, which in US dollars would amount to between $450–$750 per hour. This figure would apply to document review, consultations with attorneys, court testimony, and even travel.

Years ago, I was just as reluctant to involve myself in forensic matters as most analysts, but I got pulled into it "the old-fashioned" way. I got sued by a patient. In spite of the fact that such suits are extremely frequent in the USA because of the huge potential financial rewards to both the patient and the lawyer, needless to say I was shocked and upset. Even more so, as this was an indigent patient who I had treated at no fee.

As these things often do, the case dragged on for about four years, and eventually disappeared, because my former patient would never show up to testify. It later turned out that he had filed the case after being talked into it by his lawyer. But in the course of the proceedings, I had been represented by a law firm who did the risk management (malpractice) legal work for Harvard Medical School, where I was on the faculty.

At that point, I had been deposed (testified) a number of times in the lead up to the presumed actual court appearance. Depositions, I should say, are "dress rehearsals" for the ultimate court confrontation. They occur in the law offices of the attorneys for either side. As a point of definition, the lawyers representing the individual bringing the case are called the "plaintiff" (for "complaint") attorneys, and the lawyers representing the person being sued, are called "defense" attorneys.

As a consequence, the Harvard attorneys had had a good opportunity to see how I operated in a legal environment, including in a confrontational one, as I was often questioned by the opposing attorney. So the bottom line was that the original case disappeared, and Harvard's legal team began engaging me to render opinions and testify in an increasing number of consultations on a variety of cases. As I became known to other law firms, I also began to be engaged by them. Although, for obvious reasons, I had no further contact with my former patient, I have often ironically thought I should send him a "thank you" note!

In considering whether one would be interested in augmenting one's professional activities with forensic work, it is important to become familiar with the legal system of the particular country in which one is operating, and how expert witnesses are commonly used. As it turns out, the analytic method lends itself rather precisely to legal work. I approach the data from a legal case in exactly the same way that I would assess an individual patient, and the lawyers seem to really like the results.

In the USA, one early surprise for me was that I had assumed that the justice system was designed to try to clarify the *reality* of the claims and counterclaims, and so it is, but not in the way I had anticipated. In our profession, we are trained to try to uncover the emotional "truth" of an issue.

Not so here, or at least not in the way we are accustomed to. To my initial shock, I learned early on that the US system is strictly an "adversarial" system. What that means is that each side puts on the best "story" they can, oftentimes truth be damned. The old law school adage in training attorneys is "If you have the law on your side, argue the law. If you have the facts on your side, argue the facts. If you have neither the law, nor the facts, call the other side names!" And so it goes.

My point here is that the value system and the legal customs of a particular country have very practical implications for the psychoanalyst as an "expert witness." What I learned, for example, was that there was often great pressure from the hiring law firm to have the expert witness become an advocate for their particular position.

I have always refused to do that. I have always made it clear to any legal firm that engages me that I am going to call it exactly as I see it. If I think their side has merit, I will say so, but if I think their case is weak, I will give them that opinion, and they are free to use me in court, or not, as they wish. My feeling about it is that I am doing them a service either way, even by advising them that they have a weak case, and they should seek to settle out of court, rather than embark on an expensive, and potentially losing court battle. In the course of this work, I have seen a number of my colleagues who do not operate that way, and do fall prey to assuming inappropriate advocacy positions, often with results embarrassing to them. But I will say that I have never had a law firm dispense with my services because of my position on this matter.

The next issue is to become familiar with the types of legal cases in which a psychoanalyst might be used as an expert witness. In the USA, as I mentioned before, malpractice cases, or cases where patients allege poor treatment by a healthcare professional, which may have caused physical or emotional damage, are quite common. Even charges of poor practice on medical or surgical procedures usually allege psychological damage as well, which call for expert opinions by mental health professionals, even in those cases. The stakes are very high, as a successful judgment for the plaintiff can easily run into the millions of dollars. One consequence of this is that there is no hesitation to pay for an expert witness.

The prototypical case for a mental health expert witness in the USA is that of suicide (the legal term is "wrongful death"). Mental health hospitals in the USA are caught between pressure from insurance companies to discharge patients as soon as possible, and judgment about the safety of the patient. A typical case might be a patient hospitalized for suicidal ideation, treated for a few days to a week, put on medication, and discharged for outpatient follow-up.

Let's say a week to two weeks later, the patient commits suicide. Typically, the family engages a lawyer, sues the hospital as a corporate entity, all doctors involved as individuals, and sometimes even nurse and social workers. You can imagine the frustration of the professionals at such accusations, since the root cause of the suicide is often the family itself. A major psychological incentive for this type of case is not only the potential financial benefit, but the understandable, but misguided, need by the family, spouse, etc., to place the blame for the tragedy on anyone, and anything ("it must have been caused by the medication"), but themselves.

This is where the psychoanalyst is engaged to assess whether the "standard of care" has been met. This is the iron rule by which everything is judged. Have the professionals involved provided the average expectable quality of care, or not? As you can imagine, each side argues their own position, and each side engages "expert witnesses" to bolster their case.

The second question is the argument by each side as to what degree of damage the patient and family have suffered, and to assign a dollar amount to the alleged damage. The testimony of the psychoanalytic expert will have a very large effect on both of these determinations.

The "experts" from each side will issue a written report, which is made available to the opposition. There will often be preliminary depositions, which take place in the lawyer's office, where both sides get to question all of the witnesses, including the "experts."

At that point the two sides will negotiate back and forth to determine the relative strengths of their positions. Sometimes, they will make a "settlement," usually involving some amount of money. If no agreement is reached, the two parties then go into an actual courtroom.

Cases can be decided in court either by a judge, or by a jury of twelve citizens who have been empaneled for the purpose of this particular trial. The plaintiff side usually pushes for a full jury trial, as juries often are more sympathetic to suffering families, and the awards tend to be significantly higher.

This is also because the jury is aware that whatever financial awards they might decide are appropriate, do not come from the medical professionals themselves, but from insurance companies. Both medical professionals and hospitals are required to carry so-called "malpractice insurance," to protect against personal financial risk. Ironically, the very existence of such insurance creates even more of an incentive for bringing lawsuits. As one can see, often the major winners in this kind of system are the lawyers themselves!

However, this is where the psychoanalytic "expert witness" once again plays a crucial role. It is very important to understand that what the analyst is really doing in this situation, is playing, not to the judge or the attorneys, but to the *jury*. I have learned to address the jury directly, make eye contact with each of them, to try to avoid psychoanalytic jargon, and to keep it simple and understandable.

It takes a little thought, but it is quite possible to express psychoanalytic principles in ordinary language. I have always thought that the foundational ideas of our profession are quite powerful in themselves, and those ideas lose none of their power when explained in lay language.

But the most important principle of all, and it took me a while to learn this, is try to get the jury to *like* you. That may sound absurd, but trust me on this, how they *feel* about you is going to be at least as important as anything you say. Of course, you want the jury to respect you as an expert, but being *personable* is at least as important as being factual.

A big part of that is to convey to the jury that you respect them as well, and understand that they will have important decisions to make, that are likely to have real impact on the lives of real people. This is not just an academic or legal exercise. If you can convey to the jury that you are trying to give them important information to help them make those important decisions, they are appreciative, and even more receptive to your actual opinion. Since juries have little or no professional expertise, they can sometimes feel talked down to, or not respected by the expert. Arrogance does not play well with juries.

If a case actually does go to court, it usually follows a particular format. The plaintiff side, that is, the attorney representing the patient with the grievance, presents their side first, laying out the grounds for the complaint, and usually asking for the maximum in financial compensation. The attorney for the defense then follows, arguing as to why the grievance is either not justified at all, or only to a minimal degree. The defense attorney will present evidence that the "standard of care" was either met or exceeded.

Both sides will call witnesses to bolster their case. The plaintiff attorney will usually lead with the aggrieved patient, and then call family members, friends, etc., who have knowledge of the case, or whom have also allegedly been indirectly affected by the injury to the patient. This is obvious in the case of suicide, but not so obvious in other, less dramatic complaints. This also where the "experts" for the suing party are called. After each plaintiff witness, the attorney for the defense has the opportunity to ask questions which might strengthen the case for the defense.

The presentation by the plaintiff is then followed by the presentation by the defense attorney, who usually leads with the primary person or entities that are being sued. Similarly, relevant witnesses are called, and it is at this point that the defense expert is called and questioned about his or her opinion. That part is usually not too stressful, since the defense attorney is not challenging your opinion, since you have already gone over it with him or her, in pre-trial meetings.

The next part is where the defense expert really earns his fee. It is the opposing attorney's goal to make the opposing expert look like an idiot, and to undermine the effect of the testimony as much as possible, especially in the eyes of the jury. The grilling and the pressure is intense, and the questioning is hostile. It is combat, pure and simple. It is a bit difficult to keep in mind that it isn't personal, because it *feels* personal. This is the part that takes a bit of practice to get used to, and it is also the part where you realize that getting at the truth is not necessarily the goal of this process!

The good news, however, is that once you go through it a few times, you get past the desire to challenge the attorney to a duel, and really begin to develop some skills. At that point, as you develop more confidence, the combat actually becomes interesting. And, you get better at making and sticking to your point.

It is in this phase that both sides are likely to call on "expert" witnesses to make the case that the "standard of care" either has, or has not, been met. Unfortunately, highly paid "experts" always seem available to testify as to any claim, no matter how patently absurd such claims sometimes are. I regret to say that I have often gone up against some of my colleagues in cases that seem ridiculous.

In one case, where a patient threw himself out of a hospital window, badly injuring himself, a colleague testified that it was the professional duty of the psychiatric consultant to have checked the window locks! When I asked him afterwards how he could have taken such a position, he just shrugged, and said, "It's a living!"

What this is all about, including attorneys bringing highly dubious cases, of course, is money. Defense attorneys, such as the Harvard group that I often work with, are paid by insurance companies or by the University, and are paid on an hourly basis. Those fees can be substantial, but not monumental.

Plaintiff attorneys, on the other hand, commonly charge their clients no regular fee at all. Instead, when they agree to take a case, they depend on getting a percentage of a potential settlement, commonly between a third to a half of the awarded amount. With the kind of awards or settlements that are sometimes made, these amounts can be astronomical. For example, one of my analytic patients was a malpractice attorney, which posed a bit of a countertransference problem. One day he came to his hour, announcing that he had just settled a big case. Based on his time he had put in on the case, he figured that he had made $20,000 an hour.

As he mused about this windfall, he remarked: "Well, what I made is even more than you charge, isn't it" (My fee at that point was $125). I replied, "It *was!*" which had the desired effect. The real countertransference issue, however, was not the money, but the unsavory questionable professional ethics. Because of the potential financial rewards, some attorneys succumb to marginal professional practices, including commonly running ads on television to attract new cases.

Most of my initial work involved patients with mental health issues, although it later expanded, in ways that I will describe. In addition, almost any kind of treatment situation that results in a disgruntled patient, can result in a law suit. One interesting group of cases resulted, for example, from the treatment of so-called "Multiple Personality Disorder" where several therapists got so fascinated with the symptomatology, they kept inadvertently calling forth additional personalities, which the patients were only too happy to provide.

A very common complaint in the case of depressed or anxious patients, where the treatment hasn't gone well, is "loss of consortium." This is legal jargon for lack of sexual activity, presumably due to the continuing mental disorder. If proven, this creates more financial compensation for the aggrieved parties.

The most common legal issue in more ordinary therapy situations are negative transference reactions gone wrong, in which the patient recreates and reenacts the pathology, rather than being able to create an alliance with the therapist to examine it. Not infrequently, the patient would have acted out the negative transference by bringing a legal action. Here again, the participation of the psychoanalytic expert plays a crucial role in clarifying whether the quality of treatment was maintained, regardless of an unfortunate outcome.

Some of these cases have involved cases by students in training to become psychoanalysts. Usually these involve a patient who has developed a very intense erotic, negative, or idealized transference, which has not proved amenable to interpretation, eventually resulting in the patient suing the therapist and the analytic society. In these cases, the plaintiff lawyer will argue that the inexperience of the student analyst has resulted in damage to the patient's livelihood or relationships. The counter argument by the defense is that, generally, individuals who undertake analytic training are already skilled therapists. In addition, each case and each candidate has multiple senior supervisors. Fortunately, I have yet to see such a case result in a negative decision for the student or the society, although it is extremely stressful, and can go on for years. Obviously, the expert witness in such cases must be senior psychoanalysts themselves.

As my experience as an expert witness increased, so did the number of law firms seeking to use me as a consultant, and the nature of the cases expanded as well, to include issues beyond the specific area of mental health. One area, for example, is that of family relations, namely divorce and child custody.

Once again, these are almost always adversarial. No matter how well-intentioned and determined an estranged husband and wife might be to reach a peaceful settlement, generally by the time the lawyers get through with them, they are at each other's throats. It is very common for one of the partners, usually the wife, to claim "mental cruelty," as an argument for obtaining a larger financial settlement. In some cases, expert witnesses are called in to assess the validity of the claims, and testify accordingly.

The same goes for cases where the parent's custody rights over who gets the children, and how much time with the child each parent gets, is at issue. Here too, expert witnesses may be called, and may even be asked to evaluate the children.

These kinds of cases, in particular, bring up the issue of the privacy of the therapist's records. If one or the other, or both parents have been in therapy, those therapy records cannot ordinarily be released without the permission of the patient. But in cases where one of the parties is claiming emotional damage, since the patient has put their mental health into the financial equation, those therapy records can be subpoenaed (accessed by court order) by the other side.

On the other hand, a patient's general medical record can be rather easily accessed. It might be of interest to know that the American Psychoanalytic Association, working through our Washington representatives, has been able to obtain special protection for "psychotherapy notes," which are separated from the general medical record, and cannot be released without the express permission of the patient, except in very special circumstances.

One of those circumstances is when the patient claims damage to their mental health, including in cases that are other than exclusively psychological. This brings us to the wide range of cases that I have increasingly become involved in, that are not primarily focused on some mental health issue. These are generally cases in which some malpractice is being alleged in medical or surgical conditions.

For example, if a hysterectomy is performed because of persistent bleeding problems, and there are surgical complications, extra financial claims are likely to be made to compensate for "pain and suffering," some of which may be alleged to be emotional. Such lawsuits may be filed about just about any medical or surgical procedure with a bad result, or even a negative reaction to a medication. Such cases are often accompanied by claims of psychological damage. Here too, the role of the expert witness in assessing the validity of such claims becomes crucial. My experience has been that the vast majority of such claims result from bad outcomes, not bad practice. I do occasionally see bad practice as well, and when I do, I don't hesitate to say so. The lawyers seem to appreciate that as well, so that they can know when they have a weak case.

There is absolutely no limit to the kinds of cases in which emotional damage might be alleged, and which might require the services of a psychological "expert." Let's say someone sues about a traffic accident, an injury on the job, a reaction to a chemical substance. Almost always in such cases, there is an allegation of "PTSD," Post-Traumatic Stress Disorder, a diagnosis which has become increasingly applied, or misapplied, often for legal reasons, when there is any hint of stress.

When this diagnosis originally was developed, I was a psychiatrist in the US Navy during Vietnam, seeing US Marines straight out of combat. Based on the experience of a number of us doing this kind of work, the old diagnosis of "Combat Fatigue" seemed inadequate, and was eventually replaced with "PTSD." This new diagnosis was intended to connote a reaction to a trauma that was so extreme, ordinary defenses were overwhelmed, and the individual was lastingly traumatized.

For reasons of insurance diagnoses and especially legal cases, the diagnosis has been appropriated for just about any moderately stressful situation. But here again, the role of the expert witness becomes crucial in determining when the diagnosis is appropriate, and when it is not, and when there is psychological damage, versus the normal stresses of life.

As a typical example, let's say a young woman has been working in an urban restaurant until late at night. She goes to her car in a nearby parking garage. A strange man suddenly appears, and attempts to rape her. The attack is forestalled by a chance passerby. The woman sues the owners of the restaurant, and also the owners of the parking garage. The charge is that the owners of the restaurant, and the owners of the garage, did not provide adequate security. While there is some physical injury, the main claim for damages is for PTSD, which the woman asserts has caused her to experience constant anxiety, depression, sleeplessness, and "flashbacks" (recurrent memories of the traumatic event). She also claims that, due to these symptoms, she is unable to work, care for her children, or have sex with her husband ("loss of consortium").

In a case such as this, the claim for damages depends on the culpability that can be proven for the owners of the two establishments, the degree of physical and emotional damage that can be established for the patient, her husband and her family, the costs for medical and psychological treatment, and an estimation of her lost income, both since the event and into the future.

It becomes the responsibility of the expert witness to determine whether all of this makes psychological sense, whether it fits the criteria for the diagnosis of PTSD, and whether there have been serious attempts at appropriate treatment. Needless to say, all of these symptoms tend to get much worse as soon as the patient consults an attorney, which also becomes part of the evidence. In a case of this magnitude, the expert witness might be called upon to do a direct evaluation and assessment of the patient herself, which might involve multiple visits and written reports.

In a case such as this, the role of the psychological or psychoanalytic consultant becomes absolutely critical. Depending on how receptive the jury is to the observations of the "expert," the outcome of the case might differ, one way or the other, by quite literally millions of dollars.

There is another group of cases which might seem quite unusual, but illustrate the point that allegations of psychological damage can be made about almost any situation. My office is near Boston, Massachusetts. Boston has a large Catholic population, and extensive Catholic schools, universities, and churches. Boston has been more or less the eye of the storm in the "priest/pedophile" scandal, meaning that priests were being accused of sexually molesting children. It became even more of a scandal because it was alleged that the Archdiocese had been avoiding the issue, or possibly even covering it up, for many years.

The Archdiocese was referred to me by several law firms with whom I had consulted. Thereafter, I evaluated cases involving not only priests, but parochial schoolteachers. These cases usually involved the concept of "recovered memory." In other words, these were adults who had "suddenly remembered," usually at the suggestion of an unskilled therapist, that, as children, they had been sexually molested by a priest or teacher.

I never saw a case where I was convinced that the recovered "memory" was accurate. For the most part, these individuals seemed to be rather marginal, and easily suggestible people. Naturally, they had all been diagnosed as suffering from PTSD. Here again the role of the expert is crucial. PTSD or not? My actual feeling, for the most part, was that they had indeed been traumatized, not by their priests, but by their therapists! It seemed that the therapist had gotten caught up in an "acting out" of the transference, with a particular need to "rescue" these particularly appealing and sometimes seductive patients, and in so doing, had repeated the original trauma or the consequent wish for idealized rescuing "parents." The whole psychodrama then got further enacted in a lawsuit against the presumed "villains," the offending and disappointing caretakers, now "stand-ins" for the traumatizing original caretakers.

The dilemma of "recovered memory" of course has a long history, especially in our own profession, going all the way back to Freud discovering that so many of his patients seemed to have been sexually molested. The case of the "Wolf Man" supposedly witnessing his parents having anal intercourse is a particularly poignant example.

Freud never seemed to be able to quite decide whether such reportings by his patients were real or fantasy. Of course, that is the whole issue of the concept and use of the therapeutic technique of "reconstruction." Real or not? My own way of dealing with it, is akin to dealing with a dream. It has emotional reality, but one can never be sure about the objective reality. Fortunately, the emotional reality is the important one. As an "expert" testifying on these matters, I have followed a similar course.

To summarize, the range of human dilemmas that get recreated and "acted out" in the courtroom is truly infinite. But this, in a sense, is no different from the human dramas that we all see in our offices every day. In a very real sense, taking on the challenge of being an expert witness is yet another opportunity to bring psychoanalytic knowledge into the community, but in a practical and broad way. We need to harken back to what I think was one of the most important statements Freud ever made about psychoanalysis. What he said, to paraphrase, was that psychoanalysis as a treatment modality could never hope to reach more than a very limited number of people. The most important potential effect of psychoanalysis, in his view, was to influence public policy.

Expert witness work gives us a chance to do just that. While the work itself is not only interesting, but sometimes downright riveting, and while it is financially rewarding, the real issue is the opportunity to bring psychoanalytic principles to public attention. But even more importantly, it is an opportunity to encode those psychoanalytic principles into the body of law. The term "jurisprudence" means, in one sense, the collective wisdom represented in the body of law. But more than that, it represents the cumulative social wisdom of a culture. The way legal judgments operate in the USA, and I would guess elsewhere, is that each legal decision is supposed to be firmly rooted in the principles of prior decisions; "precedence" is the term, and it is supposed to form the foundation for future legal decisions.

Each legal case that is influenced, or decided on the basis of expert psychoanalytic testimony, represents, quite literally, an opportunity to make a lasting psychoanalytic contribution to the collective knowledge, wisdom, and principles of a social culture. And that should be an opportunity that we could all welcome and embrace.

Reference

Katz, J., Goldstein, J., & Dershowitz, A. (1967) *Psychoanalysis, Psychiatry and the Law*. New York: Free Press.

Chapter 19

The role of the forensic psychiatrist and the psychoanalyst who become double agents between clinical and judicial rationales

Andrea Marzi and Gabriele Gragnoli

Introduction

Our aim is to make an in-depth study of the psychiatric expert witness as a "double agent" in his relations with the Court.[1] We will naturally be speaking of the situation in Italy and do not know if this problem is generalizable, although we believe that there must surely be common features in the various provisions and norms across nations, despite their differing judicial systems.

It is however within the scope of the present volume to suggest the possibility of an international dialogue. We are aware that we will be presenting more problems than solutions, but this is appropriate to the complexity and uncertainty of the subject, which we will address by also offering some judicial elucidations, without which it is impossible to understand the overall picture.

The expert witness between lights and shadows

The forensic psychiatrist still finds himself having to question his actual role within the judicial system, the true scientific nature of some aspects of his work before the judge, and his substantial ambivalence, if not ambiguity, in relation to the patient who is the subject of his expertise.

Thorny dilemmas emerge out of the difficult encounter between clinical and legal rationales, where the topics of culpability and danger to society form the doctrinal fulcrum on which are articulated the most severe criticisms of them. From this emerges with dramatic clarity the figure of the forensic psychiatrist compelled to address matters which lie outside his clinical training and experience, and which do not constitute rigorously professional entities, but are demands more appropriate to the social, even socio-political sphere, despite being necessary and justified from the viewpoint of criminal law.

It is precisely the concepts of culpability and threat posed to society which determine the difficulties and ambivalences. The concept of threat in particular has for many years now been the subject of a series of profound critical studies, which have brought to light the clear "impossibility of predicting recidivism on the basis of aspects of the criminal's personality" (Bandini and Gatti, 1982). The concepts of culpability and threat continue to produce a dimension of supposed techno-scientific rigour, which frustrates a genuine approach to the rationales of clinical diagnosis (given that this is theoretically what it should be dealing with) but also, sometimes with disturbing obviousness, the rationales of justice.

Many other features tend to influence the effective role of the expert witness in the sphere of the administration of justice at the moment of the encounter with the patient under investigation: from the duty to maintain confidentiality in a milieu which requires instead that the expert–patient relationship be made public, to the further problem of patient consent to the practice of the required expertise, and lastly to the substantial change of techno-scientific horizon posed by the acknowledgment of an action – that of expert witness – which is no longer clinical and therapeutic, but exquisitely medical and legal. Here there is the high risk of a mutual overlap, which seems to confuse the roles and responsibilities of the judge and the expert witness.

Ambiguity is the essential, dramatic characteristic of the expert witness's position in this environment; an ambivalence which has for several decades been accurately defined as that of the "double agent," where the expert witness is at the centre of conflicting demands, each with their own distinctive "truths" and constantly colliding with each other.

Notes on the judicial regulations concerning expert testimony

Expert testimony is governed by article 220 of our current code of criminal procedure, which specifies the cases in which it must be deployed:

> Expertise is admitted when it is necessary to undertake investigations or to acquire data or assessments which require specific technical, scientific, or artistic competences. Except when provided for in passing sentence or assessing degrees of safety, expertise is not admissible for the purpose of establishing the habitual or professional nature of the offence, the likelihood of offending, the character and personality of the accused, and his psychological qualities in general, independent of pathological causes.
>
> (Italian Code of Criminal Procedure, 2018. Translated for the present edition)

The sole remit of the judge is therefore to assess the substance of the premises according to which, if they are confirmed, expertise must *necessarily* be applied. This is an abandonment of the faculty which – *sic et simpliciter* – had been attributed to him by the code previously in force, which imposed no obligation to give an appropriate and convincing reason for the choice made.

In open derogation of the principal provision expressed in section 1 of article 190 of the current code of criminal procedure, which allows the parties to take the initiative in requesting the admission of evidence, expertise can be called on by the judge in conformance with art. 224 of the criminal code. This initiative constitutes one of the exceptions for which the same article 190, section 2, had to provide when it was inserted into the new code of criminal procedure in 1989, because of the many speculations that have weakened the accusatorial stamp which should have characterized the new ordinance: "The law itself establishes the cases in which evidence is to be admitted." (Italian Code of Criminal Procedure, 2018; translated for the present edition).

It is "the ascertaining of the capacity of the defendant" (art. 70 of the current criminal code), which introduces one of the essential, if not the principal, themes which psychiatric investigation is called upon to address: *culpability* – that is, the capacity for understanding and volition (art. 85 of the criminal code), elements which must obtain both at the moment in which the offence was committed and during the unfolding of the trial.

The nineteenth-century concept of capacity/incapacity for understanding and volition, transformed by art. 70 of the code of criminal procedure into the more modern "being able or unable to take part consciously in the trial," represents the pivot around which the different realities of clinical practice and the trial still confront each other. The psychiatric expert witness must simultaneously inhabit both these realities, tolerating different logics and goals, distinctive languages and lexical incongruities, which represent spaces too narrow for reflection on and analysis of their meanings. These difficulties push him inexorably towards a thoroughgoing identity crisis from which it is impossible to escape.

According to the judicial lexicon, *culpability* is to be understood as possession on the part of the subject of the functions necessary for perceiving external reality and grasping the negative value of his own actions and omissions (capacity for understanding) and for controlling his impulse to act (capacity for volition). The subsistence of these elements, summed up as "culpability," is matched by the correlative criminal responsibility which becomes attributable and must be incurred in its entirety: conviction and penalty.

Nevertheless, however much the dry definition of these judicial concepts may make them appear clear and simple, the same cannot be said of any equivalents that we may seek in clinical language.

Nor is it the case if we compare the other judicial category summed up concisely as *suitas* (that is, consciousness and willed action). It can in fact come about that the acting subject, while possessing consciousness and willed action, really intends – in the grip of madness – to carry out the offence, without however being capable of comprehending the negative value and the consequences of such conduct; for these reasons he will not be culpable in the meaning of art. 85 of the criminal code (Lusa and Pascasi, 2014).

The task of the forensic psychiatrist becomes still more arduous where he has to address gradations of what it is already difficult to define in its entirety: that is, when he has to investigate, according to the provisions of art. 89 of the criminal code, whether because of "mental incompetency" – another judicial category with vague boundaries – the capacity for intention and volition has been *greatly diminished*, without being completely eliminated. The positive outcome of such an evaluation will entail an equivalent reduction in criminal responsibility. Indeed, it is anticipated that, given diminished comprehension of the crime committed for reasons of pathology, the Court must hand down a correspondingly lower level of penalty.

So it is clearer than ever that the law must obtain elements of indisputable knowledge from the clinical investigation, when it is on the contrary obvious that this cannot be the case: the overall psychiatric assessment of the subject is far too broad and complex to be easily contained within a set of paradigms and archetypes.

Indeed it is widely claimed that "beyond the diagnostic identification proper to the traditional psychiatric approach, the acknowledgement of the possible relationship between psychopathological symptoms and cerebral activity becomes of prime importance when what is cited in evidence must not only be the *capacity for understanding and volition*, in a purely judicial sense, but the functioning of the person as a whole" (Zara, 2013, p. 324; italics in original. Translated for the present edition).

The legal system's intrinsic need to reach the truth all too clearly conceals many dangers of a legal-procedural nature which directly cut across the roles of all those involved in the trial, confusing their tasks and functions.

Expert testimony acquires an attribution of ever-greater scientific exactitude, also thanks to the rapid evolution of research in the field of neuropsychiatry. These mechanisms have surreptitiously introduced practices and misdirections which radically undermine the fundamental principles on which the trial is founded: first and foremost, the adversarial system.

According to one line of jurisprudential and doctrinal thought, which has numerous proponents, expertise could be defined as a neutral means of ascertaining proof (Cass. Pen. sec. IV 4/5/2011 n. 33734). This assumption, which seems not to aim at endowing expertise with the function of obtaining decisive proof, does not depend on the cooperation of the parties, and is not classifiable as being either "advantageous" or "prejudicial" to the defendant and instead ends up obtaining the opposite result (Lembo, 2015, p. 21).

Assigning a sort of outcome *super partes* to the investigation endorses its findings in absolute terms, preventing the inquisitorial dialectic, which is the fulcrum of the criminal process.

> The definitive statement is, however, disavowed by those who instead maintain that, although the expert is a technical witness nominated by the judge because of his particular competence, and sharing with the judge a position of impartiality equidistant between the parties, the result of the appraisal depends nevertheless to a large degree on the pre-selected method and its application in practice; operations which afford a high level of discretion to the expert who, despite his being a third party in both institutional and functional terms, could also be a bad scientist, making an incorrect use of his own cognitive heritage.
>
> (Zecchinon, 2013)

Art. 468 of the criminal code confirms the impossibility of considering expertise as neutral as any other means of establishing proof: it authorizes the parties to request the examination of expert witnesses and the citation of contrary evidence from experts not included in the official list. The rule in question acts as a safeguard for the emergence of proof within the debate, the fruit of the adversarial process, the natural confrontation between the parties in the trial.

This idea could be evaluated differently: the indisputability of expertise, that neutral means of establishing proof, and the close interdependence between expert and judge end up homogenizing the commissioner and commissioned and rendering their respective positions indistinct, with understandable consequences.

The institutional reasons why a certain surreptitious form of transfer of the judicial function to the expert which would ultimately require the judge to rely no longer on the law but on science, are stated in article 101 of the Italian Constitution.

Indeed, we cannot forget that the judiciary, of which each individual judge is a representative (Barbera and Fusaro, 2016, p. 544), is that power of the state which is called on to exercise the fundamental function of giving concrete application to the judicial norms. Although not elected, the judicial organs enjoy an indirect form of legitimacy to the extent that they are answerable only to the law (Guarnieri, 1979, p. 34).

Art. 101, sec. 2 of the Italian Constitution does indeed aim at formally subordinating the judge to the principle of legality, "and formally therefore to the force and tenor, determined and positive, of the law" (Pisani, 2013, p. 562. Translated for the present edition).

The Italian Constitutional Court itself stated that art. 101, sec. 2 Const. "expresses the requirement for the judge to be directed only by the law with regard to the rules to be applied in giving judgement, and therefore that no other authority can give the judge orders or suggestions about how to pass judgement" (Const. Court n. 40, 1964. Translated for the present edition). Not even science.

In other words, the expert expresses the voice of the professional category to which he belongs, a category not embedded in the system of state and constitutional powers, and therefore has no role that might act as a guarantee, nor any independence as a third party. These considerations make it still more urgent that the judge should be placed in a position where he can evaluate the scientific data that are introduced into the trial, so as to ensure that he does not, at the most deeply judicial moment, reduce his own function to the mere certification of whatever expert testimony turns out to be most persuasive (Moccheggiani, 2017).

Expert witness, threat posed to society, and risk assessment

On the expert's side we find the further difficulty represented by the fact that the apparatus of justice has a strong desire to draw on a largely "compartmentalized" classification of the mentally ill offender, while clinical and criminological reflection has for decades insisted on the presence of so-called "degrees of psychic freedom" in the mentally ill, with sane and ill parts coexisting in the same subject (which is in line with certain important classical psychoanalytic positions: that of Bion, for example). This state of affairs continues to present itself as one of the most arduous dilemmas (at least on the theoretical level) in forensic psychiatric assessment. Faced with this reality, the individual subjected to expert assessment cannot end up being schematically and immediately inserted into a "partial" or "total" assemblage of cognitive, volitional, emotional elements which can be capable, by their presence or absence, of determining a rigid forensic diagnosis, which, in turn, might be translated into quanta of culpability, as is required by our criminal code.

The expert witness ends up fatally generalizing (or often risks doing so) what is only a part, however important and extensive, going so far in extreme cases as to treat the subject like the "Visconte Dimezzato" (Bisected Viscount), as Italo Calvino (1952) reminds us.

Furthermore, the expert examination, even when not being admitted among the means of ascertaining proof, is used on the applied side as thorough, "undoubtedly" decisive proof of character, as if it were endowed with the same characteristics, the same "evidence," as those from which the adjudicating body derives its judicial truth. Thus the expert witness risks becoming a potential judge of the accused, artificially extrapolating and decontextualizing the individual under examination.

It is moreover necessary to emphasize clearly that the expert witness cannot evaluate generic neuroanatomies or neurophysiologies, nor even chromosome maps, but internal psychic conditions which may have a bearing on illness related to criminal conduct.

We are in search of a justice that might conjoin the rigour of the scientific method with the abandonment of an approximating and reductionist method. But we must ask ourselves if the introduction of risk assessment and/or neuroscientific maps, which inevitably lead to restricted, or even ultra-specific localizations of crime-friendly potentialities, do not embody precisely that indefatigable reductionism which we are trying to avoid. Let's try to go a little deeper into this very important aspect.

We know that research has shown the validity and significance of certain risk factors in the enactment of violent and criminal behaviors. Applied research has attested to the validity of instruments designated for assessing the risk of violence and of reoffending over time. We also know that mentally disturbed people share the same risk factors and processes present in the mentally healthy population. From this point of view, a history of violence and a criminal career are key indicators.[2]

In this connection, for almost three decades a shift of emphasis has been sought away from the concept of threat posed to society towards that of risk assessment as a method of giving ever more accurate responses in a controversial field.

It is an area of research in which risk certainly has a biological, psychological, psychopathological, family or social origin, with its own temporality and dynamics.

An ever-greater precision and accuracy in the instruments used is therefore a *conditio sine qua non* for avoiding traps created by expert discretion, even though in the Anglo-Saxon world "58 per cent of experts in the forensic context use different instruments for assessing risk" (Zara, 2016, p. 18).

The integration of these heuristic models should help us say what kind of pathology affects the subject of expertise and what he has committed and what level of risk he poses, but above all who he is, how he has functioned, and how he probably will continue to function (Zara, 2016).

However, this tells us that in the end it is the clinical dimension, marginalized by this approach, which nevertheless reappears authoritatively in the necessity, for example, for assessment of what is needed to induce criminal behavior. This is a clinical dimension to which is given the not unfamiliar task of taking responsibility for rare and untypical events: in other words, those that, while rare and insignificant on the level of general understanding, have often been over-exploited in directing judgments and beliefs.

In this connection, it must be reiterated that the possibility of an unexpected event occurring – the textbook example, which is characterized by its unexpected (or apparently unexpected) character – is often not foreseeable. The proponents of risk assessment, who have brought it to such prominence, tend strangely to delegate to the "clinical sensibility" – *a posteriori*, what's more – the necessity for giving a meaning to this event.

If all this turns out to be of great interest and a helpful line of research and application in the future, then to this undoubted characteristic is added the impression that the substantially psychological/psychometric stance is directed towards an assessment that is held to be aseptic and neutral, scotomizing however the fact that the observer is no such thing, and therefore distancing oneself from the object of research with a view to obtaining heuristic purity falters badly. The idea that risk assessment is a scientific instrument and therefore "certain"

regarding the clinical fallacy (to which many taxonomic and therapeutic "problems" are nevertheless delegated), and is directed towards
avoiding contamination by the malfunctions of expertise, and avoiding
the mixing of the expert's role with that of the judge, and so on, is of
course a fine thing to wish for. However, the impression is that, along
with the innumerable scales of statistical evaluation – efficient, certainly, and ever more sophisticated – we may be creating a condition
in which we really are not sure – while promoting ourselves as being
so – that the factors selected are truly decisive, or even so precise as
to be indisputable, or at least probabilistically precise enough to offer
assessments that avoid reductionism, determinism, and evaluative bias
caused by over- or underestimating the value of the evidence.

The anxiety which seems to pervade these positions concerns the
fact that, despite strenuous efforts, it is always unlikely that absolute
certainties and truths can be achieved. Anxiety about the unknown is
highly present in the field of expertise. Moreover, a position oriented
in a different direction tends to become mechanical because it ends
up considering the individual under expert investigation as a mere
object, reifying him and putting him at a distance, in the conviction that scientific exactitude and objectivity can be achieved in
direct proportion to the distance between the subject and object of
investigation.

The "trial's truth" is moreover achieved within contingently temporal dimensions and contexts, and within the bounds of the trial procedure itself.

This offers us no comfort at all. Of course, the shift from the "plaster
cast" imposed by the prevalence of the concept of social hazard to
the evaluative dimension of the theoretical and practical world of risk
assessment is a highly significant opportunity in this field. The path it
opens must be travelled to its full extent and further refined.

And yet the impression arises that this theoretical slant – one which
slightly promotes the psychological approach over the clinical and psychiatric in the provision of expert testimony – is not exempt, in spite
of constant denials, from the attempt to obtain sufficient knowledge
to map out all human projects in an objective manner, excluding subjective factors as irritating inconveniences, and expanding a method
believed to be scientifically rigorous into the most diverse areas of

reality. This risks increasing not the certainty of the diagnosis but the ambiguity of the expert witness and the judge.

In the end, when all is said and done, it does not seem that the heart of the matter is the opposition between clinical practice – held to be inadequate, fallacious, *démodé* – and psychometric psychology, held instead to be efficient, the science of the future; rather it is the predominance of the still muddled, obscure, and endlessly misleading concept of hazard. Risk assessment, though it challenges the outworn concept of danger to society and contributes important behavioral studies, nevertheless risks showing itself to be acquiescing in the judge's usual requests, while at the same time claiming to be outside, with a sleight of hand that does not help to make matters any clearer.

Besides, together with what we have now underlined, not even the neo-positivist return to psychic biology, neuroscientific investigations, or the dogged search for organic markers which would confirm the possible, and in some respects obvious, neurobiological substratum of mental disorder, still seem to offer a certain and reliable passport towards that proposed objectivity we have previously mentioned. This is not only because, on the scientific plane, decisive, "absolute" discoveries in this field are still a long way off, but also and perhaps above all, because the subjective, dynamic, and relational element is destined to re-emerge constantly in the forensic psychiatric sphere.

The enthusiasm for the possibility of resolving many dilemmas in the field of forensic psychiatry with the ever more fascinating discoveries of the neurosciences, sometimes considered to be a sort of philosopher's stone of expertise, opens up a lasting ambivalence, if not ambiguity, when it comes to translating these elements into assessments, with regard to the increase or diminution of culpability, for example. And again: the expert witness, having to respond to the question about danger to society, finds himself faced with the well-known dilemma of the possibility of forming false positives or false negatives because of the undeniable imprecision of a clinical judgment regarding a request from a judicial source.

Lastly, it must be added that the possible increase of requests in the service of monitoring and social defence (as may be expected to result from, for example, the progressive and hasty closure of psychiatric secure units) risks creating a rise in over-prediction.

The two-faced psychiatrist

In the thorny conflict between clinical practice and the law there also emerges a certain vagueness in the ethical recommendations, so that the psychiatrist as expert witness ends up finding himself without clear, codified directives concerning what is genuinely ethical and appropriate for his function, and this contributes to the stirring up of controversial conditions around expertise and the outcomes arising from it.

So the very institution of expertise embodies characteristics of ambiguity and doubleness that are then consequently dumped on the institutional figure of the psychiatrist as expert witness, the true double agent of the situation.

Moreover, the duty to act on behalf of institutions and subjects other than the patient is another of the central components of the psychiatric expert's split loyalty, of his inevitable double dealing. This condition of splitting tends to obscure and contaminate, more or less covertly, the correct and "ideal" ethical conduct. The expert ends up being answerable to a plurality of "organizations," such as the court, the mass media, politics, public opinion, and society, with multiple and divergent interests and needs.

If his position is that of *amicus curiae*, he cannot help but act as if he were exercising a function of social control. Where he "defends interests other than those of the patient" (Halmosh, 1986, 214) or of the judge – in other words, acts as consultant to one of the parties – he can only once again adopt an ambiguous position which confuses him, sometimes even about himself. Indeed, the psychiatrist very often ends up considering himself objective, neutral, and oriented towards the best interests of everyone, entirely avoiding the recognition that he is in the risky position of double agent, a position subject to obvious denial.

Consent and confidentiality

It is the predominant presence of the public interest to permit (without however being able to justify it at all) the modification (and for some the actual violation, if even a one-off concession is made) of the private doctor–patient relationship. In this sphere it is therefore inevitable that we take the topic of consent and confidentiality into consideration.

We know that the patient in a forensic milieu presents concurrent needs and interests which conflict with those of other entities involved in the unfolding of the legal process.

Consent in this context must be obtained both in the judicial sense and in the technical and operational sense, but it is highly probable that this necessity will be experienced by the individual under investigation with ill-concealed suspicion. There is often a risk of forgetting the cardinal principle of *nemo tenetur se detegere*, in addition to which there arises the further dangerous possibility that, for the individual under investigation, the expert examination is transformed into a situation where he is unable to represent himself perfectly and to comprehend the roles, objectives, and expert "games," and for the expert a situation in which he betrays not only the patients' best interests, but also his inalienable human rights.[3]

In this sphere too, consent requires that the subject of the investigation be given information beforehand. It is a central rule for the mental health professional that he keep the patient/subject under investigation fully informed, using discernment and prudence. One of the most important rules for the psychiatrist is that of not utilizing the doctor–patient relationship in an inappropriate manner to encourage the subject to reveal information without it being clear who the psychiatrist is representing and what use will be made of the information elicited.

The problem remains open and controversial: let's take as a textbook example, the formidable problems which crop up around the validity of consent, however "informed," obtained from individuals currently in the grip of a mental illness.

Further doubts arise with regard to the problem of confidentiality. It is this, more than anything else, which highlights the contentious question of the forensic psychiatrist as double agent who, revealing and making public the personal information which the examined subject has provided, places himself on the scales which weigh, on the one hand, the expectations of the law which requires rich technical data, and on the other the indispensable *primum non nocere*, the ancient and still current foundation of correct medical action (alongside its twin *neminem laedere*, "especially binding for the doctor because of his power" (Barni, 1989, p. 12).

So the expert witness is faced with a great responsibility in discharging the task assigned to him by the judge and at the same time protecting the accused from the dissemination of information which could be used against him.

Here we come upon the need to find a delicate balance between the quantity and quality of information to be obtained, and the duty to adduce only what is relevant to specific medico-legal tasks.

The picture is further complicated if we bring psychoanalytic reflection to our aid. We know that the responsibility which psychoanalysis speaks about is quite different from that understood by justice. The fact under investigation may be the same, but not the profound objective that one is trying to clarify and bring to light. Indeed, as long ago as 1906, in the lecture "Psychoanalysis and the establishment of the facts in legal proceedings" (Freud, 1906), Freud had delineated differences and mismatches between the action of the subject on the strictly clinical level and his categorizable behavior in the judicial context.[4]

Psychoanalysis can certainly enlighten us about the motivations which sustain moral values in individuals, but it is very difficult to say something about the essence of those moral values, which only makes its participation in the judicial world still more complicated.

In essence, the gaze nurtured by psychoanalytic attention also poses once again the ethical problem which cuts across it in this field. If it becomes too difficult to achieve an absolute truth – understood as objective, factual, singular, static, certain – what emerges is the constant reinvention of a much more disturbing and, in certain respects, "catastrophic" relativity, to be understood as dynamic, changing, polygonal, and therefore the herald of uncertain values which can only conflict, dramatically, with the judicial mode of thought. It is evident that all this entails considerable "gymnastics" for both judge and psychiatrist, who find themselves as it were at cross-purposes in a confusing and dangerous way, in carrying out their respective tasks which become ever more unhelpfully mixed together.

Culpability and competency

In current practice, at least in Italy, the enquiry about competency also comes into the tasks entrusted to the psychiatric expert witness, and is linked to the central question of culpability.

It is not unusual for the technical opinion on culpability to risk being transformed by the magistrate into a moral opinion about the freedom of the subject to be judged. This dissonance between law and psychiatry gives rise to the problematic translatability of the category of in/capacity for understanding and volition in a psychiatric diagnosis.

In the attempt to find a middle ground, the choice has for a long time been made to overuse the "diagnosis" of partial mental defect, to say the least a dubious pronouncement from the psychiatric viewpoint, but one which in the past was prompted by at least three demands: that of psychiatry, according to which diagnoses of total incapacity are antitherapeutic; that put forward both by psychiatry and by substantial sectors of the civil liberties lobby, to limit as far as possible (if not to eliminate) pronouncements of danger to society, and thereby to avoid admissions to psychiatric secure units (which are now being closed down); and the complementary demand, advanced in the name of justice, for the defence and security of society, for not setting free those who have committed crimes (Pitch, 1989).

The incapacity for understanding and volition correlated to culpability, which on the theoretical/clinical level is constantly judged to be inadequate, if not incomprehensible, nevertheless still forms the fundamental *trait d'union* between law and clinical psychiatry. The forced osmosis from one nature to another in the end reveals the socio-politico-ideological rationales which have informed it.

In this context we may sometimes note warnings about the offender's personality traits, motivations, and tendencies (despite this being explicitly forbidden by art. 314 Code of Criminal Procedure).

Or else, with an inadvertent drift towards narcissism, the expert witness can try to transform the interview into a third degree foreign to the nature of his expertise, and with professional nimbleness tends to turn himself into "an absurd psycho-cop who has lost his own clinical and medico-legal coordinates" (Marzi, 1990, 1992, 2002. See also Bollas & Sundelson, 1995; Bollas, 2001).

Psychoanalytically-informed conceptions of this subject, from a range of schools, were offered even in the quite distant past. Gregory Zilboorg's (1943) well-known position was especially radical: he attended court proceedings and maintained that if in his opinion the prisoner at the bar was mad, he had to assert candidly, in order to stay true to his professional conscience and the Hippocratic Oath, that first of all he did not understand the question, and that secondly, for this very reason, he could not know whether the accused was mad or not.

Alexander and Staub (1931) showed themselves to be more accommodating, suggesting that the problem of infirmity could be addressed on cognitive bases concerning the capacity for comprehension and representation, and for freedom of choice in action, although by doing so one could only "render the conscious personality responsible for actions: which means to say that we conduct ourselves as if the conscious ego had the power over human conduct that it would like. The way we are organized is entirely without foundation from the theoretical viewpoint, but it has a practical, or rather tactical, justification" (p. 35; translated for this publication).

On their own, these concepts can only turn out to be dramatically insufficient.[5]

What constitutes the real theoretical and professional-ethical crux is the need for a concept which – though already insufficient and open to criticism in itself – should be translated into a "quantum" of punishment or into a solution with a penal character, whatever kind that may be. Although, legally speaking, this is the province not of the psychiatrist but of the judge, the former nevertheless acts as a link in a chain which is simultaneously doctrinal and procedural, two aspects which are unlikely to be reconciled.

Conclusions

If we cannot propose solutions, we can nevertheless express the conviction that such a question must certainly not be addressed by breaking it up into convenient segments with doubtful scientific status.

No directive imposed from on high can definitively solve the theoretical, operational, and ethical problems which emerge in forensic psychiatric practice and which on the contrary impose the duty to relativize on the cultural, doctrinal, historical, and lastly implementational plane what only a Manichaean outlook can consider as absolute.

All this undoubtedly multiplies the already notable complexity of the matter in hand and should compel us into a profound theoretical, judicial, and forensic-psychiatric re-elaboration, making evident the artificiality of certain schematizations of practice and the teachings which inform it, to the benefit of the possibility of accepting expert testimony as one possible outcome from the totality of scientific probability, rather than be accepted as absolute or certain (Pollack, 1973) which only produces a spuriously scientific fit between the clinical and the judicial.

The impossibility of finding a homogeneous solution underlines still further that an adequate and correct forensic psychiatric setup would have to solidly endorse the objective of seeking a "truth" (however mutable and changing), which might really assist in the comprehension of the subject and the act, but not promote its classification as a penal instrument, as is attested with disturbing frequency in practice.

So a round table is needed in which these poorly reconciled fields can enter into a dialogue by thinking the matter through deeply. Permit us to be somewhat puzzled and sceptical about the likelihood of this occurring. The present historical and socio-political conditions do not favor the composition of this encounter, leading rather towards a loss of contact between the parties, in a growing lack of interest in the rationales governing mental health. In the juvenile field, which is not the specific subject of the present study, we are probably glimpsing better collaborations, in a better mediation of the best interests of the minor, with clinical programmes which may be encouraging. And yet this mediation is achieved every time that, beyond the prescriptions of the court, there is an encounter between a mental health professional and a judge who are sensitive and open-minded in listening to each other about the psyche's side of the matter. But when this happens it arises out of the contingent, existing circumstances, not from the prescriptions of some normative procedure.

In this, psychoanalysis can make a substantial contribution, without reserve, without aloofness. It is a challenge that we cannot ignore.

Notes

1   This chapter was translated by Adam Elgar.
2   We can add, more generally this time, difficulties in anger management and aggression, lack of impulse control, being male, and early onset as also

being indicative of a possible disturbance in behavior. The consumption of narcotics is of decisive significance, as is the presence of an anti-social personality disorder, sometimes defined, using an old term, as psychopathy. Weight is also given in this to a previous history of hospitalization and the absence of family support.

3 While in general it is obviously necessary to obtain consent in an unequivocal and legally appropriate manner, and therefore with rigorous documentation which is, as far as possible, unchallengeable, it must be emphasized that in a broadly psychiatric field it is a characteristic which poses itself as necessarily diachronic. This appears to hold true both with regard to patients in general, but still more in relation to the patient who is mentally ill. From the clinical point of view, the patient's consent to treatment is a condition realized every time the patient – whatever position he may find himself in – makes himself available to enter into a relationship where he trusts and relies on the mental health professional.

4 However, it should be noted that in his lecture, Freud proposed the comparison of psychoanalytic theory and method with the particular technique which in those years was developing with dizzying speed, and which went under the name of Tatbestandsdiagnostik (translated by Strachey as "Establishment of the Facts in Legal Proceedings"), consisting in the attempt to obtain, by means of verbal associations requested from witnesses or accused, an objective ascertainment of the truth, even and especially in the juridical context. This is therefore a technique inserted into the field of the psychology of testimony. Although Freud stresses some analogies closely relevant to the comparison of the two techniques (the psychoanalytic and that of the establishment of facts), he seems in general to emphasise the profound difference between their theoretical and operational presuppositions. He will return to the problem of the criminal personality in the fundamental paper, "Criminals from a sense of guilt" (1916).

5 It is not within the scope of the present work to offer an examination of the numerous psychoanalytic positions regarding the encounter between psychoanalysis and the law.

References

Alexander F., & Staub, H. (1931). *The Criminal, the Judge and the Public.* New York: Collier. [Il delinquente, il giudice e il pubblico (1973). Giuffré, Milano.]

Bandini, T., & Gatti U. (1982). Perizia psichiatrica e perizia criminologica. Riflessioni sul ruolo del perito nell'ambito del processo penale, *Riv. It. Med. Legale, 2*, 231.

Barbera, A., & Fusaro, C. (2016). *Corso di diritto costituzionale, III ed.* Bologa: Il Mulino.

Barni, M. (1989). La deontologia medica. In AA.VV., *Guida all'esercizio professionale*. Turin: Edizioni Medico-Scientifiche.

Bollas, C. (2001). The case for confidentiality in psychoanalysis. Unpublished manuscript.

Bollas, C., & Sundelson, D. (1995). *The New Informants*. London: Karnac.

Calvino, I. (1952). *Il Visconte dimezzato (The bisected Viscount)*. Turin: Einaudi.

Const. Court n. 40 (1964). Prima Serie Speciale della Gazzetta Ufficiale.

Freud, S. (1906). Psychoanalysis and the establishment of the facts in legal proceedings, *SE, 9*, 103–109.

——— (1916). Criminals from a sense of guilt. In Some character-types met with in Psycho-analytic work. *SE, 14*, 311.

Guarnieri, C. (1979). L'indipendenza della magistratura. Rivista trimestrale di diritto e procedura civile, 1, pp. 29–56.

Halmosh, A. (1986). The expert witness: The trap of the medical certificate. In A. Carmi, S. Schneider, & A. Hefez (Eds.), *Psychiatry, Law and Ethics* (p. 214). Berlin and New York: Springer-Verlag.

Italian Code of Criminal Procedure (2018). Giuffrè, Milano.

Lembo, M.S. (2015). La perizia nel processo penale. In A.M. Casale, M.S. Lembo, & P. De Pasquali (Eds.), *La perizia psichiatrica nel processo penale*. Rimini: Maggioli.

Lusa V., & Pascasi, S. (2014). Profili Criminali e psicopatologici del reo. In A.M. Casale, M.S. Lembo, & P. De Pasquali (Eds.), *Profili criminali e psicopatologici del reo*. Rimini: Maggioli.

Marzi, A. (1990). Compiti e funzioni medico-legali. In V. Fineschi et al. *Il nuovo codice di deontologia medica*. In Giuffrè, Milano, Seconda edizione, pp. XXXII–537, 389 e segg.

——— (1992). *Deontologia e Psichiatria*, pp. XI–250. Milan: Giuffrè.

——— (2002). Confidentiality and the psychoanalytical setting in Italy: Some problematic issues. EPF Annual Conference, Prague, April 4–7, 2002.

Moccheggiani, M. (2017). Sapere scientifico e ruolo del giudice. *Il Mulino –* fasc. 3, 2017), Bologna.

Pisani, M. (2013). Il giudice, la legge e l'art. 101, co. 2, Cost., in Rivista italiana di diritto e procedura penale, 2, pp. 558–572.

Pitch, T. (1989). *Responsabilità limitate*. Milan: Feltrinelli.

Pollack, S. (1973). Osservazioni di Franz Alexander sul rapporto fra psichiatria e legge. In Alexander F e Staub H. *Il delinquente, il giudice e il pubblico*. Milan: Giuffré.

Zara, G. (2013). La validità incrementale della psico-criminologia e delle neuroscienze in ambito giuridico. Il Mulino, 2, pag. 324

—— Tra il probabile e il certo. *La valutazione del rischio di violenza e di recidiva criminale. Diritto penale contemporaeo* www.penalecontemporaneo. it/upload/1462543469ZARA_2016a.pdf

Zecchinon, G. (2013). Note to verdict. Cass. Pen. 2008, in "La rilevanza probatoria della perizia nel processo penale" by V. Mormile, 2013).

Zilboorg, G. (1943). *Mind, Medicine, and Man*. New York: Harcourt.

Index

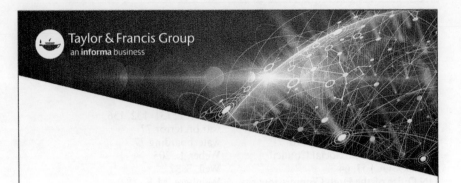

30 Jan
2022年.

プレゼント：

コリンから.

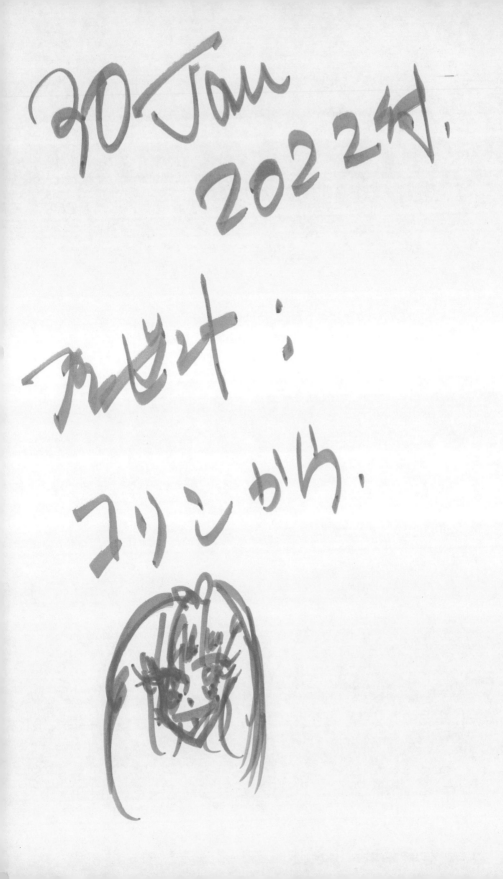